A MISSIONARY LOOK AT THE BOOK OF ACTS

EMPOWERED
for Global Mission

Forward by John York

DENZIL R. MILLER

Revised Edition

2013

Library of Congress Cataloging-in-Publication Data

Miller, Denzil R., 1946-
Empowered for Global Mission: A Missionary Look At The Book Of Acts /
Denzil R. Miller
Includes subject and scripture indices

ISBN 978-09911332-0-8

1. Pneumatology—Lukan—Pentecostal. 2. Missions—Biblical teaching—Strategy. 3. Biblical studies—Acts

Published by PneumaLife Publications
Springfield, MO, USA, 2013
Springfield, MO, U S A

Printed in the United States of America

To Sandy, my loving wife,
my friend, my companion, and my colleague in ministry.

THE KEY

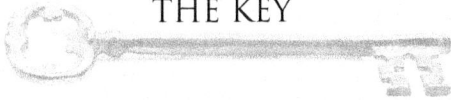

But you will receive power when the Holy Spirit has come upon you; and you shall be My witnesses both in Jerusalem, and in all Judea and Samaria, and even to the remotest part of the earth.

- Jesus -

- CONTENTS -

PART 4: APPLICATION

APPENDICES

- FOREWORD -

When I finished reading the draft for *Empowered for Global Mission*, I wrote the author my feeling that this was the best book there is on the missional purpose of Holy Spirit baptism. Three reasons for this assessment follow:

The book's message. This book clarifies the purpose of Spirit baptism without becoming argumentative or partisan. *Empowered for Global Mission* demonstrates that the recurrent pattern in Acts is one of outpourings of the Holy Spirit followed by missional evangelism. The presentation is consistent with accepted principles of biblical interpretation and is both logical and convincing.

The book's passion. Recently, a student said to me, "You know, missions classes can be so boring." This student was not referencing the content of this book! Every line is driven by a passion to demonstrate Lukan authorial intent and the relevance of that intent to our mission as Christians. *Empowered for Global Mission* shows convincingly that a book need not put the reader to sleep in order to be credible.

The book's author. For the more than thirty years that I have known Denzil R. Miller, he has consistently modeled what he teaches, first as a pastor and then as a missionary. Denzil's theme has been the same in his local church, in summer camp ministry, in mentoring Bible School students, and in teaching and preaching throughout Africa. I know of no one who has as consistently given his life for the purpose of seeing the church baptized in the Holy Spirit so that the nations may hear the Good News of the death and resurrection of Jesus Christ.

Because many are hungry for a visitation of the Holy Spirit resulting in last-day harvest, I expect *Empowered for Global Mission* to have a wide circulation. This may indeed be the most helpful book you will read on the missional purpose of the baptism in the Holy Spirit.

Dr. John V. York
April 2005
Executive Director, Africa's Hope
Assemblies of God World Missions

- INTRODUCTION -

The Bible is a missionary book. To miss this grand truth is to miss the very essence of Scripture. Beginning with the declaration that "God created man in His own image" (Gen. 1:27), and continuing through the final cry of Revelation that "whosoever will" can come and "take the water of life without cost" (Rev. 22:17), the Bible has a guiding theme. Bible scholars call this theme *missio Dei*, or the mission of God. Every Bible writer echoes this uniting theme of Scripture: the God of all creation is a missionary God, and He is on a mission to redeem and call unto Himself a people out of every tribe, tongue, and nation under heaven (Rev. 5:9).

What is true for the entire Bible is supremely true of the New Testament. It is a missions book from start to finish. Apart from a clear understanding of its missionary orientation, one cannot truly understand the message and thrust of the New Testament. In fact, the entire New Testament can be properly called a "missions manual." Every book in the New Testament, with the exception of the book of James, was written by a missionary.[1] Almost all were written in the context of missionary endeavor, to missionary churches, and with clear missional intent. Missions is the heartbeat of the New Testament.

I sometimes smile when I hear preachers describe the so-called Pastoral Epistles as "Paul, the older pastor, giving advice to Timothy and Titus, the younger pastors." Certainly, such an application can be made. However, these epistles can be more

---

1   Many Bible commentators believe that the book of James was written by James the Just, the brother of Jesus, and the pastor of the first missionary sending church, the church at Jerusalem.

accurately described as Paul, the veteran missionary, giving advice and instructions to his younger missionary colleagues.

Our primary interest in this book is the Acts of the Apostles. We ask, just how does Acts fit into the missiological intent of the Bible and, more specifically, the New Testament?

The book of Acts is in essence a handbook on missionary strategy. While the epistles were divinely inspired instructions to emerging missionary churches, Acts is a divinely inspired strategy for dynamic missionary expansion. C. Peter Wagner writes that Acts "is intended to be a paradigm of how the kingdom of God would be spread worldwide through the centuries until Jesus returns."[2] He further states, "In planning our service to God today we draw deeply on the Gospels and the later Epistles, but Acts, more than any other book, is our primary training manual."[3]

I could not agree more. Acts is the premier training manual for missions. The epistles are intended to be discipleship guides, aimed primarily at nurturing existing Christians. Their primary focus is not on reaching the lost for Christ, but on teaching and maturing those who are already in Christ. The focus of Acts, however, is clearly on evangelistic and missionary outreach. Under the inspiration of the Spirit, Luke wrote Acts to chronicle the missionary advance of the primitive church. He further wrote to inspire the church of his age—and of every age—to imitate the first church. Wagner observes, "The Gospel of Luke tells what Jesus did, and Acts tells what He expects His followers to do, both then and now. . . . [Luke] writes more about true missiology than any other biblical author."[4]

Further, Acts demonstrates the absolute necessity of divine empowerment for missionary endeavor. It demonstrates that this

---

2   C. Peter Wagner, *The Acts of the Holy Spirit* (Ventura, CA: Regal Books, 2000), 17.
3   Ibid., 18.
4   Ibid., 17.

empowering comes as a direct result of one's being baptized in the Holy Spirit. According to Luke, this uniquely empowering experience is a must for every Christian and is an essential requisite for effective missionary service.

At the beginning of the twentieth century a new movement emerged on the Christian scene. This movement came to be known as the Pentecostal Movement. The defining message of the movement was an emphasis on the experience of Spirit baptism as seen in the book of Acts. The early Pentecostals enthusiastically proclaimed that every believer should be filled with the Holy Spirit. They contended that it was an experience separate from the new birth and evidenced by speaking in tongues. A powerful dynamic of the early Pentecostals was the way they successfully married the experience of Spirit baptism to world evangelization and to the soon coming of Christ. The combining of these three theological concepts produced a powerful synergy that propelled them around the world to declare the good news of Christ. In short time Pentecostal missionaries were present on every continent. Today, more than 524 million people around the world identify themselves with some form of Pentecostalism.[5]

The Pentecostal emphasis on the baptism in the Holy Spirit as an empowering experience separate from conversion has been criticized by some as a misunderstanding of Scripture. Is it true? Is the Pentecostal insistence that every believer seek such an experience a misguided practice? Is the message of a subsequent baptism in the Holy Spirit a non-issue, or at best, a side issue? Is it a perversion of Scripture to teach that there is a second empowering experience apart from conversion? As some would put it, is it useful but not essential, normal but not normative? Or is the message of the baptism in the Holy Spirit at the very heart of the Christian message?

---

5   David Barrett, "The Worldwide Holy Spirit Renewal" in *The Century of the Holy Spirit: One Hundred Years of Pentecostal and Charismatic Renewal, 1901-2001,* ed. Vinson Synan (Nashville, TN: Thomas Nelson Publishers, 2001), 388.

This book will attempt to answer these questions. It will seek to demonstrate, based on the book of Acts and the writings of Paul, that the empowering experience of the baptism in the Holy Spirit is an essential requisite for optimum evangelistic and missionary ministry.

The book will thus examine the issue of Spirit baptism as it relates to global missions. It has been divided into four parts: Part 1 deals with hermeneutical issues involved in interpreting the book of Acts. It addresses the unique challenges one encounters when seeking to interpret historical narrative. A key concern will be authorial intent. Part 1 will attempt to answer the questions: Does Luke reveal his intent in writing Acts? If so, what was that intent, and how is it demonstrated? Also, how does that intent affect how one is to interpret Acts?

Part 2 will examine the first six of seven key outpourings of the Spirit in Acts. Those seven outpourings are as follows:

- Pentecost, the First Jerusalem Outpouring (2:1-4)
- The Second Jerusalem Outpouring (4:31)
- The Samaritan Outpouring (8:14-17)
- The Damascene Outpouring (9:15-18)
- The Caesarean Outpouring (10:44-48)
- The Antiochian "Outpouring" (13:1-3)
- The Ephesian Outpouring (19:1-7).

How each of these outpourings of the Spirit contributes to the fulfillment of Luke's intent in writing Acts will be discussed. It will be observed how, in each instance, Luke consistently returns to what we are calling his *empowerment–witness motif.*

Part 3 will examine the Pauline perspective on empowerment for mission. It will do this in two ways: First, it will investigate the seventh key outpouring of the Spirit in Acts, the Ephesian Outpouring. We will discover how the outpouring of the Spirit on twelve disciples was a key component of Paul's greater missionary strategy for reaching Ephesus and all of Asia Minor with

the gospel. It is a strategy we are calling a "Strategy of the Spirit."
Further, Part 3 will look into Paul's epistles and examine how he
viewed the role of the empowerment of the Holy Spirit in missionary
work, and how his view complemented that of Luke.

Finally, Part 4 will apply the truths learned in the first three
parts. One way this will be done is by examining the role of spiritual
gifts in missions. We will attempt to define and classify the nine gifts,
or "manifestations," of the Spirit listed in 1 Corinthians 12:8-10, and
then to identify them in operation in Acts. We will discuss the use of
these same gifts in the work of missions today. Further application
will be made by discussing pertinent issues regarding the role of the
Holy Spirit in missions, including receiving the Spirit, ministering
the Spirit, and ministering spiritual gifts. The final chapter will
address the issue of evidential tongues as it applies to the subject of
world missions today.

It is my sincere desire that, as you read this book, you will
come to a new appreciation of the role of the Holy Spirit in the work
of missions, and that you will more fully realize the need for the
Spirit's power and presence in your own life and ministry. Further,
I hope you will understand in a fuller way the need for the church
you are planting—or the church with which you are working—to be
empowered by the Spirit for the task of global mission.

PART ONE

HERMENEUTICAL
ISSUES

- CHAPTER 1 -

INTERPRETING

ACTS

Returning home from work one evening Bill spied a folded piece of paper lying on his doorstep. Stooping down, he picked it up, unfolded it, and read, "I will get you tonight at midnight!"

"What could it mean?" Bill wondered, "Who could have written such a note? Who wants to *get* me?" He shivered at the thought. "What could I have done to deserve such a callous threat?" Entering his house, he immediately shut the door, double-locked it, and switched on his burglar alarm. Menacing thoughts plagued his mind.

Later that evening, as he sat huddled in his bedroom with the lights turned low, he received a phone call. It was from his friend, John. "Did you get my note?" John asked. "I left it on your doorstep. I hope you didn't forget our fishing trip. I will be by to get you tonight at midnight."

AUTHORIAL INTENT

This fictitious story illustrates the importance of a key principle of biblical interpretation, the principle of authorial intent. Had Bill known who wrote the note, and the reason he had written it, he would have never reacted the way he did. Once he knew who wrote it, and why he wrote it, he understood clearly what it meant. His fears evaporated.

So it is in interpreting Scripture. The more one knows about the author of the work and his intent in writing, the more accurately he can interpret the meaning of what is written. One must, therefore, ask two principle questions in interpreting a passage of Scripture: "To whom was it written?" and "Why was it written?" Other pertinent questions could include, "What particular situation prompted the author to write at that particular time?" and "What did the author hope to accomplish in writing?" These questions speak to issue of authorial intent. Determining their answers is crucial in interpreting the message of a biblical work.

Authorial intent can be determined in a number of ways. An understanding of what is often referred to as *external evidence* can be very helpful. Here, the interpreter seeks to determine the historical and cultural circumstances surrounding the writing of the book. An understanding of both sacred and secular history can be of benefit. Knowing these circumstances help in understanding the condition and needs of the people to whom the biblical author wrote. For example, an understanding of the culture and religious practices of the ancient city of Corinth is an invaluable help in interpreting Paul's Corinthian letters.

Another way an interpreter of Scripture can gain clues concerning an author's intent in writing is by examining *internal evidence*. Internal evidences are those clues contained within the work itself. They include statements made by the author that give insight into why he wrote the book. These statements can be in the form of either explicit or implicit statements of intent. Explicit

statements of intent are those statements made by the author in
which he clearly states his reason (or reasons) for writing. For
example, in his gospel John states clearly why he wrote:

> Therefore many other signs Jesus also performed in the
> presence of the disciples, which are not written in this book;
> but these have been written so that you may believe that
> Jesus is the Christ, the Son of God; and that believing you
> may have life in His name (John 20:30-31).

John, according to his own testimony, wrote so his readers might
believe in Jesus and find life in Him. John follows the same literary
strategy in his first epistle. Early in the book he states three reasons
why he wrote the epistle (see 1 John 1:3-4; 2:1). In the same manner,
Jude, in his small letter, clearly states his purpose in writing: "I felt
the necessity to write to you appealing that you contend earnestly for
the faith which was once for all handed down to the saints" (v. 3).
When seeking to interpret a particular biblical book, an interpreter
will do well to read and reread the book, carefully looking for explicit
statements of authorial intent.

Unfortunately, however, most biblical writers do not
explicitly state their reasons for writing. One should not despair,
however, for there is another way to discover authorial intent:
through a thoughtful examination of the author's implicit statements
of intent. Implicit statements of intent are those statements made by
the author which give indirect indications of his reason (or reasons)
for writing.

Biblical authors often employ certain literary devices to help
give insight into their reasons for writing. These literary devices
include repetition, inclusion-exclusion, and source redaction.
Whether studying the more didactic or the so-called "purely
narrative" portions of Scripture, understanding these devices can aid
in determining authorial intent. While Luke, the author of Acts, does

not state explicitly why he wrote,[1] he does use all three of these literary devices. Let's take a moment to look briefly at each.

REPETITION

Discovering repeated words, phrases, and themes can help in determining authorial intent. Biblical writers often use repetition to emphasize certain truths. If an author returns again and again to some particular theme, it can be safely assumed that the theme is important to him. For example, the writer of Hebrews returns repeatedly to the theme of "something better," using the word "better" thirteen times in the thirteen chapters of his book. He speaks of Jesus being "better than the angels" (1:4), of "better things" (6:9), a "better hope" (7:19), a "better covenant (7:22, 8:6), "better promises" (8:6), "better sacrifice(s)" (9:23, 11:4, 12:24), a "better possession" (10:34), a "better country" (11:16), a "better resurrection" (11:35), and "something better for us" (11:40). In reviewing these texts one gets the idea that the theme of "something better" is important to the writer of Hebrews. Certainly, this understanding can help the interpreter to more accurately understand the author's purpose in writing. In our investigation of the book of Acts, we will look for such repeated themes and actions. These will help us to determine Luke's authorial intent.

INCLUSION-EXCLUSION

A second literary device that can help in determining authorial intent is *inclusion-exclusion*. By its very nature, historical writing is selective and subjective. Based on his purpose in writing,

---

1   Some contend (and I believe correctly) that in Luke 1:1-4 Luke introduces both volumes of his work, Luke-Acts, where he states that he wrote to "compile an account of the things accomplished among us" so that his readers might know "the exact truth about the things you have been taught." His intent thus appears to have been both historical and theological. These two statements naturally suggest a follow-up question: "Why did Luke want his readers to know these things at this particular time?"

the historian, either consciously or unconsciously, chooses those events he will include in (or exclude from) his history. He includes materials that further his purpose, and excludes materials which do not.

Understanding this literary technique is especially helpful in determining authorial intent in a historical narrative such as Luke-Acts. This is true because biblical histories, whether found in the Old Testament or the New, are episodic in form. This means that the biblical historians did not, nor did they intend to, record exhaustive histories of Israel (Old Testament), the life of Jesus (the gospels), or the church (Acts). They rather chose particular historical episodes that helped them to advance their purpose in writing.[2] The history covered in Acts spans about thirty years.[3] During that time, thousands of memorable events must have taken place in the church and in the ministries of the apostles. To paraphrase what John said about Jesus, "There are many other things *which the apostles and the early church did*, which if they were written in detail, I suppose that even the world itself would not contain the books which were written." Yet, out of those thousands of events, Luke chose only about seventy episodes, contained in only about fourteen episodic series, to tell his story.[4] He was thus very selective, choosing only those stories which helped him to fulfill his Spirit-inspired agenda for writing the book. As we look closely at which stories Luke chose to include in his narrative, we gain clues as to his intention in writing.

2   An episode is a story that is complete in itself, and yet fits into the overall thematic flow of a larger narrative. An episodic series is a series of stories which together form a complete story in themselves, but are also part of a yet larger narrative.
3   W. Graham Scroggie, *The Unfolding Drama of Redemption: The Bible as a Whole*, 2d ed., vol. 2 (Grand Rapids, MI: Zondervan Publishing House, 1976), 174-175.
4   See Appendix 1. These episodes are often connected by a number of summary statements made by Luke throughout the book.

REDACTION

Authorial intent can also be deduced by observing how a writer redacts (or edits) his sources in order to fulfill his purpose. Carefully observing how Luke uses his Old Testament sources[5]— adding a word or phrase here, or subtracting or changing a word or phrase there—gives us clues as to what he wants to emphasize or de-emphasize.

At this point I should insert an explanation. When I speak of redaction, I am not talking about the radical redaction criticism theories of the more liberal biblical scholars who deny the verbal inspiration of Scripture. The redaction theory I am proposing holds securely to the belief that all Scripture is verbally inspired by God and is inerrant in its original autographs. I further believe that the redactor's choices were guided by the Spirit of God. Also, it is very possible that what often seems to be redaction to us on the part of the author, could instead be selective inclusion-exclusion. Luke could have had a number of sources to choose from, some of which we remain totally unaware today. He simply chose the ones that best suited his purposes. For instance, when Luke, or any gospel writer, quotes a saying of Jesus, it could be that Jesus actually made the same statement on several different occasions and in a number of slightly different ways. One gospel writer quotes it in one of its forms, another quotes it in another.

Be that as it may, it is significant which form the author chooses, or the way in which he, under the Spirit's guidance, edits the source to fit his purpose. A careful scrutiny of his choices gives us insight into why he wrote. As we progress through this study, we will see how, in writing Acts, Luke carefully employed this literary technique.

---

5   The Scriptures used by Luke were the Greek translation of the Old Testament known as the Septuagint, or LXX.

MULTIPLE AND PRIMARY INTENT

It is also important to understand that an author often writes with multiple intents. Some have argued that Acts was written only as a historical record of the beginnings of the Christian church. These interpreters contend that Luke wrote history from a purely objective standpoint. They claim that he had only one intent in writing, which was to faithfully chronicle the beginnings of the early church in Jerusalem and its eventual spread to Rome. It is highly improbable, however, that Luke, or for that matter, anyone else, could write a history that is purely objective. It is also highly improbable that anyone can write with only one purpose in mind. A critical reading of Acts reveals that Luke did indeed write with multiple intents, as will be discussed later in this chapter.

BIBLICAL THEOLOGY

Recent developments in hermeneutics also impact the way biblical narratives are being interpreted. One is the emergence of the biblical theological approach to interpreting Scripture. Historically, theologians have taken a systematic approach to formulating doctrine. In doing systematic theology, a selection of the biblical texts is interpreted synchronically, that is, all at the same time. In applying this method, a topic is first chosen. Next, texts relating to the topic are gathered from throughout the Bible. These texts are then laid out side by side for investigation, often with little or no consideration given to their historical or contextual realities. The theologian then seeks to interpret and harmonize what these texts teach on the subject.

In biblical theology, however, the Bible is approached diachronically, or across time. The biblical theologian seeks to discover how God has progressively revealed Himself and His plan throughout history. A key feature of biblical theology is that it does not seek to harmonize Scripture as in systematic theology, but rather seeks to allow each biblical author to speak for himself, out of his own theological agenda and his own historical and cultural milieu. In this study I will employ the biblical theological method, thus allowing Luke to speak for himself without unduly imposing upon him the theological agenda of either Paul or John.

NARRATIVE THEOLOGY

Another recent development in biblical interpretation is the growing acceptance of the theological significance of the biblical narrative. Robert P. Menzies has called this growing acceptance a "quiet revolution" in evangelical hermeneutics.[6] He writes,

> The revolution has also challenged older, well-established principles of interpretation. No longer can we, as a matter of principle, give priority to didactic portions of Scripture. No longer can we engage in theological reflection without giving due place to all of the evidence from an author's hand.[7]

Our stories define who we are and what we ideally should be as a people. Americans remind themselves of who they are by telling stories of the Pilgrims and the founding fathers. Africans remind themselves of who they are by telling stories of their ancestors. According to Joseph M. Williams, "Storytelling is fundamental to human behavior. No other form of prose can communicate large amounts of information so quickly and persuasively."[8] Donald A. Johns says that people use stories "to promote behavior and experience consistent with the group's identity."[9] A group will often

---

6   William W. Menzies and Robert P. Menzies, *Spirit and Power: Foundations of Pentecostal Experience* (Grand Rapids, MI: Zondervan Publishing House, 2000), 37.
7   Ibid., 44.
8   Joseph M. Williams, *Style: Toward Clarity and Grace* (Chicago: The University of Chicago Press, 1995), 19-20.
9   Donald A. Johns, "Some New Directions in the Hermeneutics of Classical Pentecostalism's Doctrine of Initial Evidence," in *Initial Evidence: Historical and Biblical Perspectives on the Pentecostal Doctrine of Spirit Baptism*, ed. Gary B. McGee (Peabody, Mass.: Hendrickson Publishers, Inc., 1991), 153-154.

remember the stories of its beginnings or crucial events in its history to remind itself of its fundamental ethos. According to Johns, in interpreting Acts, it works something like this:

> "How can the church preach the Good News about Jesus so powerfully?" I can hear Theophilus asking. "Well," Luke says, "Let me tell you a story. On the day of Pentecost . . . ." This function of stories is relevant because the stories of Acts tell the church about itself, about its essential qualities, and concerning Pentecost itself, about a pivotal point that inaugurates a new essential quality, being filled with the Spirit, which has as a goal effective, powerful, God-directed service.[10]

Craig S. Keener further notes that "most cultures in the world teach lessons through stories. Westerners are the ones who are odd in finding themselves unable to follow the point of narratives in the Bible."[11]

NARRATIVE RHETORIC

One important aspect of narrative theology is the concept of *narrative rhetoric*. Luke, like the other biblical historians, uses this narrative device in telling his story. Narrative rhetoric is a conscious attempt on the part of the author to influence the thinking and attitudes of his readers. He does this, however, not through overt moral or theological pronouncements, but through the application of certain narrative techniques. Through these techniques he constructs a world based on his predetermined values and beliefs. Robert C. Tannehill comments,

---

10   Ibid., 154.
11   Craig S. Keener, *Three Crucial Questions about the Holy Spirit* (Grand Rapids, MI: Baker Book House, 1999), 188.

A Gospel story exercises influence in a much richer way than through theological statements, which might be presented in an essay. Readers are led to believe or reaffirm their belief in the central character, Jesus, and are thereby influenced in complex ways—in their attitudes, controlling images, patterns of action, feelings, etc.[12]

He continues, "The message of Luke-Acts is not a set of theological propositions but the complex reshaping of human life, in its many dimensions, which it can cause."[13] Thus, Luke, like other narrative writers, uses narrative rhetoric in an attempt to reshape his reader's attitudes, beliefs, and practices.

Nevertheless, traditional Reformed evangelicals have historically attributed scant significance to the value of historical narrative in formulating theology. John R. W. Stott voices the opinion of most of these scholars when he speaks of "the importance of allowing the didactic to control our interpretation of the narrative."[14] As a result, these interpreters staunchly maintain that doctrine—at least in any normative sense—can never flow directly from the so-called "purely narrative" portions of Scripture, such as Acts. Since, in their view, Luke wrote with historical rather than theological intent, Acts is largely stripped of its theological utility. Such theologizing is, of course, a direct attack on Pentecostal theology, since the distinctive Pentecostal doctrines of subsequence and normative tongues are derived largely from the book of Acts.[15] Pentecostals have countered by noting that evangelicals have created

---

12   Robert C. Tannehill, *The Narrative Unity of Luke-Acts: A Literary Interpretation*, vol. 1, *The Gospel According to Luke* (Philadelphia, PA: Fortress Press, 1991), 8.

13   Ibid.

14   John R. W. Stott, *The Message of Acts* (Leichester, Eng: Inter-Varsity Press, 1990), 7.

15   The doctrine of subsequence says that the baptism in the Holy Spirit is an experience separate from and logically subsequent to the new birth. The doctrine of normative tongues says that all who are baptized in the Holy Spirit will speak in tongues as the Spirit gives utterance.

a "canon within a canon." That is, they have elevated one portion of
Scripture above another, saying it is legitimate to read one portion of
Scripture when formulating doctrine, but illegitimate to read
another. Keener speaks of the danger of such an approach to
Scripture:

> Although few would dismiss the doctrinal value of narrative
> altogether, many suggest that one should find in narrative
> only what is plainly taught in "clearer," more "didactic"
> portions of Scripture. Although some of these scholars are
> among the ablest exegetes in other portions of Scripture,
> I must protest that their approach to Bible stories violates the
> most basic rule for biblical interpretation and in practice
> jeopardizes the doctrine of biblical inspiration. Did not Paul
> say that all Scripture was inspired and therefore useful for
> "doctrine," or teaching (2 Tim. 3:16)?[16]

THE THEOLOGICAL CHARACTER OF ACTS

Today's consensus among theologians is that the gospel
writers were indeed theologians in their own right, each writing with
his own theological agenda. The same is of course true for Luke when
he wrote Acts. As far back as 1984, Roger Stronstad challenged the
prevailing methodology utilized in interpreting Acts.[17] He called for a
new theological paradigm based on three hermeneutical concepts:
First, he called for the literary and theological homogeneity of Luke-
Acts, declaring the two books comprised a single two-volume work.
They, therefore, should be studied as a literary unit. He stated, "This

---

16   Keener, 186-187. See also his book, *Gift and Giver: The Holy Spirit for Today*
(Grand Rapids, MI: Baker Academic, 2001), 210.
17   Roger Stronstad, *The Charismatic Theology of St. Luke* (Peabody, MA:
Hendrickson Publishers, Inc., 1984), 2-12.

homogeneity is no less true for the charismatic theology of St. Luke than for his other distinctive doctrines and motifs."[18]

Next, Stronstad called for biblical interpreters to recognize the theological character of Luke's historical method. When interpreting Acts, Pentecostals have emphasized the theological character of the book. Conversely, traditional evangelical and Reformed interpreters have emphasized the narrative character of Acts, minimizing its theological value. Stronstad said that such a fragmented view of Scripture "is alien to the general New Testament understanding of biblical, that is, Old Testament historiography."[19] He noted that Paul himself understood Old Testament historical narrative to have didactic purpose, citing Paul's statement in 2 Timothy 3:16, "All Scripture is inspired by God and profitable for teaching, for reproof, for correction, for training in righteousness" (see also Rom. 15:4; 1 Cor. 10:11).

Finally, Stronstad contended that Luke must be given theological independence from Paul. That is to say, Luke must be afforded the right to speak on his own, and his words must not be interpreted as though they were written by Paul. Luke used his own terminology and had his own intent in writing; therefore, he must be interpreted on his own terms. Stronstad noted that while Paul relates "Spirit baptism" to conversion-initiation (1 Cor. 12:13), Luke sees it as empowerment for witness (Acts 1:8).[20] We will develop some of these thoughts at greater length in succeeding chapters.

---

18   Ibid., 5.
19   Ibid., 6.
20   A closer reading of 1 Corinthians 12:13 reveals that Paul is indeed speaking of conversion- initiation; however, he is not talking about baptism in the Holy Spirit as presented by Luke in Acts. He is rather talking about baptism into Christ (see Rom. 6:3). In the baptism in the Holy Spirit, Jesus (the "baptizor") immerses the believer (the "baptizee") into the Holy Spirit (the element). In 1 Corinthians 12:13 the Holy Spirit is the "baptizor," the new believer is the "baptizee," and the body of Christ is the element. In his epistles Paul thus refers to believers as being in Christ over 80 times. Luke, however, never uses this terminology, with the possible exception of Acts 24:24 where Paul spoke to Felix about "faith in Christ."

PENTECOSTAL PRESUPPOSITIONS

Pentecostal theologian Anthony D. Palma cites several presuppositions that guide his personal hermeneutics in interpreting Acts. It is fair to say that these presuppositions can be generally viewed as the guiding principles of a contemporary Pentecostal approach to interpreting Acts. They are as follows:

- All Scripture (including the historical portions) is inspired by God.

- Exegesis of Scripture must be controlled by a proper understanding of the discipline of biblical theology.

- Each biblical writer must be understood on his own terms.

- Different biblical writers have different emphases.

- A biblical writer must first be understood on his own terms, and only then should his teachings be related to those of other writers and the whole of Scripture.

- The seeming differences between biblical writers are appropriately characterized by complementariness rather than competition or contradiction.

- Luke's writings belong to the literary genre of history.

- Redaction criticism, within the framework of the historical-critical method, can be useful in interpreting Scripture.

- In writing his histories, Luke, under the guidance of the Holy Spirit, was selective and subjective in his choice of material.

- Narrative theology is useful in interpreting the Acts narratives.

- Induction is a legitimate form of logic, and historical precedent is useful in interpreting Acts. This is especially

true in regards to being filled with the Spirit, since it is a
divinely rather than a humanly initiated activity.

- Luke's intent for writing Acts is encapsulated in Acts 1:8.[21]

Other Pentecostal scholars, such as Howard Ervin, speak of the role
of the Holy Spirit in illuminating the text.[22] According to Ervin, since
the Bible is inspired by the Spirit, the Spirit-indwelt believer can elicit
His aid in interpreting Scripture. The new birth, therefore, becomes a
precondition for understanding the word of God (2 Cor. 2:9-15).
Further, the experience of the baptism in the Holy Spirit opens up
one's spirit to a greater sensitivity to the Spirit of God, and can thus
open the way to greater insight into certain portions of Scripture.

French L. Arrington further speaks of the dialogical role that
experience can play in interpreting Scripture. According to him, both
Scripture and experience inform one another—with Scripture, of
course, having the final word on the matter. William W. Menzies
says that experience can also serve to "verify" truth that has been
derived from cognitive reasoning. He asserts, "If biblical truth is to be
promulgated, it must be demonstrable in life."[23] While some accuse
Pentecostals of reading their personal experience into Scripture,
Pentecostals counter by saying that non-Pentecostals read their non-
experience into Scripture. While not abandoning their view of the
supremacy of Scripture in determining faith and conduct, and while

---

21   Anthony D. Palma, *The Holy Spirit: A Pentecostal Perspective* (Springfield, MO:
Logion Press, 2001), 91-96.

22   Howard M. Ervin, "Hermeneutics: A Pentecostal Option," *Pneuma* 3, no. 2,
(1981): 11-25. See also Roger Stronstad's evaluation of Ervin in *Spirit, Scripture, and
Theology: A Pentecostal Perspective* (Baguio City, Philippines: Asia Pacific Theological
Seminary Press, 1995), 24-27.

23   William W. Menzies, "The Methodology of Pentecostal Theology: An Essay on
Hermeneutics," in *Essays on Apostolic Themes: Studies in Honor of Howard M. Ervin
Presented to Him by Colleagues and Friends on His Sixty-fifth Birthday*, ed. Paul Elbert,
(Peabody, MS: Hendrickson Publishers, 1986), 13; "Synoptic Theology, An Essay on
Pentecostal Hermeneutics," *Paraclete* 13, no. 1, (Winter 1979): 20; Roger Stronstad,
Spirit, Scripture, and Theology: A Pentecostal Perspective (Baguio City, Philippines: Asia
Pacific Theological Seminary Press, 1995), 29.

holding firmly to the grammatico-historical approach to interpreting Scripture, Pentecostals contend that one's experience can rightly impact his understanding of the text.

THE MISSIOLOGICAL CHARACTER OF ACTS

In addition to writing as a historian and theologian, Luke also wrote as a Spirit-inspired missiologist. Missiology is the area of scholarly study that concerns itself with an understanding of the biblical and philosophical foundations of missions, and then seeks to apply that understanding to the actual practice of missions in the field. It combines the disciplines of theology, history, sociology, anthropology, and psychology as each applies to missions. In Acts, Luke's theology and his historiography are both eminently missiological. Acts is an account of the missionary advance of the first century church and a presentation of how that advance was accomplished. Missiological themes dominate the book. This truth is evidenced by Luke's repeated interest in the Gentile nations, the *ethne*.[24] It is further demonstrated by his obvious interest in missionary strategy. This interest of Luke's is shown in, among other things, his structuring the book around Jesus' strategic pronouncement in Acts 1:8 and by his depiction of Paul's missionary strategy in Acts 19. The missiological character of Acts offers an important clue as to Luke's primary intent in writing the book.

DIDACTIC SEGMENTS

Clues as to an author's purpose in writing can also be found in certain "didactic segments" which he embeds into his story. These didactic segments often appear as propositional statements spoken by the characters of the story. The author thus uses the words of the

---

24   The *ethne* are mentioned 44 times in Acts, including 2:5; 4:25, 27; 7:7, 45; 8:9; 9:15; 10:22, 35, 45; 11:1, 18; 13:19, 42, 46, 47, 48; 14:2, 5, 16, 27; 15:3, 7, 12, 14, 17, 19, 23; 17:26; 18:6; 21:11, 19, 21, 25; 22:21; 24:2, 10, 17; 26:4, 17, 20, 23; 28:19, 28.

characters to teach the lessons he wants taught. Much like a news reporter who quotes the statements of those individuals who express the opinions he wants aired, the narrative writer sometimes quotes his characters saying the things he wants said. New Testament examples of such didactic statements include the teachings and sermons of Jesus and the apostles. Didactic segments can also be inserted in a narrative in the form of parenthetical comments made by the author.

Luke employs both of these narrative techniques in Luke-Acts. For example, Jesus' encouragement to His disciples to ask their "heavenly Father" for the gift of the Spirit in Luke 11:9-13 has clear didactic value. It also has evident normative implications for Christians of all ages.[25] According to Robert Menzies, "This text, then, reflects Luke's intent to teach a Spirit-baptism distinct from conversion," which, he says, "for Luke meant open access to the divine Spirit—the source of power that would enable them to be effective witnesses for Christ (Luke 12:12; Acts 1:8)."[26] Some, however, object, saying that such teachings of Jesus and the apostles, since they are directed toward specific audiences in specific historical contexts, do not contain normative features. Keener disagrees, noting that "a few hundred years ago Protestants explained away the Great Commission in just such a manner."[27]

Another example of a didactic segment contained within a narrative portion of Scripture is Acts 2:38-39:

> Peter said to them, "Repent, and each of you be baptized in the name of Jesus Christ for the forgiveness of your sins; and you will receive the gift of the Holy Spirit. For the promise is for you and your children and for all who are far off, as many as the Lord our God will call to Himself."

---

25   It should be noted that this injunction of Luke's was to post-Pentecostal disciples since Luke wrote his gospel in about A.D. 60.

26   Menzies and Menzies, 117.

27   Keener, 189.

Although the Pentecostal and the non-Pentecostal would interpret the meaning of this text differently, both can agree as to its normative character. In like manner, Jesus' promise in Acts 1:8 has clear normative value for the church and for individual Christians today. As will be demonstrated in this book, this verse serves as Luke's interpretive key for the entire book of Acts, and it is the key to understanding Luke's intent for writing the book.

PARENTHETICAL COMMENTARY

Authorial intent is also evidenced in certain parenthetical comments made by Luke in Acts. A parenthetical comment is an explanatory or informational insight inserted by the writer into the narrative to help the reader better understand the meaning of an event. It can involve as little as a single phrase or as much as a full sentence or two. Parenthetical commentary can be omitted without changing the basic meaning and construction of the sentence or affecting the flow of the story. It may or may not be enclosed in parentheses. A classic example of parenthetical commentary is found in John 7:37-40:

> Now on the last day, the great day of the feast, Jesus stood and cried out, saying, "If anyone is thirsty, let him come to Me and drink. He who believes in Me, as the Scripture said, 'From his innermost being will flow rivers of living water.'" *(But this He spoke of the Spirit, whom those who believed in Him were to receive; for the Spirit was not yet given, because Jesus was not yet glorified.)* Some of the people therefore, when they heard these words, were saying, "This certainly is the Prophet."[28]

---

28   Italics and parentheses added. A similar parenthetical comment is found in verse 50 (KJV).

Note how verse 39, which the KJV rightly puts in parentheses, functions as parenthetical commentary. In this side comment John explains to his readers the historical context of Jesus' statement and how that context impacted its full meaning.

Three parenthetical comments in Acts function in much the same manner. The first is found in Acts 5:26, "Then the captain went along with the officers and proceeded to bring them back without violence (for they were afraid of the people, that they might be stoned)." In this parenthetical comment Luke is helping his readers understand why the Jewish leaders refrained from maltreating the apostles in public, as well as emphasizing the respect the apostles had gained among the populace of Jerusalem. Another parenthetical comment is found in Acts 8:14-17,[29]

> Now when the apostles in Jerusalem heard that Samaria had received the word of God, they sent them Peter and John, who came down and prayed for them that they might receive the Holy Spirit. (*For He had not yet fallen upon any of them; they had simply been baptized in the name of the Lord Jesus.*) Then they began laying their hands on them, and they were receiving the Holy Spirit.

In this paragraph, verse 16 (which I italicized and enclosed in parentheses) functions as parenthetical commentary. In the context of his greater purpose in writing Acts, Luke wanted his readers to know that these Samaritans did not receive the Holy Spirit when they were converted or baptized in water. They had a further need for divine empowering in order that they too might fully participate in the *missio Dei*. This passage serves as a strong argument for an empowering experience for Christians subsequent to conversion.

A second example of Luke's use of parenthetical commentary is found in Acts 10:44-48:

---

29   See Acts 17:16 for a similar example.

> While Peter was still speaking these words, the Holy Spirit
> fell upon all those who were listening to the message. (*All the
> circumcised believers who came with Peter were amazed,
> because the gift of the Holy Spirit had been poured out on the
> Gentiles also. For they were hearing them speaking with
> tongues and exalting God.*) Then Peter answered, "Surely no
> one can refuse the water for these to be baptized who have
> received the Holy Spirit just as we did, can he?" And he
> ordered them to be baptized in the name of Jesus Christ.
> Then they asked him to stay on for a few days.

In this paragraph, all of verse 45 and most of verse 46, ending in the
words "exalting God" (which I again italicized and enclosed in
parentheses), function as parenthetical commentary. Luke inserted
this explanatory statement because he felt it was important for his
reader to know exactly how the baptism in the Holy Spirit was
experienced in Caesarea—that is, with speaking in tongues and
prophetic speech. He also wanted his readers to know that tongues
serve as a normative sign that the baptism in the Spirit has occurred.
Johns agrees: ". . . the comments of the narrator often evaluate or
explain an event narrated. This is significant for the classical
Pentecostal, because the narrator in Acts 10:46 explicitly assigns
evidential value to speaking in tongues and states that this was the
view of Peter and his associates."[30]

APPLICATION TO ACTS

Let's now apply some of these interpretive principles to Acts.
We will begin by listing those things we know about the book,
including insights from both external and internal sources. For
instance, we know that Acts is the second in a two-part work, often
called Luke-Acts (Luke 1:1-4; Acts 1:1). We know that both the
gospel and Acts were written by Luke, the physician and missionary

companion of Paul (Col. 4:14; Phil. 2:3), and that both were
addressed to "Theophilus" (Luke 1:3; Acts 1:1), the friend and
possible patron of Luke. We also know that both deal with
beginnings: Luke with the beginnings of the gospel and Acts with the
beginnings of the church (Luke 1:2, Acts 1:1). And finally, we know
that both were meant for a wider audience than just one man. Luke
meant for them to be read by all "lovers of God."

We can be fairly certain that Luke wrote Acts around
A.D. 65, more than thirty years after the Day of Pentecost. He,
therefore, wrote to a second generation of Christians, many of whom
were not yet alive when the early events of Acts occurred. We can
also be reasonably sure that Luke's audience lived remotely from
Jerusalem. Arrington notes that Luke wrote "to instruct people who
are removed in geography and time from the ministry of Jesus," and
thus from the beginnings of the church.[31] Some have suggested that
Luke wrote from Rome, others say Achaia, Antioch, or Caesarea.[32]
His original audience likely lived in a Roman province somewhat
removed from Judea. From the internal evidence we can deduce that
Luke's audience was probably comprised of predominantly Gentiles
and Hellenized Jews. Also, from the internal evidence, two further
conclusions can be drawn.

WANING MISSIONARY VISION

First, there was a waning missionary vision among the
Christians comprising Luke's original audience. It is possible that this
waning vision was caused, at least in part, by the persecution they
were experiencing. People enduring persecution have a tendency to
look inward and focus on their own plight and suffering rather than
looking outward to the spiritual needs of others. Luke viewed this

---

31   French L. Arrington, "Luke," in *The Full Life Bible Commentary to the New
Testament,* eds. French L. Arrington and Roger Stronstad (Grand Rapids, MI:
Zondervan Publishing House, 1999), 379.
32   Ibid.

situation with alarm, and he set out to remind his readers that, in spite of severe persecution, the early Pentecostal believers triumphed and remained focused on their evangelistic mission.[33] Those to whom he wrote could expect the same results, if they too would be empowered by the Spirit.

DE-EMPHASIS ON PENTECOSTAL EMPOWERING

Secondly, we can infer from the internal evidence that there was a de-emphasis on Pentecostal empowering among Luke's original audience. Luke wrote to call these "second generation" Christians back to their Pentecostal roots and to demonstrate to them the absolute necessity of pneumatic empowering for witness to the nations. This purpose of Luke's will become clearer as we proceed through this book.

SECONDARY PURPOSES

I should digress for a moment to point out that Luke also wrote with other secondary purposes in mind. These included historical, theological, evangelistic, pastoral, and apologetic purposes.

Luke obviously wrote with *historical intent*. He felt it important that his readers have a clear understanding of the beginnings of the church. This purpose in writing is stated in Luke 1:3-4:

> . . . it seemed fitting for me as well, having investigated everything carefully from the beginning, to write it out for

---

33   The reader will note that I use the word "Pentecostal" in a number of ways in this book. Sometimes I am speaking of those contemporary churches and Christians who are part of the renewal movement that began at the turn of the 20th century and is generally known as "Pentecostalism." At other times I am speaking of those early first century Christians who experienced the power of the Holy Spirit on the Day of Pentecost or shortly thereafter. The third way I use the word is more theological. I am speaking of the unique approach to interpreting Acts espoused by those in the Pentecostal movement. How the word is used in each case can be determined by the context.

you in consecutive order, most excellent Theophilus; so that you may know the exact truth about the things you have been taught.

Luke's historical intent is also implied in Acts 1:1: "The first account I composed, Theophilus, about all that Jesus began *to do* and teach . . ." (emphasis added).

Also implied in these two introductory statements is Luke's *theological intent.* He wrote so that his readers might know "the exact truth about the things [they had] been taught" (Luke 1:4) and to emphasize, not only the "doings," but also the "teachings" of Jesus and the early church (Acts 1:1).

Luke also wrote with *evangelistic intent.* A major theme running through Luke-Acts is the nature and importance of salvation. Luke repeatedly emphasizes God's offer of salvation to all humankind: Jew and Gentile, man and woman, young and old, wealthy and poor (Luke 2:30-32; Acts 2:17-21). According to Luke, this salvation is available only through Christ (Acts 4:12), and is received through faith and repentance (Acts 2:38- 39; 16:31).

It is clear that Luke also wrote with *pastoral intent.* He sought to encourage and strengthen the Christians by ensuring them that they could triumph over opposition and persecution as did the first Christians. Through the power of the Spirit they could not only stay true to Christ, they could be powerful witnesses of His grace.

Finally, Luke wrote with *apologetic intent.* In interpreting Acts one is faced with the question, why did Luke include the lengthy trial episodes in Acts? (chaps. 22-26). As some have suggested, it was because he was concerned with the attitude of the Roman authorities toward Christianity. He thus included these episodes to demonstrate to the Roman magistrates that Christianity was no threat to Rome. In each trial, Paul is found to be legally innocent, and Christianity is represented as a religion of high ethical and moral standards. While encouraging the persecuted Christians to endure, and even triumph in the power of the Spirit, Luke is also calling on the Roman authorities to stop persecuting them.

Primary Intent

Having said these things, it is evident, however, that none of the above represents Luke's *primary intent* in writing Acts. Luke's primary intent was, rather, prophetic and missiological. He writes as a Spirit-inspired prophet calling the church of his day back to its Pentecostal and missionary roots. William Barclay, after stating other possible reasons for Luke's writing Acts, said, "But these are merely secondary aims. Luke's chief purpose is set out in the words of the Risen Christ in Acts 1:8, 'You shall be my witnesses in Jerusalem and in all Judea and Samaria and to the end of the earth.'"[34] This we will investigate further in succeeding chapters.

Conclusion

In this chapter we have discussed some of the hermeneutical issues surrounding the interpretation of Acts. We have noted that Acts, which belongs to the literary genre of historical narrative, must be approached somewhat differently from other New Testament genre, such as gospel, epistle, or apocalyptic writing. We have stated that understanding a writer's authorial intent is an essential ingredient in interpreting Scripture, and we have concluded that Luke's primary purpose in writing Acts was at the same time prophetic and missiological. He thus wrote as a prophetic voice calling the church of his day back to its Pentecostal and missionary origins.

In the chapters which follow we will look more closely at Luke's intent in writing Acts. Especially pertinent is 1:8, the interpretive key to the book. We will see how the *empowerment-*

---

34   William Barclay, *The Daily Study Bible: The Acts of the Apostles,* rev. ed. (Edinburgh, Eng: The Saint Andrew Press, 1976), 4.

witness motif established in that verse is repeated throughout the entire book, giving Acts its cohesion and dynamic impact.

CHAPTER 2

THE NARRATIVE
BRIDGE

ACTS 1:1-11

*The first account I composed, Theophilus, about all that Jesus
began to do and teach, until the day when He was taken up to heaven,
after He had by the Holy Spirit given orders to the apostles whom He had
chosen. To these He also presented Himself alive after His suffering,
by many convincing proofs, appearing to them over a period of forty days
and speaking of the things concerning the kingdom of God. Gathering them
together, He commanded them not to leave Jerusalem, but to wait for
what the Father had promised, "Which," He said, "you heard of from Me;
for John baptized with water, but you will be baptized with the
Holy Spirit not many days from now."*

*So when they had come together, they were asking Him, saying,
"Lord, is it at this time You are restoring the kingdom to Israel?" He said to
them, "It is not for you to know times or epochs which the Father has fixed
by His own authority; but you will receive power when the Holy Spirit has
come upon you; and you shall be My witnesses both in Jerusalem, and in all
Judea and Samaria, and even to the remotest part of the earth."*

And after He had said these things, He was lifted up while they
were looking on, and a cloud received Him out of their sight.
And as they were gazing intently into the sky while He was going,
behold, two men in white clothing stood beside them. They also said,
"Men of Galilee, why do you stand looking into the sky? This Jesus,
who has been taken up from you into heaven, will come in just the
same way as you have watched Him go into heaven."

In Chapter 1 we looked at the hermeneutical principles that
will guide our present study. In this chapter we will focus our
attention on Luke's introduction to Acts found in Acts 1:1-11. These
eleven verses serve two literary purposes for the book: First, when
taken with the last ten verses of the gospel of Luke, they serve as a
sort of narrative bridge, linking the two volumes. Secondly, they
serve as a programmatic introduction to the book of Acts,
functioning much as a literary or legal abstract, outlining the major
elements of what is to follow in the rest of the book. Let's look more
closely at each of these two functions.

A NARRATIVE BRIDGE

The first eleven verses of Acts 1 serve as a narrative bridge,
providing a literary connection between Luke and Acts. A
comparison of Luke 24:44-53 and Acts 1:1-11 reveals that these
passages record the same events, and represent an overlapping of the
two books, the first passage concluding Luke and the second
introducing Acts. Contained in these two passages are eight direct
parallel statements, as I have diagramed in the chart below.

EIGHT PARALLEL STATEMENTS
(FIGURE 2.1)

LUKE 24:44-53	ACTS 1:1-11
1 [The Gospel of Luke]	[1]The first account I composed, Theophilus, about all that Jesus began to do and teach, [2]until the day when He was taken up to heaven, (see v. 9 below)
2 [45]Then <u>He opened their minds to understand the Scriptures,</u> [46]and He said to them, " Thus it is written, that the Christ would suffer and rise again from the dead the third day, . . .	. . . after <u>He had by the Holy Spirit given orders</u> to the apostles whom He had chosen.
3 [44]Now He said to them, "<u>These are My words which I spoke to you</u> while I was still with you, that all things which are written about Me in the Law of Moses and the Prophets and the Psalms must be fulfilled.	[3]To these He also presented Himself alive after His suffering, by many convincing proofs, appearing to them over a period of forty days and <u>speaking of the things concerning the kingdom of God</u>. (See v. 6 below)

LUKE 24:44-53	ACTS 1:1-11
4	[49a]"And behold, I am sending forth <u>the promise</u> of My Father upon you; but <u>you are to stay in the city</u> . . ."	[4]"Gathering them together, <u>He commanded them not to leave Jerusalem</u>, but to <u>wait for what the Father had promised</u>, "Which," He said, "you heard of from Me; [5]for John baptized with water, but you will be baptized with the Holy Spirit not many days from now."
		[6]So when they had come together, they were asking Him, saying, "Lord, is it at this time You are restoring the kingdom to Israel?" [7]He said to them, "It is not for you to know times or epochs which the Father has fixed by His own authority;
5	[49b]. . . <u>until you are clothed with power from on high</u>."	[8]but <u>you will receive power when the Holy Spirit has come upon you</u>
6	[48a]<u>You are witnesses of these things</u>.	. . . and <u>you shall be My witnesses</u>
7	[47]and that repentance for forgiveness of sins would be proclaimed in His name <u>to all the nations, beginning from Jerusalem</u>."	. . . both <u>in Jerusalem</u>, and in all Judea and Samaria, and <u>even to the remotest part of the earth</u>.

LUKE 24:44-53	ACTS 1:1-11
8 ⁵⁰And He led them out as far as Bethany, and He lifted up His hands and blessed them. ⁵¹While He was blessing them, He parted from them and was carried up into heaven.	⁹And after He had said these things, He was lifted up while they were looking on, and a cloud received Him out of their sight. ¹⁰And as they were gazing intently into the sky while He was going, behold, two men in white clothing stood beside them. ¹¹They also said, "Men of Galilee, why do you stand looking into the sky? This Jesus, who has been taken up from you into heaven, will come in just the same way as you have watched Him go into heaven."

The eight parallels presented in Figure 2.1 can be summarized as follows:

1. The book of Acts is the second volume of Luke's two volume history of Christian beginnings, with the gospel of Luke being the first (Acts 1:1).

2. Even after His resurrection Jesus continued to move under the Spirit's guidance (Acts 1:2). This Spirit-directed ministry included opening the minds of the disciples to understand the Scriptures, especially those prophecies that spoke of His death and resurrection (Luke 24:44-45).

3. During the forty days between His resurrection and His ascension, Jesus taught His disciples about the kingdom of God (Acts 1:3). Part of His kingdom teaching included an explanation of how His life was a fulfillment of the Old Testament Scriptures (Luke 24:44, see also vv. 25-27).

4. Jesus promised His disciples that He would soon send forth the promise of His Father upon them. They were therefore to stay in the city of Jerusalem until the promise

was fulfilled. This promise of the Father was none other than the baptism in the Holy Spirit about which John the Baptist had spoken (Luke 3:15-16).

5.   This baptism would come as "power from on high," and it would occur when the Holy Spirit came upon the disciples. They were thus to wait in anticipation of this dynamic experience from heaven. The experience would be, at the same time, a clothing with and a baptism in God's presence and power.

6.   As a result of this dramatic spiritual experience, the disciples would receive power to bear witness to the death and resurrection of Christ (cf. Acts 4:33).

7.   Their witness was to begin in Jerusalem; however, it was not to end there. It would be a global mission that would continue to expand into all Judea and Samaria, and until it reached "even the remotest part of the earth."

8.   Jesus ended His earthly ministry by blessing His disciples and then ascending bodily into heaven (Acts 1:2, 11; Luke 24:50). His ascension was the final preparatory step before He would fulfill His promise to pour out the Spirit on His waiting disciples (cf. Acts 2:33).

This overlapping of Luke and Acts demonstrates the narrative unity of the two books. It is therefore clear that Luke meant for Acts to be seen as a continuation of his gospel.

These two passages not only have several parallel features, each passage has its own unique features. Let's take a moment to note some of these special features of each account.

Concluding Luke

The last ten verses of the gospel of Luke serve as a fitting conclusion to the book (24:44-53). Throughout his gospel Luke has given his readers repeated indicators of God's concern for all peoples. For instance, he begins the book by addressing it, not to a Jew, but to a Gentile by the name of Theophilus, meaning "lover of God," thus suggesting that the message of the gospel is not for Jews only, but for Gentiles as well, and that all people of all nations can become lovers of God. Early on Luke includes the Spirit-inspired prayer of Simeon over the infant Jesus: "For my eyes have seen Your salvation, which You have prepared in the presence of all peoples, a light of revelation to the Gentiles and the glory of Your people Israel" (Luke 2:31-32). Note the inclusiveness of Simeon's prayer, how it emphasizes the idea that God's salvation is for "all peoples," Gentiles as well as Jews.

Luke's concern for the nations is indicated in other ways. For instance, while all four gospels record John the Baptist's ministry of preparing the way for Jesus, only Luke chooses to quote the words of Isaiah: "And all flesh will see the salvation of God" (3:6). Thus, by way of narrative inclusion, Luke emphasizes God's concern for all peoples. Unlike Matthew, who in his genealogy traces Jesus' lineage back to Abraham, the father of the Jews (1:2), Luke traces His lineage back to Adam, the father of all mankind (3:38), inferring that Jesus is not only the Savior of Israel, but the Savior of all nations.

Of the four evangelists, only Luke records Jesus' attempt to reach out to the mixed-raced people of Samaria, stating that He had come to "save them" (9:51-56). Further, Luke alone records Jesus' parable about the Good Samaritan, thus indicating that righteous works were not the exclusive prerogative of the Jews (10:30-36). Again, only Luke records Jesus' words, "And they will come from east and west and from north and south, and will recline at the table in the kingdom of God" (13:29). It is, therefore, fitting that Luke ends his gospel with Jesus commissioning His disciples, stating that "repentance for forgiveness of sins would be proclaimed in His name to all the nations [*panta ta ethne*], beginning at Jerusalem" (24:47).

Also fitting is Luke's record of the combination promise/command of Jesus which immediately follows His commission: "And behold, I am sending forth the promise of My

Father upon you; but you are to stay in the city until you are clothed with power from on high" (24:49). Throughout his gospel Luke presents Jesus as the Spirit-anointed Christ (3:16, 22; 4:1, 14, 17-19, 36; 5:17; 6:19; 11:20). It is therefore appropriate that he concludes his book with Jesus' promise to His disciples that they, too, would soon be clothed with the Spirit's power, and with His command that they wait for that promise. His followers would participate in His mission to the nations, not in their own strength, but, just as He had done, in the power of the Spirit. In these ways Luke's gospel clearly parallels the missiological and pneumatological emphasis of Acts.

The conclusion to Luke's gospel is open-ended (24:53), just as the book of Acts is open-ended (28:31), as if both books end anticipating something to come. The gospel concludes with the disciples anxiously waiting for the "the promise of the Father" (vv. 49-53), a promise yet unfulfilled. Something remains for Jesus' followers to do. John Michael Penney comments on the closing of Luke, connecting it with the opening of Acts:

> The narrative expectation engendered at the close of Luke, of an inaugurated world mission and Spirit-empowered ministry of word and deed by Jesus' disciples, is further intensified and illuminated by the opening chapter of the book of Acts. The first main section (1:1-2:42) is a careful statement by Luke of the ultimate reality underlying the mission or "acts" of the apostles which enables the reader to understand the material that follows.[1]

Luke thus ends his gospel by leaving the reader in a state of anticipation. Jesus has departed, leaving His emerging church with the task of completing the work He began. He also leaves them with a promise of "power from on high" so that they might rise to the task of proclaiming repentance and forgiveness of sins to all nations.

---

1   John Michael Penney, *The Missionary Emphasis of Lukan Pneumatology* (Sheffield, Eng.: Sheffield Academic Press, 1997), 64.

INTRODUCING ACTS

While Luke 24:44-53 serves as a fitting conclusion for the Gospel of Luke, Acts 1:1-11 serves as an appropriate introduction to his second volume. Luke presents Acts as a continuation of the Spirit-anointed ministry of Jesus. This is indicated by his statement in verse 1: "The first account I composed, Theophilus, about all that Jesus *began* to do and teach" (italics added). The word "began" indicates that Jesus' ministry was not completed in Luke but continued into Acts. Luke's gospel thus records the deeds of the Spirit-anointed Jesus, while Acts records the continuing work of Jesus through His Spirit-anointed witnesses. Arrington concurs:

> Acts, then, records the continuation of the ministry of Jesus. From the outset to the conclusion of His earthly ministry, all that Jesus did and said was directed and empowered by the Spirit. Luke's second volume narrates a similar story, which focuses on a Spirit-anointed community of disciples continuing to do and teach the things Jesus has begun to do and teach during this time on earth.[2]

A PROGRAMMATIC INTRODUCTION

Not only does Acts 1:1-11 serve as a narrative bridge between Luke's first and second volumes, it also serves as a programmatic introduction to the book of Acts. These eleven verses function as an introductory unit outlining Luke's intent in writing Acts. This introductory unit is comprised of a prologue and two brief episodes as follows:

- Prologue, giving a brief summary of the first volume (14)

---

2   French, L. Arrington, "Acts of the Apostles," in *The Full Life Bible Commentary to the New Testament,* eds. French L. Arrington and Roger Stronstad (Grand Rapids, MI: Zondervan Publishing House, 1999), 535.

- Jesus' last instructions to His disciples (5-8)

- Jesus' ascension into heaven (9-11).

Taken together, these three literary elements provide a programmatic introduction to the entire book, serving much as would a literary or legal abstract.[3] Abstracts normally contain three parts: (1) a statement of the context and problem to be addressed in the work, (2) an announcement of its key themes, and (3) a statement of its main point.[4] The first eleven verses of Acts serve these same three functions for the book.

KEY THEMES

In narrative form the first eleven verses of Acts announce five key missio- pneumatological themes that will characterize the work. They thus set the tone for the entire book, as Luke will continue to develop them throughout the entire book. They are as follows:

1. The Kingdom of God

> *"speaking of the things concerning the kingdom of God" (v. 3)*
> *"Lord, is it at this time You are restoring the*
> *kingdom to Israel?" (v. 6)*

Twice in verses 1-11 Luke mentions the kingdom of God (1:3, 6). This concept, in turn, provides the overarching context for the entire book of Acts. In Acts the kingdom of God is mentioned eight times (1:3, 6; 8:12; 14:22; 19:8; 20:25; 28:23, 31) and Jesus is portrayed as royalty three times (2:30; 5:13, 31). In addition, Luke

---

3   An abstract is a brief summary statement of the essential thoughts of a book, article, speech, or court record. It is used by researchers to preview the purpose and contents of a work before they delve into it more exhaustively.
4   Wayne C. Booth, Gregory Colomb, and Joseph M. Williams, *The Craft of Research,* 2d ed. (Chicago: University of Chicago Press, 2003), 219-220.

employs a narrative device known as *inclusio*.[5] In applying this
narrative device an author frames his story with key parallel
statements revealing a concept or idea that is to be superimposed
onto all that occurs between them. In Acts Luke frames the entire
book with key statements concerning the kingdom of God. Having
done this, it is no longer necessary for him to mention the kingdom
each time it is applicable. It is assumed that the kingdom of God is
the context of everything within the frame.

Notice how Luke first mentions the kingdom of God is at the
very beginning of the book:

> The first account I composed, Theophilus, about all that
> Jesus began to do and teach, until the day when He was taken
> up to heaven, after He had by the Holy Spirit given orders to
> the apostles whom He had chosen. To these He also
> presented Himself alive after His suffering, by many
> convincing proofs, appearing to them over a period of forty
> days *and speaking of the things concerning the kingdom of
> God* (1:1-3, italics added).

Then, notice how he again speaks of the kingdom of God in the very
last verse of Acts:

> And he stayed two full years in his own rented quarters and
> was welcoming all who came to him, *preaching the kingdom
> of God* and teaching concerning the Lord Jesus Christ with
> all openness, unhindered (28:30-31, italics added, see also
> v. 23).

Luke thus frames the entire book within the context of the kingdom
of God. The reader can, therefore, assume that this is the overarching
context of the entire book.

---

5   Not to be confused with inclusion-exclusion discussed in Chapter 1.

The kingdom of God represents God's sovereign rule over His creation. It is the divine agency through which He fulfills His will on the earth, and executes His mission (*missio Dei*) among the nations. John V. York has demonstrated that *missio Dei* is, in fact, the central theme of all Scripture.[6] God's mission is to redeem and call unto Himself a people out of every tribe, tongue, and nation on earth (cf. (Rev. 5:9; 7:9; 11:15).

Notice again how, in verse 3, Luke states that during the forty days between Jesus' resurrection and ascension, He spoke "of things concerning the kingdom of God." An investigation of Jesus' post-resurrection teachings reveals three key main "kingdom themes":

- Jesus as the fulfillment of the Old Testament Scriptures (Luke 24:25-27, 44-48)

- The church's commission to take the gospel to all nations (Matt. 28:18-20; Mark 16:15-16; Luke 24:47-48; John 20:21; Acts 1:8)

- The need for pneumatic empowering to accomplish the missionary task (Matt. 28:20; Mark 16:17-18; Luke 24:49; John 20:22; Acts 1:3-8).

These kingdom themes are repeated again and again through the entire book of Acts.

2. The Global Mission of the Church

> *"You shall be My witnesses both in Jerusalem, and in all Judea and Samaria, and even to the remotest part of the earth" (v. 8).*

A second key theme introduced by Luke in his programmatic introduction is the global mission of the church.

---

6   John V. York, *Missions in the Age of the Spirit* (Springfield, MO: Logion Press, 2000).

When in verse 6 Jesus' disciples asked Him if He would immediately restore the kingdom to Israel, He answered that the time of Israel's restoration was not for them to know. He then revealed to them two primary kingdom issues at hand: (1) the task of global witness and (2) the need for divine empowering to accomplish the task. In reference to the task of global missions, Jesus told His disciples, "You shall be My witnesses both in Jerusalem, and in all Judea and Samaria, and even to the remotest part of the earth." In the parallel passage in Luke, Jesus said that they would be His witnesses "to all the nations, beginning from Jerusalem" (24:47).

Acts 1:8 is a restatement of Jesus' Great Commission as recorded in each of the four gospels, each of which speak of the church's global mission (Matt. 28:18-20; Mark 16:15-18; Luke 24:46-49; John 20:20-23). Here in Acts Jesus is echoing His call for world evangelization.

Further indication of the global mission of the church is found in 1:4 where Jesus tells His disciples to wait in Jerusalem for "what the Father had promised." Other versions of the Bible translate this phrase as "the promise of the Father."[7] We ask, "To which promise of the Father is Jesus referring?" He is referring to the promise of a universal outpouring of the Spirit, including the prophecy of Joel 2:28-29. Peter confirmed this when he cited this prophecy on the Day of Pentecost (Acts 2:16-21). Jesus was at the same time referring to the prophecy of John the Baptist that Jesus would baptize believers in "the Holy Spirit and fire" (Luke 3:16). Some have further suggested that Jesus could also have been referring to God's promise to Abraham to bless "all the families of the earth" (compare Gen. 12:3 with Gal. 3:14). Stanley Horton writes,

> The story of God's dealings with His people is a step-by-step revelation: First was the promised defeat of that old serpent, the devil, through the seed of the woman (Genesis 3:15).

---

7   i.e., ASV, NKJV, and NRSV.

Next, the promise was given to Abraham, to Isaac, and to
Jacob. The chosen line was then narrowed down to Judah,
then to David. This led to Jesus, David's greater Son. Now
through Jesus would come the Promise of the Father, the gift
of the Spirit.[8]

Jesus individualized the promise in Luke 11:9-13 where He
said that the Holy Spirit would be given to any child of God who
would simply ask. The promise is thus universal in scope, extending
to every ethnic group worldwide, yet individual in application,
applying to anyone who will ask.

3. The Necessity of Pneumatic Empowering

> "He commanded them not to leave Jerusalem, but to wait for
> what the Father had promised" (v. 4)
> "But you will receive power when the Holy Spirit has come upon
> you" (v. 8)

A third key theme introduced in Acts 1:1-11 is the need for
pneumatic empowering in order to accomplish the task of global
witness. As we progress through this study we will observe how Luke
returns again and again to this all-important theme. The work of
world evangelization comes with a question: How is the work to be
accomplished? Jesus answers that it can only be accomplished with
God's help, and that help comes when one is empowered by the
Spirit.

Acts 1:1 describes the missionary method of Jesus as one of
both doing and teaching. In the Emmaus Road episode, Luke has
Cleopas describing Jesus as "a prophet mighty in deed and word"
(Luke 24:19). These two elements—anointed proclamation and
powerful demonstration—characterized the entire ministry of Jesus:

---

8   Harris, Ralph W., gen. ed., *The Complete Biblical Library*, vol. 5, *Acts* by Stanley
M. Horton (Springfield, MO: The Complete Biblical Library, 1991), 21.

"Jesus was going through all the cities and villages, teaching in their synagogues and *proclaiming* the gospel of the kingdom, and *healing* every kind of disease and every kind of sickness" (Matt. 9:35, italics added; cf. Matt. 4:23; Acts 10:38). Jesus told His disciples that they too would have the same two-fold ministry of proclamation and demonstration (Luke 9:1-2, cf. 10:8-9). Their *modus operandi*, like that of their Master, would include both "doing" and "teaching." They would, therefore, need the same anointing as He had. He thus commanded them "not to leave Jerusalem, but to wait for what the Father had promised." This same power is needed today. How can we ever hope to fulfill Christ's Great Commission without the power of the Spirit?

In his gospel, Luke tells the story of what Jesus *began* to do and teach (Acts 1:1). The story ends with His task as yet unfinished. The world remained in need of His message and His healing touch. His disciples were to be His agents, assigned to finish His work and take these blessings to the nations. Like Him, they too would need to be empowered by the Spirit. As the next chapter will reveal, empowerment for mission is the overarching theme of the entire book of Acts.

4.   The Role of the Holy Spirit in Superintending the Harvest.

"after He had by the Holy Spirit given orders to the apostles" (v. 2)

A fourth key theme introduced by Luke in his programmatic introduction to Acts is the role of the Holy Spirit in superintending the work of global harvest. In verse 2 Luke notes that Jesus "by the Holy Spirit" gave orders to the apostles. This reveals that, even after His resurrection, Jesus was still anointed by the Spirit, and that He was still being guided by the Spirit, just as He had been during His pre-resurrection ministry (Luke 4:18-19; Acts 10:38). In his gospel, Luke portrays the Holy Spirit as the One who led and directed Jesus in His work.

At the beginning of Jesus' earthly ministry we read of His being "led around by the Spirit in the wilderness for forty days" (Luke 4:1-2). Now, at the end, we see Him giving orders "by the Holy Spirit." Here is another example of Luke's use of *inclusio*, where he frames Jesus' entire ministry in the work of Holy Spirit. He was anointed with, and directed by, the Spirit at the very beginning of His ministry (Luke 3:22; 4:18-19). Then, at the end, we see Him still being guided by the Spirit (Luke 24:49; Acts 1:2-3). We can thus assume that Jesus was anointed and directed by the Spirit throughout His entire ministry.

In the same way that the Spirit superintended the ministry of Jesus, He now, in the book of Acts, superintends the missionary outreach of the church. Shelton writes:

> Luke even begins the book of Acts with a reference to the Holy Spirit superintending the work of Jesus: "He [Jesus] had given commandments through the Holy Spirit to the apostles whom he had chosen" (1:2). . . . Thus, Luke sees Jesus' entire mission as directed by the Holy Spirit. Following this same pattern established for the ministry of Jesus, Luke portrays the Holy Spirit as the director and enabler of the activities of the church."[9]

Divine guidance thus emerges as a major theme in Acts, where we often see the Spirit directing the missionary activities of the church.[10] On this subject Shelton writes:

---

9   James B. Shelton, *Mighty in Word and Deed: The Role of the Holy Spirit in Luke-Acts* (Peabody, MA: Hendrickson Publishers, 1991), 125.

10   Five clear examples in Acts of the Spirit directing the missionary enterprise of the church are as follows: (1) Philip is guided by the Spirit to witness to the Ethiopian (8:26-30); (2) Peter is directed to go to the household of Cornelius (10:9-16; 19; 11:12); (3) Paul's missionary band is led into Europe to preach the gospel (16:6-10); (4) Paul is encouraged to remain in Corinth (18:9-10); (5) Paul goes "bound by the Spirit" to Jerusalem (20:22).

In addition to the frequent references to the Holy Spirit's tactically directing the mission of the church, Luke also presents the Holy Spirit as the strategist and director of the larger mission. That is to say, the Holy Spirit not only enabled the believers to witness, but he also directed when and where the witness was to take place.[11]

Further, Jesus' command to His disciples to stay in Jerusalem until they were empowered by the Spirit (1:4-5), and His promise of power for global mission (1:8), must also be included in the "commandments" that Jesus gave "through the Holy Spirit" (1:3). These words thus represent the Holy Spirit as directing the missionary work of the church from its very onset.

5. The Eschatological Urgency of the Missionary Task

> *"Why do you stand looking into the sky?" (v. 11)*
> *"This Jesus ... will come ..." (v. 11)*

A final key theme introduced by Luke in his programmatic introduction is the theme of eschatological urgency. Listen to the words of the two angels to the disciples as they stand watching Jesus ascend into the clouds: "Men of Galilee, why do you stand looking into the sky? This Jesus, who has been taken up from you into heaven, will come in just the same way as you have watched Him go into heaven" (1:11). Sense the urgency in their voices. Time is wasting; Jesus is coming again; be about your business of receiving the Spirit and preaching the gospel to the nations! Of all the gospel writers, only Luke records this urgent exhortation of the angels.

Verse 11, with its promise of Christ's coming again, thus introduces the reader to the eschatological context of the book of Acts. This context is again emphasized in Peter's message on the Day of Pentecost. In explaining the meaning of the miraculous events that

---

11   Shelton, 126.

had just occurred, Peter declares, "But this is what was spoken of
through the prophet Joel: 'And it shall be in the last days,' God says,
'That I will pour forth of my Spirit on all mankind; . . .'" (Acts 2:16-
17).[12] He was announcing that the Last Days had arrived, and that
they would be an era characterized by the outpouring of the Spirit of
God. The Last Days were inaugurated by the first coming of Jesus,
and confirmed by the outpouring of the Spirit. They will continue
until Jesus comes again. For Luke, the Last Days were a time of great
eschatological urgency. This sense of urgency characterized the
missionary outreach of the primitive church as presented in Acts.

The disciples' question concerning the restoration of the
kingdom to Israel (v. 6) also has strong eschatological connotations,
for this restoration is yet in the future, at the time of Christ's second
coming. Jesus replied that it was not for them know the "times"
(*chronoi*) and "epochs" (*kairoi*), which were set by the Father's
prerogative. The urgent issue at hand, rather, was the evangelization
of the nations (v. 8).

Luke also uses the story of Christ's ascension to narratively
"set up" Peter's Pentecostal declaration that the Spirit had been
poured out by the ascended Christ (2:33). Christ's ascension, and His
subsequent outpouring of the Spirit, signified the completion of His
work on earth. At the same time, the Spirit's outpouring signaled the
beginning of His disciples' work, which would continue until He
came again at the end of the age. Stott writes on the subject:

> . . . although they were not to know the times or dates, what
> they should know was that they would receive power so that
> between the Spirit's coming and the Son's coming again, they
> were to be witnesses in ever-widening circles. In fact, the
> whole interim period between Pentecost and the Parousia

12   Other eschatological references in Acts include 1:11; 3:20-21; 10:42, 17:31, and
24:25. The Gospel of Luke sets the eschatological stage for Acts with many references to
Christ's second coming: 12:35-40, 41-48; 17:22-37; 18:28-30; 19:11-27; 20:9-18, 27-40;
21:7-36; 22:14-18, 28-30.

(however long or short) is to be filled with the world-wide mission of the church in the power of the Spirit.[13]

He continues,

> We have no liberty to stop until both ends have been reached [i.e., the end of time and the ends of the earth]. Indeed the two ends, Jesus taught, would coincide, since only when the gospel of the kingdom has been preached in the whole world as a testimony to all nations, only then "will the end come" (Matt. 24:14).[14]

CONCLUSION

Much like an abstract, Luke's introduction to Acts announces the main themes of the work. It also strategically and succinctly states the main point. This main point is found in Jesus' statement in Acts 1:8: "But you will receive power when the Holy Spirit has come upon you; and you shall be My witnesses both in Jerusalem, and in all Judea and Samaria, and even to the remotest part of the earth." In this verse, Luke reveals his main reason for writing the book of Acts: to show the absolute necessity of the empowering of the Holy Spirit in order to fulfill the mission of God. We will discuss this verse and its implications for world missions in detail in the next chapter.

---

13   John W. Stott, *The Message of Acts: The Spirit, the Church and the World* (Downers Grove, IL: Inter-Varsity Press, 1990), 44.
14   Ibid.

CHAPTER 3

THE INTERPRETIVE
KEY

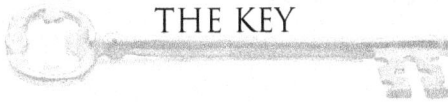

THE KEY

ACTS 1:8

*But you will receive power when the Holy Spirit
has come upon you; and you shall be My witnesses . . .
. . . in Jerusalem, and in all Judea and Samaria,
and even to the remotest part of the earth.*

In the last chapter we described the first eleven verses of the book of Acts as a narrative bridge between the gospel of Luke and the book of Acts. By overlapping the ending of his first volume with the beginning of his second, Luke created a literary connection between the two, establishing the fact that the one is indeed the continuation of the other. We noted that Acts 1:1-11 also serves as a programmatic introduction to the book, functioning much as would a literary or legal abstract. Thus, in the first eleven verses of Acts 1, Luke introduces the reader to the key themes which will dominate the book: the kingdom of God, the global mission of the church, the necessity of pneumatic empowering, the Holy Spirit's role in superintending the harvest, and the eschatological urgency of the missionary task. This chapter will focus particularly on Acts 1:8, the interpretive key to the entire book, and the key to understanding Luke's authorial intent in writing Acts. After first reviewing how interpreters have traditionally approached the text, I will suggest what I believe to be a better way.

THE TRADITIONAL WAY OF VIEWING ACTS 1:8

The great majority of commentaries on Acts correctly cite Acts 1:8 as the key or structuring verse of the book.[1] Commentators often err, however, in the way they approach the text. Rather than focusing their attention on the first and relatively more important part of the verse, they focus on the second and relatively less important part. In doing this they, in effect, get the hermeneutical cart before the horse. By concentrating their attention on the geographical progress of the church, they often ignore—or at best downplay—the first and more important part, which deals with empowerment for witness. As a result, Luke's primary intent in writing Acts is overlooked. That intent, as will be demonstrated in the following pages, was not merely to chronicle the church's westward geographical progress to Rome, as some have suggested. It was rather to call the church back to its Pentecostal and missionary beginnings, and to present a strategy for renewed missionary

---

1   e.g., F. F. Bruce, *The Book of the Acts,* rev. ed. (Grand Rapids, MI: William B. Eerdmans Publishing Co., 1988), 36-37; Stanley M. Horton, *The Book of Acts: The Wind of the Spirit* (Springfield, MO: Gospel Publishing House, 1996), 11; John R. W. Stott, *The Message of Acts: The Spirit, the Church and the World* (Leichester, Eng: Inter-Varsity Press, 1990), 43; Clifton J. Allen, ed., *The Broadman Bible Commentary,* vol. 10, *Acts—1 Corinthians,* by T. C. Smith (Nashville, TN: The Broadman Press, 1970), 19.

outreach for the church of Luke's day—and ultimately for the church of every age.

A BETTER WAY

A more profitable way of viewing 1:8 is to place the weight of emphasis on the beginning of the verse where it belongs, rather than on the end. When this is done, an entirely new perspective on the book of Acts emerges. The table below (Fig. 3.1) helps to demonstrate this truth.

COMPARISON OF THE FIRST AND SECOND PARTS OF ACTS 1:8
(FIGURE 3.1)

Acts 1:8	Character	Duration	Scope	Reveals
First Part: "But you will receive power when the Holy Spirit has come upon you; and you shall be my witnesses . . ."	Spiritual	Timeless	Paradig-matic	Luke's Purpose for Acts
Second Part: ". . . both in Jerusalem, and in all Judea and Sa-maria, and even to the remotest part of the earth."	Geogra-phical	Time bound	Program-matic	Luke's Program for Acts

Notice from the table the difference between the first and second parts of Acts 1:8. The first part is spiritual, dealing with spiritual realities; the second part is geographical, speaking of more earthly matters. The first part is timeless, and speaks to Christians of all ages; the second part is time bound, speaking only of the first thirty or so years of the New Testament church. The first part is paradigmatic, meaning that it is a model of how things ought to be for believers of every age. The second part, however, is programmatic, simply laying out a plan of advance for the book of

Acts. The first part reveals Luke's primary purpose in writing Acts. The second part reveals his programmatic outline for the book. As Roger Stronstad has pointed out, "the geographical focus of missions changes with each generation, the need for the Spirit's empowering does not."[2]

The first part of Acts 1:8 thus serves as an interpretive key to the entire book of Acts. It lays out a pattern, or motif, that will be repeated over and over throughout the work. I call this pattern Luke's *empowerment–witness motif.* As we progress through the book of Acts, we will note how every evangelistic and missionary advance of the church is preceded by one or more empowerings with the Holy Spirit in which the church is equipped for the task ahead. This is to be the church's pattern for witness during the entire Age of the Spirit, until Jesus comes again.

Those who interpret Luke's writings within the framework of the Pauline epistles would disagree with this assessment of Luke's intent in writing Acts. They would rather emphasize the soteriological aspects of the Spirit's work in believers, saying that Spirit baptism in Acts is to be viewed as initiation-conversion rather than as empowerment for witness. James D. G. Dunn, a chief proponent of this view, writes, "The high point in conversion-initiation is the gift of the Spirit, and the beginning of the Christian life is to be reckoned from the experience of Spirit-baptism."[3] Pentecostal commentator James B. Shelton disagrees with Dunn:

> Paul is addressing the ontological question: How is one a
> Christian? It is often assumed that Luke is addressing that
> same question. In reality however, this is not the issue that

---

2   Spoken in a conversation with the author in Springfield, MO, on October 29, 2003.

3   James D. G. Dunn, Baptism in the Holy Spirit: A Re-examination of the New Testament Teaching on the Gift of the Spirit in Relation to Pentecostalism Today (Philadelphia, PA: The Westminister Press, 1970), 4.

Luke is addressing here. Luke relates the events of Pentecost to answer the question, How do we witness?[4]

In a similar manner, D. Martin Lloyd-Jones sees empowerment for witness as the dominating theme of Acts. He writes, "Go through Acts and in every instance when we are told either that the Spirit came upon these men or that they were filled with the Spirit, you will find that it was in order to bear a witness and a testimony."[5] Roland Allen, Anglican missionary and missiologist of the early twentieth century, was also impressed by Luke's pneumatological and missiological intent in writing Acts:

> St. Luke makes the revelation of the Spirit clear to us by setting before us the acts of those men in the early Church whose lives were devoted to what we, today, call "missionary work." If he had dwelt upon the labors of those others who were not engaged in this special missionary work the revelation would have been less clear. . . If He had written at length of church organization we should probably have missed the revelation of the Spirit as the Spirit which labors for the salvation of the world. When by the insistence of St. Luke upon the missionary aspect, we have learnt to know the Spirit as the Spirit who inspires active zeal for the salvation of others.[6]

In Acts 1:8 Luke clearly states his reason for writing the book. He wants his readers to know that in order to fulfill Christ's command to take the gospel to all nations, the church, and each

---

4   James B. Shelton, *Mighty in Word and Deed: The Role of the Holy Spirit in Luke-Acts* (Peabody, MA: Hendrickson Publishers, Inc. 1991), 127.
5   D. Martin Lloyd-Jones, *Joy Unspeakable* (Eastbourne, Eng: Kingsway, 1984), 75; quoted in David Shibley, *Once in a Lifetime: Seizing Today's Opportunities for World Harvest* (Kent, Eng: Sovereign World, 1997), 78.
6   David Paton and David Charles H. Long, eds., *The Compulsion of the Spirit: A Roland Allen Reader* (Grand Rapids, MI: William B. Eerdmans Publishing Co., 1983.), 92-93.

believer in the church, must be empowered by the Holy Spirit. This empowering comes as a result of one's being baptized in the Holy Spirit. As we will see, the rest of Acts is Luke's Spirit-inspired endeavor to prove this thesis.

BOOK PREVIEW

In the pages that follow, we will be applying to the book of Acts the concepts we have been discussing. We will do this by examining seven key outpourings of the Spirit in Acts. Although other outpourings are mentioned—and even more are implied— these seven have special significance in the Acts narrative, and serve to set the thematic tone for the rest of the work. As we proceed through this study, we will note how each instance of the Spirit's outpouring results in powerful missionary witnesses, and contributes to Luke's missio-pneumatological intent in writing Acts. Further, we will observe how each empowering results in an ever-widening expansion of the church's missionary witness. These seven events will be discussed in detail in the following chapters; however, for now, in order that we may see them all together, and get a mental picture of what is to come, I have summarized them as follows:

1.   The First Jerusalem Outpouring (2:1-4)
         Luke begins Acts by describing two powerful outpourings of the Holy Spirit which took place in the city of Jerusalem. The first occurred on the Jewish festival of Pentecost (2:1-4). This dramatic outpouring resulted in immediate Spirit-empowered witness in the city (vv. 5-36), leading to a great harvest of souls (vv. 37-41), the birthing of a dynamic prophetic community (vv. 42-46), and vigorous ongoing witness (v. 47). With this episode Luke first illustrates his *empowerment–witness motif* introduced in 1:8. As we will see, this motif is repeated again and again throughout Acts.

2.   The Second Jerusalem Outpouring (4:31)
     A second powerful outpouring of the Spirit in Jerusalem
took place within weeks of the first. Like the first, this outpouring
resulted in immediate and powerful witness. Luke states, "they were
all filled with the Holy Spirit and began to speak the word of God
with boldness" (4:31). This outpouring is the second key example of
Luke's *empowerment–witness motif.*

3.   The Samaritan Outpouring (8:14-17)
     A third key outpouring occurred about three years later in
the nearby city of Samaria. As a result of persecution, the church in
Jerusalem was scattered. One of the scattered, a Spirit-filled disciple
by the name of Philip, found his way to the city of Samaria where he
preached the gospel with dramatic results. When the apostles in
Jerusalem heard about these events, they sent Peter and John to
Samaria to pray with the new believers to receive the Holy Spirit. As
a result of these believers receiving the Spirit a new center of
missionary outreach was born, and the gospel continued to spread to
the region and beyond (8:40; 9:31).

4.   The Damascene Outpouring (9:15-17)
     A fourth key outpouring of the Spirit occurred a couple of
years later in the Syrian city of Damascus. It was there that Saul of
Tarsus (later to become Paul the apostle) was filled with the Spirit
(9:17-18). True to his missio-pneumatic intent in writing Acts, Luke
notes that, Paul "immediately . . . began to proclaim Jesus in the
synagogues" of Damascus (vv. 20-22). By including this account in
his narrative, Luke prepares the reader for the apostle's Spirit-
anointed missionary career that will dominate the last sixteen
chapters of Acts. This outpouring is yet another example of Luke's
empowerment–witness motif.

5.   The Caesarean Outpouring (10:44-47)
     The showering of the Holy Spirit on the household of
Cornelius in Caesarea is the fifth key outpouring of the Spirit in Acts.

As with each of the other six outpourings, this one also resulted in witness. First, it bore witness to the church in Jerusalem that the door of salvation had been opened to the Gentiles. Secondly, it served to empower the newly-birthed Caesarean church for its own Spirit-empowered missional witness. The message of this account is thus twofold: not only can Gentiles receive the gospel and be saved; they can also, through the empowering of the Holy Spirit, become full participants in the mission of God to proclaim the gospel to the nations.

6.   The Antiochian "Outpouring" (13:1-4)

        A sixth key "outpouring" of the Spirit occurred in Antioch, Syria, about seventeen years after the Day of Pentecost. This powerful move of the Spirit in the church in Antioch resulted in the launching of Paul and Barnabas into their first missionary journey. Luke includes this special move of the Holy Spirit to reemphasize the Spirit's role in empowering and directing the missionary enterprise of the early church. As before, Luke's *empowerment–witness motif* is clearly demonstrated.

7.   The Ephesian Outpouring (19:1-7)

        The Ephesian Outpouring is the final outpouring of the Spirit in the book of Acts. It occurred about 25 years after Pentecost, and demonstrates how God continued to empower the church for witness many years after the initial outpouring of the Spirit on the Day of Pentecost. As a result of this outpouring, the Ephesian church is empowered for witness, and the gospel spreads quickly to the entire province of Asia. As before, Luke's missio-pneumatic intent in writing Acts is evidenced.

CONCLUSION

        In the following seven chapters we will take a more detailed look at each of these seven outpourings of the Holy Spirit. We will closely observe how Luke consistently presents Spirit baptism as an empowering experience given to believers to enable them to participate in the mission of God. In the next chapter we will investigate in greater detail the first outpouring of the Holy Spirit, which took place in Jerusalem on the Day of Pentecost. We will see how this outpouring resulted in immediate and powerful witness in Jerusalem and beyond, and how it introduces and establishes Luke's *empowerment–witness motif*, which he continues to emphasize throughout the entire book of Acts.

PART TWO

A MISSIO-
PNEUMATOLOGICAL
LOOK AT ACTS

CHAPTER 4

THE FIRST
JERUSALEM
OUTPOURING

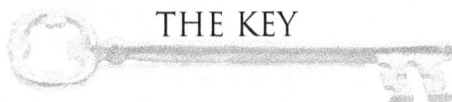

THE KEY

ACTS 1:8

But you will receive power when the Holy Spirit has come upon you;
and you shall be My witnesses ... in Jerusalem ...

THE FIRST JERUSALEM OUTPOURING

ACTS 2:1-4

When the day of Pentecost had come, they were all together in one place.
And suddenly there came from heaven a noise like a violent rushing wind,
and it filled the whole house where they were sitting. And there appeared to

them tongues as of fire distributing themselves, and they rested on each one
of them. And they were all filled with the Holy Spirit and began to speak
with other tongues, as the Spirit was giving them utterance.

Some people organize their day with a checklist. On a piece of paper they list the tasks they hope to complete on a given day. Then, as they move through their day, they put a check mark by each item as it is completed. In Acts 1:8, Jesus gave the emerging church a sort of "missiological checklist" when He told His disciples that they would be His witnesses "in Jerusalem, and in all Judea and Samaria, and even to the remotest part of the earth." The book of Acts is the divinely-inspired story of the church's completing that checklist. It is, however, much more than that. It is the story of how the emerging church was enabled to accomplish the task in Pentecostal power. The first item on their list was the proclamation of Christ in Jerusalem. Before they attempted that task, however, they were to wait until they had been "clothed with power from on high" (Luke 24:49). Then, and only then, were they to start working on their check list.

In this chapter we will examine the first outpouring of the Holy Spirit in Acts, where the disciples were clothed in the power of the Spirit. This outpouring took place in the city of Jerusalem on the Day of Pentecost (2:1-4). It enabled the church to complete the first item on its checklist—the evangelization of Jerusalem. It also helped to prepare the church for its subsequent assignments of reaching Judea, Samaria, and the ends of the earth (1:8).

As we look into this powerful outpouring of the Spirit, we will ask and seek to answer three important questions:[1] First, we will ask, "What happened?" A maxim of interpreting biblical narrative is that one must know exactly *what* happened before he can determine *why* it happened. We will, therefore, begin our investigation of this, and each of the other outpourings of the Spirit in Acts, by focusing our attention on the actual events of that particular outpouring,

---

1   In the chapters that follow, we will ask these same three questions about the six other key outpourings of the Holy Spirit in Acts.

seeking to determine precisely what happened. Once we have done this, we will ask a second question, "What resulted?" Here, we will seek to discover the cause and effect relationships, if any, between the outpouring of the Spirit and the missionary advance of the church. Then, once we have determined what happened and what resulted, we will ask a final question, "So what?" That is, what implications do these truths have for the church of the twenty-first century? With these things in mind, let's now turn our attention to the events of the Day of Pentecost.

THE FIRST JERUSALEM OUTPOURING

Pentecost was a special day on the Jewish religious calendar, being one of three annual pilgrim festivals in which all males living in and around the city of Jerusalem were required to attend.[2] The feast of Pentecost occurred each year on the fiftieth day after Passover—*pentecostos* meaning "fiftieth" in the Greek language. The day was also known by other names. It was sometimes called the Feast of Weeks (Exod. 34:22), since it occurred a week of weeks after the Passover feast. It was also known as the Feast of Harvest (Exod. 23:16) and the Feast of First Fruits (v. 19), because on Pentecost the people brought the first fruits of their barley harvest and presented them as an offering to God. Because Pentecost occurred in the warmer season of the year when travel was easier, thousands of Palestinian and Diaspora Jews attended. In Luke's words, they came from "every nation under heaven" (Acts 2:5).

The outpouring of the Spirit on the Day of Pentecost likely occurred in late May or early June of A.D. 28.[3] Two possibilities exist concerning the actual venue of the event. Popularly, it is believed that

---

2   The other two pilgrim festivals were Passover and Tabernacles.

3   This determination is made in the following manner: Accepting 6 B.C. as the year of Jesus' birth, and knowing that He began His public ministry at the age of 30 years (Luke 3:23), and that His ministry continued for about three and one half years, we deduce that He was crucified in A.D. 28. The Day of Pentecost occurred 50 days later in the same year.

the 120 were in an "upper room" in some undisclosed location in the city of Jerusalem when the outpouring occurred. This was possibly the same room where Jesus ate the Passover meal with His disciples (Luke 22:12). Acts 1:13 is cited as proof for this view: "When they had entered the city, they went up to the upper room where they were staying; . . ." This verse, and the one following, tells us that the eleven, along with a group of other select individuals, were residing in this second story room. It was there that the disciples also spent time praying (v. 14) and conducting church business (vv. 15-26).

A second possible location for the outpouring of the Spirit was on the temple mount in Jerusalem. This location seems more plausible than the first for several reasons: First, Luke tells us that, after Jesus' ascension, the disciples "were continually in the temple praising God" (Luke 24:53). They apparently continued this practice for at least a time, even after the outpouring of the Spirit on the Day of Pentecost (2:46; 3:1). Since the outpouring occurred during the celebration of the Feast of Weeks, it is also probable that the disciples spent much of their time at the temple with the other Jewish worshipers. Further, Luke indicates that the outpouring occurred at "the third hour of the day" (2:15), or nine o'clock in the morning. This was the time of the morning prayers (3:1). The disciples, being faithful Jews, would likely have attended these prayers.

Another indication that the outpouring of the Spirit occurred in the temple is the size of the crowd present on that day. Luke tells us that, following Peter's message, "about three thousand souls" were added to the church (2:41). These three thousand converts in all probability represented only a small percentage of the throng who had gathered to observe the wonders and hear the preaching of Peter. If the three thousand represented ten percent of the crowd, then 30,000 people were gathered. If the three thousand represented twenty percent of the crowd, then 15,000 were present. The only venue in Jerusalem that could have accommodated such a large crowd is the expansive Court of the Gentiles in the temple (see

Fig. 4.1). It has been estimated that the Court of the Gentiles could accommodate over two hundred thousand worshipers.

COURT OF THE GENTILES
(FIGURE 4.1)

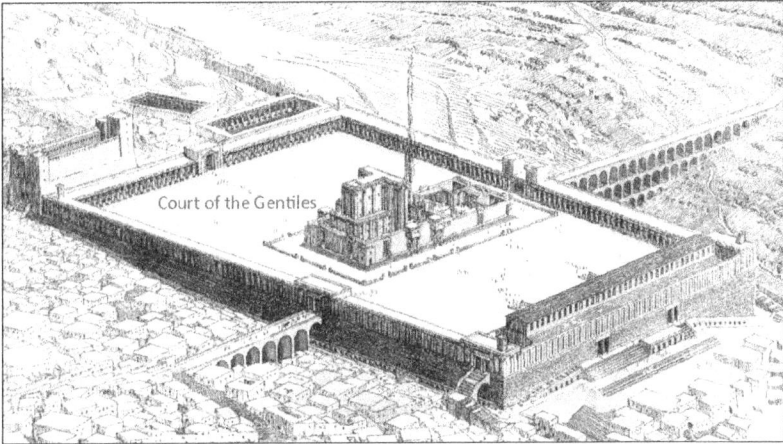

Some have objected to this view, noting Acts 2:2, which says that the disciples were sitting in a "house" when the Spirit was poured out. However, in his two volume work, Luke cites both Jesus and Stephen as referring to the temple as a "house" (Luke 19:46; Acts 7:47). The Greek word translated "house" (*oikon*) can also carry the generic meaning of "building." Wherever the outpouring occurred, it was a never-to-be-forgotten event.

There are two possible ways of viewing the outpouring of the Spirit on the Day of Pentecost: as an *epochal-universal* outpouring and also as a *local-vocational* outpouring.

AN EPOCHAL-UNIVERSAL OUTPOURING

Scholars have long commented on the epochal nature of the outpouring. For example, James D. G. Dunn has written,

"Pentecost is a new beginning—the inauguration of the new age, the age of the Spirit—that which had not been before."[4] Clark H. Pinnock agrees, "Pentecost was an act of God that initiated the new age. . . . It was a historical turning point and the beginning of the end-time harvest."[5] John R. W. Stott writes that Pentecost was "the final act of the saving ministry of Jesus before the Parousia."[6] He continues, "In this sense the Day of Pentecost is unrepeatable . . ."[7] There is, then, a sense in which the Pentecost event was a once-and-forever, never-to-be-repeated occurrence. It ushered in a new epoch of God's dealing with mankind—the Age of the Spirit. Pentecost, understood in this way, is one of seven pivotal events in salvation history.[8] As such, it is not repeatable. It was at Pentecost that a new era in God's dealing with mankind was inaugurated.

Viewed this way, the outpouring of the Spirit on the Day of Pentecost was also a universal outpouring, at least potentially. Quoting Joel, Peter noted that the Spirit had been poured out on "all mankind" (Acts 2:17, cf. Joel 2:28). The gift of the Spirit was thus made available to every person in every nation of the world. It would no longer be limited to certain individuals or certain occasions. Two powerful implications flow from this fact: First, because the Holy Spirit has been poured out universally, every person can be saved. Note how Peter ends his quotation from the prophecy of Joel with

---

4   James D. G. Dunn, *Baptism in the Holy Spirit: A Re-examination of the New Testament Teaching on the Gift of the Spirit in Relation to Pentecostalism Today*, (Philadelphia, PA: The Westminister Press, 1970), 44.

5   Clark H. Pinnock, *Flame of Love: A Theology of the Holy Spirit* (Downers Grove, IL: InterVarsity Press, 1996), 142.

6   John R. W. Stott, *The Message of Acts: The Spirit, the Church and the World* (Downers Grove, IL: Inter-Varsity Press, 1990), 61.

7   Ibid.

8   Those seven pivotal events are: (1) The creation of man (Gen. 1:26-27); (2) The call of Abraham (Gen. 12:1-3); (3) The giving of the Law and the Mosaic Covenant (Exod. 19:5-8, 20:1-17); (4) The Davidic Covenant (2 Sam. 7:4-17); (5) The death and resurrection of Christ (Matt. 27-28; Mark 15-16; Luke 23-24; John 18-20); (6) The outpouring of the Spirit at Pentecost (Acts 2:1-4); (7) The second coming of Christ (Rev. 19:11-16)

the glad pronouncement: "And it shall be that everyone who calls on the name of the Lord will be saved" (Acts 2:21). Because the Holy Spirit has been universally given, any person, of any ethne, from anywhere on earth, can call on Jesus' name and be given a new heart and a new spirit within (Ezek. 36:22, 27). Thus, all nations have become God's chosen people.

There is a second implication of the universal outpouring of the Spirit: Not only can everyone who calls upon the Lord be saved, but everyone who calls on His name for salvation can also participate fully in the mission of God. In anticipation of the Pentecostal outpouring, Jesus promised that the Holy Spirit would come upon believers to empower them to be His witnesses (1:8). No matter how weak or marginalized by others, anyone who receives the Pentecostal baptism can thus become an effective participant in reaching the nations with the gospel.

A final point. Not only does the outpouring of the Spirit on the Day of Pentecost have soteriological and missiological implications, it also has powerful eschatological meaning. Again quoting Joel, Peter pointed out that the outpouring of the Spirit served as proof that the last days had arrived: "'And it shall be in the last days,' God says, 'that I will pour forth of My Spirit on all mankind . . .'" (2:17). It is significant that Peter, by the Spirit's inspiration, changed Joel's phrase "after this" (2:28) to "the last days." Some have proposed that the outpouring of the Spirit at Pentecost marked the beginning of the last days. It seems more plausible that the last days began with the appearance of Jesus, the Messiah. Be that as it may, the Pentecostal outpouring, including Peter's pronouncement, was a clear indication that the last days had indeed dawned and that they would be an age characterized by a universal outpouring of the Spirit on all mankind.

A LOCAL-VOCATIONAL OUTPOURING

While the outpouring of the Spirit on the Day of Pentecost can be properly viewed as a once-and-forever epochal event, it can also be correctly viewed as a local-vocational outpouring.[9] Stott recognizes this two-fold characteristic of the day: "Pentecost," he writes, "was the inauguration of the new era of the Spirit . . ." In the same paragraph he also describes Pentecost as "the first 'revival'" in history, when the people of Jerusalem became "vividly aware of [God's] immediate, overpowering presence."[10] The outpouring at Pentecost was *local* since it was an outpouring of the Spirit on a local congregation of believers—the church in Jerusalem. It was *vocational* since it enabled this local church to fulfill its Christ-given vocation of being His witnesses in Jerusalem (1:8). In this sense, the outpouring of the Spirit on the Day of Pentecost is like any other outpouring of the Spirit in Acts. Stronstad notes that "the gift of the Spirit to the disciples on the day of Pentecost is not an isolated and unique event. It is but one of several occasions, both prior to and following Pentecost, when people were filled with the Spirit."[11]

Let's now look more closely at this "First Jerusalem Outpouring" and ask the question: How does this outpouring of the Holy Spirit help to fulfill Luke's *empowerment–witness motif*

---

9   Roger Stronstad, *The Charismatic Theology of St. Luke,* (Peabody, MA: Hendrickson Publishers, Inc., 1984), 23, 24. Here Stronstad discusses the "vocational motif" of the gift of the Spirit in Old Testament historiography. He defines this vocational giving of the Spirit as the Spirit's endowment of the appropriate skills needed for leaders to fulfill their divine calling. These skills include, among other things, knowledge, perception, craftsmanship, leadership, military prowess, and physical strength. According to Stronstad, Luke applies this same vocational motif to the charismatic ministry of Jesus as depicted in his gospel, and to the primitive church as depicted in Acts. He discusses these things further from a Christological and pneumatological point of view in *Spirit, Scripture and Theology: A Pentecostal Perspective,* pages 150-152 and 159-167 respectively.

10   Stott, 61.

11   Stronstad, 53.

established in 1:8? We will do this by asking our three questions: "What happened?", "What resulted?" and "So what?"

WHAT HAPPENED?

Exactly what happened on the Day of Pentecost? Let's see if we can recreate the scene. Jesus had commanded His disciples to "stay in the city" until they were empowered by the Holy Spirit (Luke 24:49; Acts 1:4-8). In obedience to His command, they had returned to Jerusalem, where they gathered together a group of about 120 committed followers of Jesus, and began their time of waiting (1:12). Their days were filled with prayer and praise, sometimes in the upper room (Acts 1:14) and sometimes in the temple courts (Luke 24:53). Keen expectation must have filled their hearts. Finally, on the Day of Pentecost the120 gathered in the temple at the hour of prayer. Weaving their way through the mass of worshipers, they found their way to the appointed place—possibly under one of the covered porticoes to one side of the expansive Court of the Gentiles. There, they sat down together, and, as the festive crowds milled around them, they began their prayers. Then it happened . . .

Suddenly from heaven there came a sound like the roar of a raging gale. Instinctively, the people's eyes shot skyward. Some reeled in fright and astonishment. Others clasped their hands over their ears to mute the deafening sound. And yet, strangely, though there was the howling sound of a mighty wind, there was no accompanying movement—no blowing of the hair, no fluttering of the hemlines. The anomaly confounded the people's senses. Then, as suddenly as it had begun, the roar stopped, soon to be followed by a second great wonder. Luke describes it like this: "And there appeared to them tongues as of fire, distributing themselves, and they rested on each one of them. . . ." (v. 3). Stanley M. Horton elaborates: "A mass of flames appeared above the heads of the whole group. Then it broke up, and a single tongue that looked like a flame of fire settled on the head of each one of them, both men and women."[12] This supernatural phenomenon may have continued for several minutes. The onlookers stood motionless, eyes wide, mouths agape. And yet, God was not yet finished with that day's mighty works.

From all around, those who had heard the great "sound" rushed into the Court of the Gentiles (v.6). The gathering mob quickly grew into thousands. As the bewildered crowd marveled, God worked yet another wonder: "They were all filled with the Holy Spirit and began to speak with other tongues, as the Spirit was giving them utterance" (v. 4). To some it seemed as if these poor Galileans were drunk or demented. "They are full of sweet wine!" someone shouted (v. 13). However, as the people listened more closely, one by one they began to hear these uneducated Galileans speaking in their own native languages (v. 6). Travelers from Arabia heard them speaking Arabic; those from Egypt heard them speaking Coptic; visitors from Rome heard them speaking Latin, and so it went (vv. 7-11). What were they saying? They were joyously proclaiming the mighty deeds of God! (v. 11). Dumbfounded, the people began to ask one another, "What does this mean?" (v. 12).

In answer to their inquiry, Peter, who just a few weeks earlier had fearfully denied even knowing Jesus (Luke 22:54-62), stood with the eleven and began to boldly proclaim His name (Acts 2:14ff). As a result of the mighty demonstrations of God's presence and power, and Peter's Spirit-inspired proclamation of the gospel, three thousand repented of their sins and came to know Christ as Lord and Savior (v. 41). That same day they were baptized in water and added to the church—and possibly, judging from the context, baptized in the Holy Spirit (vv. 38-41).

---

12   Stanley M. Horton, *The Book of Acts: The Wind of the Spirit* (Springfield, MO: Gospel Publishing House, 1996), 30.

WHAT RESULTED?

The immediate results of the disciples being filled with the Spirit on the day of Pentecost were twofold: The first was a remarkable inner change that occurred in the 120 disciples themselves. The second was the powerful Spirit-anointed witness that went out to the city of Jerusalem. Roland Allen describes the first result:

> In the Acts there is revealed a most curious change in the conduct of the apostles before and after Pentecost. . . . Before Pentecost the apostles are represented as acting under the influence of an intellectual theory; after Pentecost they are represented as acting under the impulse of the Spirit"[13]

He explains further, "The coming of the Spirit at Pentecost was the coming of a missionary Spirit . . . [and He] stirred in the hearts of the disciples of Christ a great desire to impart that which they had received."[14] Thus, according to Allen, the coming of the Spirit "revealed to them the need of men for that which he alone could supply."[15] With the reception of the Spirit a new urgency and inner boldness came into the lives of the disciples—boldness to fearlessly and aggressively proclaim Christ to their home city, along with an overwhelming desire to do it.

The most conspicuous result of the disciples being filled with the Spirit, however, was outward witness rather than inward transformation. This witness included immediate powerful Spirit-inspired proclamation of the gospel, followed by astonishing evangelistic success. According to J. B. Lawrence, after Pentecost,

---

13   David Paton and Charles H. Long, eds., *The Compulsion of the Spirit: A Roland Allen Reader* (Grand Rapids, MI: William B. Eerdmans Publishing Co., 1983), 76.
14   Ibid.
15   Ibid, 91.

> [The disciples] were as men moved beyond themselves by a
> mighty inward impulse. . . . the passion of divine urging was
> within their souls, and the freedom of a divine utterance was
> upon their lips. They had been told to wait for power and the
> power had come. The Spirit, like a mighty breath from
> heaven, had filled them with divine energy. Their tongues
> were touched with the fire from off the altar, and when they
> began to speak the thousands who were present at the feast
> felt the influence of the divine enthusiasm and were moved
> by the divine presence.[16]

The disciples' reception of the Spirit resulted in a dramatic
outbreak of Spirit-inspired proclamation, both in unlearned
languages and in the local vernacular, each of which served as an
impressive witness to the gathered multitude. The first occurrence of
prophetic speech was the 120 disciples' speaking in tongues "as the
Spirit was giving them utterance" (Acts 2:4). In verses 16-18 Peter
identified this inspired tongues speech as prophecy by declaring to
the crowd, "*This* [the disciples' speaking in tongues] is *that* [the
fulfillment of the prophecy of Joel, which said] . . . your sons and
your daughters shall prophesy" (KJV, italics added). Peter thus
identified speaking in tongues as the fulfillment of Joel's prediction
that all of God's people would someday be prophets.

Luke says that they were "speaking of the mighty deeds of
God" in the native languages of their listeners (v. 11). Some have
interpreted this activity of the disciples as Spirit-anointed praise to
God.[17] A closer examination of the text, however, reveals that their
words were not directed to God but to the multitude. It was, rather,
Spirit-inspired proclamation. The New International Version more
appropriately translates this phrase, "we hear them declaring the

---

16   J. B. Lawrence, *The Holy Spirit in Missions* (Atlanta, GA: Home Missions Board
of the Southern Baptist Convention, 1947), 39-40.
17   i.e., French L. Arrington, *The Acts of the Apostles: An Introduction and
Commentary* (Peabody, MA: Hendrickson Publishers, 1988), 22.

wonders of God." Menzies comments, "Luke's account highlights the missiological significance of the Pentecostal gift . . . the gift of the Spirit enables the disciples to communicate with people 'from every nation under heaven' (Acts 2:5). The product of this divine gift should not be understood simply as praise directed to God. It is, above all, proclamation."[18]

The Greek word here translated "speaking of" is *laleo*. It is the generic word for speaking (i.e., "to utter words") and can be used in various ways and contexts. A survey of Luke's use of the word, however, reveals that, in the vast majority of cases, he uses it for declaration or proclamation, that is, in words addressed directly to people. In Acts, when the context dictates, *laleo* is often translated into English as "preached" (8:25, 11:19, 13:42, 14:25, 16:6). A typical use of the word is 4:31: "And they were all filled with the Holy Spirit and *spoke* the word of God boldly" (italics added). This is not to say that there is no such thing as Spirit-directed praise. There certainly is, as is indicated in Luke 1:64,[19] 1 Corinthians 14:15-17, and Ephesians 5:18-19. The point is, that here, in accordance with his *empowerment–witness motif* laid out in 1:8, Luke presents this Spirit-inspired speech as miraculous proclamation of the wonders of God in the languages of the gathered Gentile nations. Whether praise or proclamation, the purpose of the speaking in tongues was undeniably witness. Otherwise, why would the Spirit have caused them to speak in the languages of those who had gathered to see what was happening?

The fact that Luke points out that the pilgrims had gathered from "every nation under heaven," and that the disciples spoke in Gentile languages as a result of their being filled with the Spirit, is significant to Luke's missio-pneumatological intent in writing Acts. Stott points out, "Although all the nations of the world were not

---

18   Robert P. Menzies, *Empowered for Witness: The Spirit in Luke-Acts* (Sheffield, Eng: Sheffield Academic Press, 2001), 177.
19   In all of Luke-Acts, Luke 1:64 is the only time the word *laleo* is used for praise.

present *literally*, they were *representatively*. For Luke includes in his list descendants of Shem, Ham and Japheth, and gives us in Acts 2 a 'Table of the Nations' comparable to the one in Genesis 10."[20]

The outpouring of the Spirit at Pentecost has clear missiological purpose. The implication is clear: God was demonstrating His global purposes and empowering His church so that the gospel could be preached in power to every nation under heaven. Concerning the disciples' speaking in Gentile tongues, Don Richardson comments,

> Seen in the context of Jesus' ministry and His clearly articulated plans for the whole world, the bestowal of that miraculous outburst of *Gentile* languages could have only one main purpose: to make crystal clear that the Holy Spirit's power was and is bestowed with the specific goal of the evangelization of all peoples in view.[21]

Beyond the speaking in tongues, there was a second example of prophetic witness immediately following the disciples' reception of the Spirit at Pentecost. This example is found in what is commonly known as Peter's Pentecost "sermon." However, it was not a sermon at all, at least not in the traditional sense. It was, rather, a prophetic utterance—a *pneuma* discourse.[22] Byron Klaus comments, "Peter then experienced a most important result of empowerment through Spirit baptism: He became the mouthpiece of the Holy Spirit . . ."[23] Horton, more detailed in his explanation, writes,

> Still anointed by the Spirit, [Peter] raised his voice and proceeded to "utter forth" or speak out to them. The word

---

20   Stott, 68.
21   Don Richardson, *Eternity in Their Hearts,* rev. ed. (Ventura, CA: Regal Books, 1984), 198-199.
22   A *pneuma* discourse is a Spirit-inspired address. It is characterized by spiritual illumination, keen insight, and persuasive power.
23   Byron D. Klaus, "The Mission of the Church," in *Systematic Theology,* rev. ed., Stanley M. Horton, ed. (Springfield, MO: Logion Press, 1995).

used for this speaking [*apephthengxato*] is from the same
verb used of the utterance in tongues of Acts 2:4
[*apophthengesthai*]. It suggests that Peter spoke in his own
language (Aramaic) as the Spirit gave utterance. In other
words, what follows is not a sermon in the ordinary sense of
the word. . . . Rather, this is a spontaneous manifestation of
the gift of prophecy (1 Cor. 12:10; 14:3).[24]

Peter interprets the events of Pentecost missiologically.
Standing before the crowd (which figuratively represents all the
nations of the earth), Peter takes his "sermon text" from Joel 2:28-32,
thus setting the tone for his entire message to follow. In his message
he explains the meaning and importance of what had just occurred.[25]
The outpouring of the Spirit was a graphic sign that the last days had
indeed commenced, and that this latter day outpouring was not for
Jews only but for all mankind. Therefore, every person, whether Jew
or Gentile, who will call on the name of the Lord will be saved (v. 21).
This promise alludes to Jesus' earlier promise that the disciples would
be empowered to be witnesses "to the remotest part of the earth"
(1:8).

Pentecost is Luke's first example in Acts of his
empowerment–witness motif. The disciples' reception of the Spirit at
Pentecost resulted in divine empowerment, which in turn resulted in
immediate and effective witness. As a result of this Spirit-empowered
witness, those who heard Peter's words were deeply affected: "Now
when they heard this, they were pierced to the heart, and said to
Peter and the rest of the apostles, 'Brethren, what shall we do?'" Peter
answered that they were to repent of their sins, and be baptized as a
sign of that repentance, then they too could receive the gift of the
Spirit (Acts 2:37-38). This they did, and three thousand people were
added to the church. Reasoning from the context, it is probable that

---

24   Horton, 37.
25   Just as in Luke 4:18-19 Jesus explained what happened to Him when He was
anointed by the Spirit at His baptism (3:21-22).

those who were saved were also filled with the Spirit.[26] This is evidenced by the fact that a dynamic witnessing community was created, for "the Lord was adding to their number day by day those who were being saved" (2:47).

So What?

We now ask our third question about this passage: "So what?" So what if the disciples were filled with the Spirit at Pentecost? So what if Peter preached prophetically and a great number of people were saved? What do these first century events mean to us today as twenty-first century believers?

The events of Pentecost, as we shall see with greater and greater clarity as we proceed through this study, are both programmatic and paradigmatic. To be *programmatic*, a narrative episode must point forward to the unfolding events of the narrative. Thus, when we say that the events of Pentecost are programmatic, we mean that those events establish a significant pattern that will be repeated throughout the work. To be *paradigmatic* an episode must have normative features which apply to all of Gods' people at all times and in all cultures. Therefore, when we speak of the outpouring of the Spirit at Pentecost as being paradigmatic, we mean that we can expect the Holy Spirit to be poured out today in the same way, and with the same general outcomes, as on the Day of Pentecost, as Jesus first indicated in 1:8.

With these things in mind, it becomes apparent that we, as Christians living in the twenty-first century, do indeed have much to learn from what happened on the Day of Pentecost. I will briefly mention four important lessons:

---

26   Peter told them if they would repent and be baptized they would receive the gift of the Holy Spirit. They repented and were baptized. The implication is, therefore, that they also received the gift of the Spirit. James Shelton concurs with this view, stating, ". . . it is apparent that the new converts of 2:38 were empowered for ministry." *Mighty in Word and Deed,* 130.

THE NECESSITY OF PNEUMATIC EMPOWERING

First, we learn of the absolute necessity of pneumatic empowering in fulfilling Christ's Great Commission. Twice Luke records Jesus' command to His disciples that they were not even to attempt missionary work until they had first been empowered by the Holy Spirit (Luke 24:49; Acts 1:4-5). Jesus then promised them sufficient power for the task. This power would come "after that" the Holy Spirit had come upon them (1:8, KJV). The disciples obeyed Jesus' command explicitly, and on the Day of Pentecost they were empowered for the task ahead. In like manner, if we today expect to effectively execute Christ's command to preach the gospel to all nations, we must first obey His equally binding command to "stay in the city" until we are "clothed with power from on high."

THE HOLY SPIRIT IS THE SOURCE

Another lesson we learn from the outpouring at Pentecost is that the Holy Spirit is the source of missionary empowering. Much is said today about missionaries empowering national leaders and churches to do the work of ministry. This is an important issue; however, there is an even more fundamental empowerment issue—the divine empowering that results from one's being baptized in the Holy Spirit. This fact is dramatically illustrated in the story of Pentecost.

THE PATTERN OF PENTECOST

Thirdly, from the Pentecost account we learn how we can expect that empowering to occur. According to the pattern of Pentecost, Spirit baptism is received suddenly, powerfully, personally, pervasively, and verifiably, just as it happened with the 120. Those seeking Spirit baptism are not to anticipate a bland or insipid experience, but a powerful life-changing encounter with God.

INNER CHANGE, EVANGELISTIC EFFECTIVENESS

Finally, we learn something about the results we can expect if we, too, will be empowered by the Spirit. If will allow the Spirit to fill and empower us, we can expect the same dramatic inner change and marked increase in evangelistic effectiveness that was experienced by the disciples at Pentecost.

CONCLUSION

In this chapter we have examined the outpouring of the Spirit on the Day of Pentecost. We have discovered that, although it was an epochal-universal outpouring, it was also a local-vocational outpouring. As a result of being filled with the Spirit, the church in Jerusalem became a powerful witnessing force. In the next chapter we will discover that a second outpouring of the Spirit occurred in Jerusalem, an outpouring that was, in some ways, even more dramatic and powerful than the first. And, as we shall see, like the first, the second outpouring resulted in powerful Spirit-anointed witness.

CHAPTER 5

THE SECOND
JERUSALEM
OUTPOURING

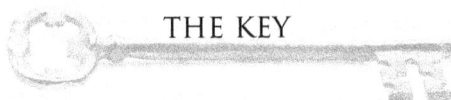

THE KEY

ACTS 1:8

*But you will receive power when the Holy Spirit has come upon you;
and you shall be My witnesses … in Jerusalem …*

THE SECOND JERUSALEM OUTPOURING

ACTS 4:31

*And when they had prayed, the place where they had gathered
together was shaken, and they were all filled with the Holy Spirit
and began to speak the word of God with boldness.*

It cannot be denied, the Day of Pentecost was a watershed moment in salvation history. It inaugurated a glorious new day in God's dealings with mankind. The enabling presence of His Spirit, which for ages had been reserved for select individuals and special occasions, was now freely poured out on all. Now, because of Pentecost, anyone can call on the name of the Lord and be saved (2:21), and through a subsequent baptism in the Holy Spirit, these same people can be empowered to become full participants in God's redemptive mission to the nations (1:8). While all of this is true, we must not forget that the Pentecostal outpouring was also an outpouring of the Spirit on a specific local congregation of believers in a specific place to accomplish a specific purpose—the evangelization of Jerusalem.

A Second Jerusalem Outpouring

It is significant, therefore, that a second outpouring of the Holy Spirit occurred in Jerusalem a few weeks after the first. Luke reports this outpouring with an economy of words: "And when they had prayed, the place where they were gathered together was shaken, and they were all filled with the Holy Spirit and began to speak the word of God with boldness" (4:31). What shall we think of this second outpouring of the Holy Spirit in Jerusalem? In answering this question, we will, as we did with the first outpouring, ask three questions:

What Happened?

After the Day of Pentecost the newly Spirit-empowered church became a powerful witnessing force in the city of Jerusalem. Luke notes that "the Lord was adding to their number day by day those who were being saved" (2:47). By the time of the Second Jerusalem Outpouring, the number of disciples had grown from about three thousand men and women to "about five thousand men" (4:4), plus women and children. This evangelistic success (as well as the stir caused by healing of the lame man at the Beautiful Gate) greatly disturbed the Jewish authorities. They, therefore, summoned the apostles, and threatened them, warning them "to speak no longer to any man in [Jesus'] name" (v. 17). Then they released them.

Upon being released, the apostles returned to the company of disciples and reported what had happened to them. Stronstad locates the "place" (4:31, *topos*) of their gathering as the temple mount.[1] After the apostles gave their report to the congregation, they all "lifted up their voices to God with one accord" and began to pray. As they prayed, they acknowledged God's sovereign rule over the affairs of men (vv. 24-28), and they entreated Him to take note of the threats of the Jewish leaders and to give them boldness to continue their witness for Jesus in the face of these threats (v. 29). They concluded their prayer by calling upon God to confirm the truth of His gospel by extending His hand to heal the sick, and to perform signs and wonders in the name of Jesus (v. 30). It was then that it happened, suddenly, as on the Day of Pentecost . . .

The stone pavement began to tremble under their feet. The vibrations migrated upward through their legs and into their bodies, causing their very insides to quiver. The Holy Spirit was again manifesting His presence in their midst, just as He had done a few weeks earlier on the Day of Pentecost. In was second theophany— another powerful manifestation of God's power and presence. Just as had happened on the Day of Pentecost, "they were all filled with the Holy Spirit."[2] Some were filled for the first time; others were refilled with the Spirit—for they had already been filled on the Day of Pentecost or at some other time since then. And, just as on the Day of Pentecost, those who were filled with the Spirit were empowered

---

1   Roger Stronstad, *The Prophethood of All Believers: A Study of Luke's Charismatic Theology* (Irving, TX: ICI University Press, 1998), 54. See 6:13-14 and 7:49-50 where the temple is called a "place," also *topos*.
2   Compare 2:4 and 4:31 where the wording in the Greek is exactly the same (*epleestheesan pantes*).

for witness, for, says Luke, "they began to speak the word of God with boldness."

It is quite probable that the great majority of the thousands of believers living in Jerusalem was present on this occasion. Stronstad notes:

> . . . the antecedent for the phrases "they had gathered together" and "they were all filled with the Spirit" is ultimately Luke's earlier reference in the same chapter to 5000 men who have believed (Acts 4:4). Thus, Luke informs Theophilus and all subsequent readers of his narrative that more than 5000 men were filled with the Holy Spirit.[3]

If there were, in fact, over five thousand men, plus their wives and children, present on this occasion, what a powerful prayer meeting it must have been. What a triumphant roar must have risen from their midst!

WHAT RESULTED?

The results of this Second Jerusalem Outpouring mirrored those of the first outpouring at Pentecost: great spiritual energy was released resulting in powerful and persuasive witness in word and deed. Verse 33 describes that witness: "And with great power the apostles were giving testimony to the resurrection of the Lord Jesus, and abundant grace was upon them all." Luke identifies the source of the apostles' "great power" (*dunamei megal*) as "abundant grace" (*charis megal*). The context reveals that the source of that abundant grace was the empowering presence of the Holy Spirit (v. 31).

Going from that place, these freshly-empowered believers "filled Jerusalem with [their] teaching" (5:28). Three times in this same chapter Luke connects bold witness with the coming of the Spirit (vv. 13, 29, 31). What was their message? It was the

---

3   Ibid.

resurrection of the Lord Jesus (v. 33). Another notable result of this outpouring of the Spirit was the reinvigorating of the dynamic community life that was born on the Day of Pentecost (vv. 34-37; cf. 2:44-47).

Although we are calling this outpouring of the Spirit the Second Jerusalem Outpouring, it was probably just one of many such outpourings that must have occurred throughout Jerusalem in the days following the initial outpouring at Pentecost. As a result of these repeated outpourings of the Spirit, the witness of the church in Jerusalem continued to prosper and gain momentum (5:12-16).

These outpourings also served a second important purpose. Not only were the Jerusalem Christians empowered for further witness in the city, they were also being prepared for the persecution and scattering that was soon to occur. When the persecution did come, they would be ready to spread the word into Judea, Samaria, and beyond. By almost immediately including in his narrative a second outpouring of the Spirit in Jerusalem, Luke reinforces his missio-pneumatic intent in writing Acts, and again illustrates the importance of the Spirit's empowering for effective witness.

So What?

What lessons can be learned from this episode that can be applied to the church today? In answering this question, another must first be asked: Why did Luke include this episode in his narrative in the first place? Its inclusion in Acts is significant. This significance is shown by the fact that several weeks have passed since the Day of Pentecost, and yet, this is only the seventh episode Luke chose to recount.[4] Luke, under the guidance of the Holy Spirit, included this incident in his narrative because it so clearly advanced his authorial intent as stated in 1:8: "You will receive power when the Holy Spirit has come upon you; and you shall be My witnesses . . ."

---

4   See Appendix 1.

Luke wanted his readers to know that one outpouring—or one infilling—of the Spirit is not enough, no matter how powerful or how dramatic it may have been.

No one can deny the greatness and power of the outpouring of the Spirit on the Day of Pentecost, and the impact it had on the lives of those who received the Spirit. However, the effects of even that experience, as powerful and life changing as they were, could not sustain the disciples' spiritual lives and ministries indefinitely. To retain their spiritual fervor, and to maintain the dynamic witness mandated by Jesus, they had to experience fresh infillings of the Spirit. These repeated infillings were experienced both corporately, as with the gathered community of believers (4:31), and individually, as with Peter (4:8). Neither can we rely on past experience in the Spirit to sustain our ministries today. We, like the early disciples, must seek and experience repeated infillings of the Spirit.

OTHER ACTS OF SPIRIT-EMPOWERED WITNESS IN JERUSALEM

While this study is limited to seven key outpourings of the Spirit in Acts, there are many other examples of Spirit-initiated witness in the book. Before proceeding to the third outpouring in Chapter 6, let's look briefly at seven other acts of Spirit-empowered witness that occurred in Jerusalem, each as a result of the various outpourings of the Spirit in the city.

1.   Witness at the Beautiful Gate

The healing of the lame man at the Beautiful Gate (3:1-10), and Peter's subsequent prophetic address (vv. 11-26), are further examples of Spirit-empowered witness resulting from the outpouring of the Spirit at Pentecost. In this story, Luke is citing a specific example of the apostles' ministry, which he had earlier described in more general terms in 2:43: "Everyone kept feeling a sense of awe; and many wonders and signs were taking place through the apostles."

Peter's declaration to the lame man, "What I do have I give to you" (3:6), is a confession concerning the power of the Spirit he had received at Pentecost. His sermon which follows is his second *pneuma* discourse in Acts, the first occurring on the Day of Pentecost. The context of the sermon, including the manifestation of the gift of healing that preceded it, indicates that Peter was operating under the Spirit's influence. Shelton writes that in this, as well as in other passages

> ... where authoritative speaking occurs, but the Holy Spirit is not explicitly named as the agent behind the speaking, the work of the Spirit is often implied by the presence of particular items in the context [such as a healing miracle]. Luke does not feel compelled to preface every statement of the faithful with a reference to the Holy Spirit. He is content to let the reader understand this implicitly. Once he mentions the presence of the Holy Spirit in a speaker, Luke does not repeat this each time he introduces one of that individual's speeches. He considers the first reference as adequate ... [5]

Shelton further notes that in 1:8 Luke establishes a dominant theme for the book, and that this theme serves as a precedent for all subsequent witness in Acts:

> In the first chapter of Acts, Luke establishes this precedent, "You shall receive power when the Holy Spirit has come upon you; and you shall be my witnesses" (v. 8). .... Thus the dominant theme of Luke's pneumatology in this presentation of the early church is: "We are witnesses of these things, and so is the Holy Spirit" (5:32).[6]

---

5   Shelton, 146-147.
6   Ibid., 147.

Again, as on the Day of Pentecost, Peter's Spirit-anointed witness results in a great harvest of souls: "But many of those who had heard the message believed; and the number of the men came to be about five thousand" (4:4).

2.   Witness to the Jewish Leaders

Another example of Spirit-empowered witness in Jerusalem is Peter and John's witness to the Jewish religious authorities (4:5-22). Luke characteristically prefaces Peter's words by noting that he was "filled with the Holy Spirit" (v. 8). Again, as on the day of Pentecost, Peter's infilling with the Spirit results in a clear Spirit-anointed proclamation of the saving power of Jesus' name (vv. 10-12). And once again, Luke carefully attributes the apostles' witness to the empowering work of the Holy Spirit in their lives.

3.   A Conspiracy is Unmasked

Not only did the empowerment of the Spirit enable the church to withstand persecution from without (4:5-22), it also enabled it to counter malfeasance from within, as is illustrated in the story of Ananias and Sapphira (5:1-11). Because he was full of the Spirit, Peter was able to discern the hand of Satan in the couple's conspiracy (vv. 3, 9). Luke, according to pattern, shows that the end result of Peter's Spirit-prompted action is witness: "And great fear came over the whole church, and over all who heard of these things" (v. 11).

4.   Ongoing Witness in Jerusalem

In 5:12-16 Luke summarizes and reveals the nature of the church's ongoing witness in Jerusalem. It was a witness characterized by miraculous signs and wonders, unity, and continued Spirit-anointed public proclamation "among the people," resulting in "all the more believers in the Lord, multitudes of men and women, [being] constantly added to their number" (v. 14). Luke presents this witness as the continued consequence of the empowering by the Spirit at Pentecost and in subsequent outpourings of the Spirit in

Jerusalem. By now, the church's witness has expanded beyond the city of Jerusalem into the surrounding areas: "Also the people from the cities in the vicinity of Jerusalem were coming together, bringing people who were sick or afflicted with unclean spirits, and they were all being healed" (v. 16).

5. Imprisonment, Release, and Witness

     The apostles' miraculous deliverance from jail and subsequent bold witness is yet another example of how the empowering presence of the Spirit enabled the church in Jerusalem to fulfill its evangelistic mandate (5:17-42). The angel's command to the apostles to "go, stand and speak to the people in the temple the whole message of this Life" (v. 20), clearly reflects Luke's *empowerment–witness motif*, as does the apostles' Spirit-garnered courage to continue preaching, even after being harassed and threatened by the Jewish authorities (vv. 21-31). Peter attributed their witness to the work of the Spirit in their lives: "And we are witnesses of these things: and so is the Holy Spirit, who God has given to those who obey Him" (v. 32).

6. A Spirit-Guided Decision

     The apostles' appointment of seven men to aid them in the church's ministry to the widows (6:1-7) also bears witness to Luke's missio-pneumatic intent in writing Acts, for in Luke's view, it is a Spirit-guided, mission-oriented undertaking. The dispute concerning the care of the hellenized widows threatened to subvert the church's evangelistic mission. The apostles, still operating under the Spirit's influence, formulate a plan (much as happens again at the Jerusalem Council in 15:1-29). Seven Spirit-filled men are chosen and commissioned to serve in this capacity, thus freeing the apostles to focus on prayer and ministry of the word (vv. 5-6).

     As usual, Luke makes it very clear that these seven men were filled with the Holy Spirit (v. 3). He also uses this episode to introduce two men who will later give powerful Spirit-anointed witness in Acts, Stephen and Philip. True to his intent in writing, Luke notes that, as a result of this action, "the word of God kept spreading; and the number of the disciples continued to increase greatly in Jerusalem, and a great many of the priests were becoming obedient to the faith" (v. 7).

7. Stephen's Spirit-Empowered Witness

A final example of Spirit-empowered ministry in Jerusalem is the ministry of Stephen, one the seven chosen to help with the neglected widow issue (6:1-8:1). He, along with the six others chosen, is identified as "a man full of faith and the Holy Spirit" (v. 5). He is further described as being "full of grace and power" (v. 8). His witness in Jerusalem was marked by anointed proclamation and miraculous demonstrations of God's power (v. 8). Luke notes that, because of his powerful prophetic witness, his distracters "were unable to cope with the wisdom and the Spirit with which he was speaking" (v. 10). When he was captured and brought before the Jewish Council, he again witnessed with power (7:1-53). His message is yet another example of a *pneuma* discourse and a fulfillment of Jesus' prophetic promise of Luke 21:12-15. Even in martyrdom Stephen ministered in the Spirit's power. He is again described as being "full of the Holy Spirit" (v. 55). His testimony served as a powerful witness to the inhabitants of Jerusalem. More importantly, it profoundly affected a young Pharisaic Jew by the name of Saul, who participated in Stephen's martyrdom (v. 58). As Saul witnessed the grace with which Stephen died, he was deeply moved. This experience contributed to his eventually becoming a follower of Christ. By including this detail in his narrative, Luke prepares the reader for Saul's eventual conversion, Spirit baptism, and missionary ministry. Luke's *empowerment–witness motif* is clearly reflected in each of these seven accounts.

CONCLUSION

As a result of two powerful outpourings of the Spirit in Jerusalem, the church quickly became a powerful evangelistic force in the city, with thousands of new members being added to its ranks. Jesus, however, had said that the church was to be His witness, not in Jerusalem only, but in "Jerusalem and in all Judea and Samaria . . ." In the next chapter we will see how that witness spread from Jerusalem into Judea and Samaria by the Spirit's power. We will also see how the apostles acted to ensure that the gospel would continue to spread in Pentecostal power from Samaria "to the remotest part of the earth."

- CHAPTER 6 -

THE
SAMARITAN
OUTPOURING

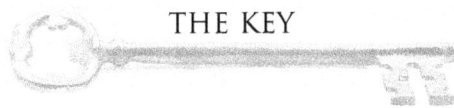

THE KEY

ACTS 1:8

*But you will receive power when the Holy Spirit has come upon you;
and you shall be My witnesses . . . in all Judea and Samaria . . .*

THE SAMARITAN OUTPOURING

ACTS 8:14-18

*Now when the apostles in Jerusalem heard that Samaria had
received the word of God, they sent them Peter and John, who came
down and prayed for them that they might receive the Holy Spirit.
For He had not yet fallen upon any of them; they had simply been
baptized in the name of the Lord Jesus. Then they began laying
their hands on them, and they were receiving the Holy Spirit.*

In Chapters 4 and 5 we investigated two powerful outpourings of the Holy Spirit in Jerusalem which resulted in a mighty surge of evangelism in the city and in the surrounding areas. These same outpourings prepared the church for what was to come. Unknown to the followers of Jesus, a frenzy of violent persecution would soon break out against the church in Jerusalem. The persecution would be so intense that many believers would have to flee for their very lives. In this chapter we will focus our attention on the expanding evangelistic outreach that resulted from that persecution, and from the outpouring of the Spirit in Samaria that facilitated an even wider outreach. We are referring to this outpouring as the Samaritan Outpouring. It is the third of the seven key outpourings of the Spirit.

One of those scattered by the persecution was Philip, whom Luke has already introduced in 6:5 as one of the seven Spirit-filled "deacons." Luke says that Philip "went down to Samaria and began proclaiming Christ to them" (8:5). His Spirit-empowered evangelistic ministry in Samaria resulted in a great soul harvest. In this chapter we will look briefly at that successful campaign. We will, however, focus most of our attention on the outpouring of the Spirit that followed when the apostles visited the work. The apostles' decision to send Peter and John to Samaria demonstrates the high value they placed on every believer receiving the Spirit in order that he or she may be a witness for Christ as promised in 1:8.

GEOGRAPHICAL AND CHRONOLOGICAL RELATIONSHIPS

To more fully grasp the context surrounding the seven key outpourings in Acts, it is helpful to understand the geographical and chronological relationships of these events. The geographical relationships are shown in the map below (Fig. 6.1). The chronological relationships are shown in Figure 6.2. In this chart the dove symbol represents the outpouring of the Spirit, the "speaking head" symbol represents the Spirit-empowered proclamation that resulted, and the number and arrow symbols represent the number of the outpouring and the forward advance of the church that followed. The times are approximate.

Note the significant time spans between each outpouring. In reading Acts one tends to get the impression that the events of the first few chapters happened over a relatively short period of time. Figure 6.2, however, gives us a more accurate picture of the time gaps between the individual outpourings—months and years rather than days and weeks.

SEVEN KEY OUTPOURINGS OF THE SPIRIT IN ACTS
(FIGURE 6.1)

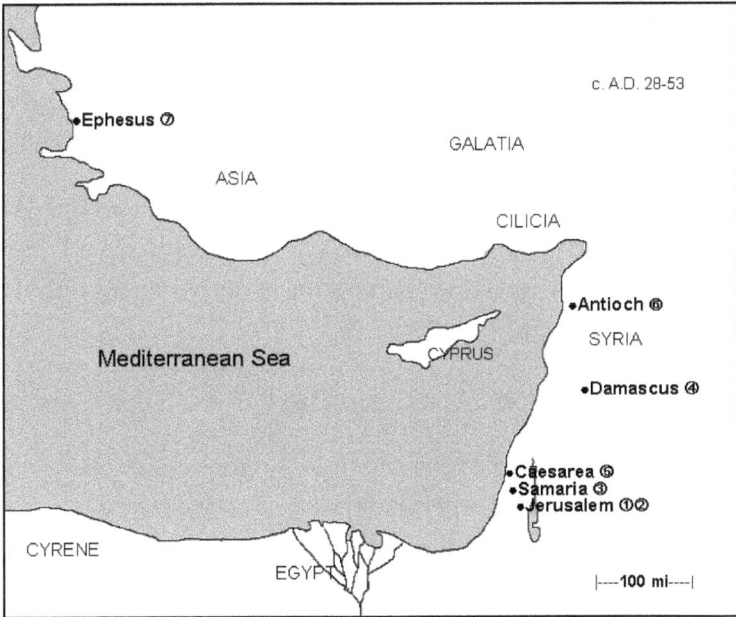

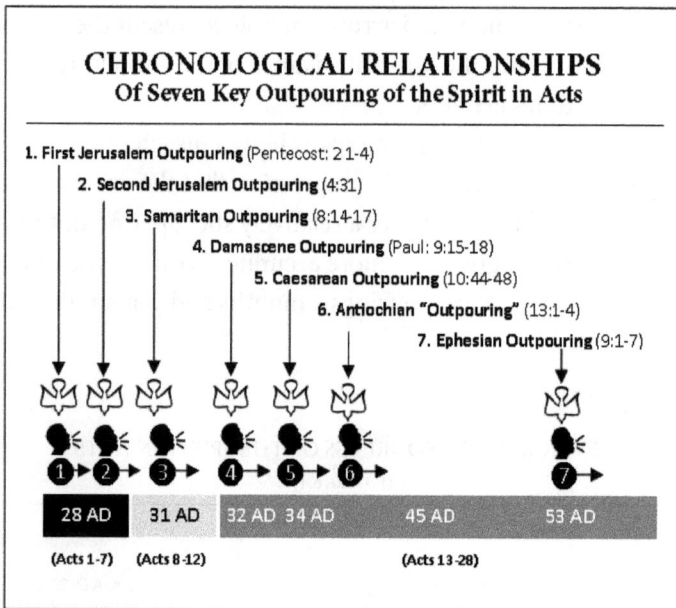

Figure 6.2

in Luke's thinking. When we consider the fact that he choe very few episodes to tell the story of the church's beginnings, we more fully realize the significance of each outpouring in furthering his authorial intent.

THE SAMARITAN OUTPOURING

The Samaritan Outpouring (8:14-17) took place about three years after the initial outpouring of the Spirit on the Day of Pentecost. After Pentecost, the newly Spirit-baptized believers filled Jerusalem with their teaching about the resurrected Jesus (5:28). In a very short time, thousands of new disciples populated the ranks of the burgeoning church. The influence of the church began to reach into the surrounding areas (5:16), and yet, three years after Pentecost, the overall geographical expansion of the church seemed to have stalled—at least temporarily.

Some scholars, such as Don Richardson, have suggested a lack of willingness on the part of the apostles to obey Jesus' command to take the gospel to the nations. He writes, "Hundreds of millions of Christians think that Luke's Acts of the Apostles records the 12 apostles' obedience to the Great Commission. Actually it records their reluctance to obey it."[1] Richardson's assessment, however, seems to be a misreading of the text. It is true, there were geographical and cultural barriers that had to be crossed in order for the church to fulfill Jesus' global mandate, and humans are, by nature, reluctant to cross either. Before the early church could fulfill its obligation to evangelize the ethne, long-held racial and cultural prejudices needed to be broken down, and new more inclusive mental paradigms formulated. However, in emphasizing these processes, Richardson overstates his case, and, I believe, misses Luke's point: Because the disciples had been filled with the Spirit they were able to learn the hard missiological lessons they might otherwise never have learned.

Since Luke doesn't specify, we can only speculate as to why, after three years, the church remained in Jerusalem. Was there a misunderstanding (or at least an underdeveloped understanding) of the mission? Probably so. Was the church undergoing strategic regrouping? This could also have been the case. Had they been providentially delayed? This is also possible. Whatever the reason, Luke voices no criticism towards the church on the matter. He simply says, "A great persecution began against the church in Jerusalem" (8:1). It seems more plausible that Satan, rather than God, was the author of the persecution, since it involved Christians being beaten, imprisoned, and even killed. It is only because the church was endowed by the Spirit that it was able to triumph in spite of

---

1   Don Richardson, *Eternity in their Hearts,* rev. ed. (Ventura, CA: Regal Books, 1981), 197.

persecution. This, after all, was Jesus' promise to the disciples in Luke 12:11-12. Citing this same passage John Michael Penney notes, "Thus, in times of persecution and opposition, fillings of the Spirit are sovereign-enablements for bold proclamation, as seen with Peter (Acts 4:8), Stephen (8:55), Paul (13:9), and the disciples at Pisidian Antioch (13:52). The word of God thereby spreads despite persecution . . ."[2] The message of Acts 8:1-4 is not what God can do providentially through persecution that the Holy Spirit cannot do through empowering willing believers, but rather, what the Holy Spirit can do in and through disciples who, although severely persecuted, have been filled with the Holy Spirit.

Whatever interpretation one may place on these events, the witness of the church was about to move out of the confines of the city of Jerusalem. Jesus had said that, as a result of receiving the Holy Spirit, the church would be His witness "in Jerusalem, *and* in all Judea and Samaria, . . ." (1:8). The time had come for the church to expand its witness.

WHAT HAPPENED?

The story of the Samaritan outpouring can be characterized as a play in three acts, with Act I entitled "The Scattering"; Act II, "The Ingathering"; and Act III, "The Outpouring." Let's look at how this exciting story developed.

ACT I: THE SCATTERING (8:1-3)

In Jerusalem, from the very beginning, the church's ministry was carried out in an atmosphere of smoldering resentment and continual harassment. Soon, however, this harassment was to burst into a blaze of full-blown persecution.

---

2   John Michael Penney, *The Missionary Emphasis of Lukan Pneumatology* (Sheffield, Eng.: Sheffield Academic Press, 1977), 113.

As the Day of Pentecost dawned, the bitter memory of the disturbances caused by Jesus of Nazareth remained fresh in the minds of the Jewish religious leaders. They thought that by plotting His execution, they had rid themselves of this Galilean pest. Then arose the persistent rumors of His resurrection, and before they had time to respond to these rumors, the extraordinary events of Pentecost, followed by the church's stunning evangelistic success. Fear of losing hold of the reins of power grew with each passing day. This fear began to manifest itself in escalating acts of antagonism against the church.

The first overt act came after the healing of the lame man at the Beautiful Gate, and the massive defection that followed. Seeing what was happening right under their very noses—in the temple courts themselves!—the Jewish elite became angry. Capturing Peter and John they imprisoned, threatened, and released them, hoping this would end the matter (4:5-22). However, when the two apostles returned to the company of believers and gave their report, another powerful outpouring of the Spirit occurred (4:31), resulting in an even more potent witness to the city.

Day by day the church grew stronger. And, all the while, apprehension grew in the hearts of the Jewish leaders. Luke says, "They were filled with jealousy" (5:17). "What will it take to stop these people?" they wondered. The followers of Jesus, however, continued to spread their teachings throughout Jerusalem. Tension continued to mount until it had reached a flash point.

The spark that ignited the flames of full-blown persecution was the Spirit-anointed ministry of Stephen. Spurred on by a young Jewish rabbi of Cilician birth named Saul of Tarsus, and enraged by Stephen's inspired apologia (7:2-51), a group of radical Jews, known as the Synagogue of the Freedmen (6:9), moved into action. They seized Stephen and stoned him to death. At that moment the pent up rage that had been thus far held in abeyance, suddenly erupted into a firestorm of savage persecution against the church. Luke says, "On that day a great persecution began against the church in Jerusalem"

(8:1). At the forefront of the persecution was Saul, who "began ravaging the church, entering house after house, and dragging off men and women, he would put them in prison" (v. 3).

As a result of this outbreak of violent persecution, the Jerusalem Christians "were all scattered throughout the regions of Judea and Samaria" (8:1).[3] The apostles, however, for reasons unstated, remained in Jerusalem, taking upon themselves the full brunt of the persecution.

This violence against the church did not, however, have the effect the Jewish authorities had hoped for. In fact, it had just the opposite effect. Instead of snuffing out the new movement, it served only to scatter it throughout the entire region. Like stamping on a fire, the embers of evangelism were scattered round about, only to start new fires in various places. Luke puts it like this: "Those who were scattered went everywhere preaching the word." Thus the curtain closes on Act I of our drama.

ACT II: THE INGATHERING (8:4-13)

As Act II begins, Luke focuses his readers' attention on Philip, one of the scattered. This is not Philip, the apostle (Luke 6:14), for he had remained in Jerusalem with the other eleven, but Philip, the "deacon" (sometimes called Philip, the evangelist) was previously introduced by Luke as one of the seven Spirit-filled men chosen to serve tables (6:5). Luke tells us that Philip "went down to the city of Samaria and began proclaiming Christ to them" (8:5).

Philip's ministry among the Samaritans was a milestone in the history of Christian missions, for it was the church's first post-Pentecostal venture into cross-cultural missions. Although the Samaritans lived in the region adjacent to and just north of Judea, they had, through the centuries, developed their own separate cultural identity. The Jews despised them and considered them half-

---

3   Note how Acts 8:1 echoes Acts 1:8, both of which speak of witness in Judea and Samaria.

breeds and heretics, and, in response, the Samaritans hated the Jews
because for their pride and arrogance.

Philip's charismatic ministry in Samaria was, nevertheless, a
breathtaking success. Luke states that "the crowds with one accord
were giving attention to what was said by Philip, as they heard and
saw the signs which he was performing" (v. 6). Demoniacs were set
free, cripples threw away their crutches and walked, many were saved
and baptized in water, and joy filled the city. Then, in a stroke of
unsuspected drama, the most powerful witch doctor in the region
confessed Christ and was baptized in water. What happened in
Samaria was a wonderful "revival" by almost anyone's standards!
And so ends Act II, with a great ingathering of souls from among an
outcast people group. The "internationalization" of the church had
begun.

ACT III: THE OUTPOURING (8:14-17)

The curtain rises on Act III with the apostles in Jerusalem,
where they receive a report from Samaria concerning a great harvest
of souls that was taking place under the ministry of Philip. How they
must have rejoiced when they heard the encouraging news. Upon
closer consideration, however, they noticed that something was
disturbingly amiss in the Samaritan revival. It was, in fact, something
so serious that it needed their immediate attention— none of the
Samaritan converts were being filled with the Spirit. The apostles,
therefore, chose Peter and John and sent them to Samaria so they
could pray with the new believers "that they might receive the Holy
Spirit," for, as the text adds, "He had not yet fallen upon any of them"
(v. 16). It is likely that, upon arriving in Samaria, the apostles took
time to encourage and instruct the Samaritans. They then laid hands
on them and, one by one, "they were receiving the Holy Spirit"
(v. 17), just as had the believers at the first and second outpourings of
the Spirit in Jerusalem.

WHY DID IT HAPPEN AS IT DID?

In addition to the question, "What happened?" we must, at this point, insert another important question. Why did the Samaritan Outpouring happen as it did? This second question suggests four others:

- Why did the scattered Jerusalem disciples do as they did?

- What qualified Philip to do what he did?

- Why did the apostles send Peter and John to Samaria?

- Why did Peter and John lay hands on the Samaritan believers?

As we seek answers to these questions, it is important to remember that these events occurred approximately three years after the Day of Pentecost. It is also significant that this story is contained in only the twelfth, thirteenth, and fourteenth episodes (and only the second episodic series) in the book of Acts.[4] Again, this insight emphasizes the episodic character of Acts, and highlights how selective Luke was in choosing the events he included in his book. Imagine, out of three full years of dynamic ministry, Luke has only included fourteen events in his story thus far. Each event was chosen to advance his purpose in writing the book. We will therefore seek to answer each of the above four questions in light of Luke's intent in writing Acts as revealed in Acts 1:8.

WHY DID THE SCATTERED JERUSALEM DISCIPLES DO AS THEY DID?

In other words, what gave the persecuted Christians the moral and spiritual fortitude needed to preach the gospel under such trying circumstances? We must bear in mind that these scattering believers were political and religious refugees, fleeing for their very

---

4   See Appendix 1

lives. Luke writes, "Saul began ravaging the church, entering house after house, and dragging off men and women, he would put them in prison" (8:3). Years later Paul would testify, "I persecuted this Way to the death, binding and putting both men and women into prisons" (22:4-5). The early believers had been threatened, abused, and driven from their homes. Some had been separated from family members. Many had lost their businesses, their possessions, and their lives' savings. A twentieth-century account can help us to understand how these first century refugees must have felt:

In the summer and fall of 1994 the world watched as hundreds of thousands of traumatized refugees streamed out of the small central African country of Rwanda into the surrounding countries. We were witnessing one of the great human tragedies of history, as one ethnic group tried to totally eradicate another. In his book, *Rwanda: A Walk Through Darkness . . . Into Light*, Carl Lawrence describes a scene that was repeated many times during those horrific days:

> Farmers who ordinarily would have been in their fields evaluating their crops, mothers who should have been in front of their little houses building fires to cook breakfast, children who normally would have been laughing and talking while putting on their best clothes to go to school were instead coming out of the bushes carrying on their backs or heads everything they owned. As they stared at the river, they realized they now would lose everything. There was no question about what they must do. They set their meager belongings at their feet and stood at the river, the last obstacle before reaching some sort of safety. They didn't know what was on the other side, but they knew it couldn't be as bad as what they had just left.[5]

---

5   Carl Lawrence, *Rwanda: A Walk Through Darkness . . . Into Light* (Gresham, OR: Vision House Publishing, Inc., 1995), 62.

Those first century believers who fled Jerusalem must have experienced much of the same trauma these Rwandan refugees would experience centuries later. With this in mind, it is all the more amazing what these first Christian refugees did. In the midst of great persecution and personal deprivation, they "preached the word wherever they went" (8:4, NIV).

What enabled them do this? What gave them the moral courage and will to preach the gospel under such trying circumstances? Luke's answer is simple and direct: they had been filled with the Spirit, and that ongoing experience made a radical difference in their response to persecution. Their filling could have happened during one of the two Jerusalem outpourings, either on the Day of Pentecost, when 120 were filled with the Spirit, or a few weeks later when five thousand plus were filled, or at some other undisclosed time. Jesus had promised power to witness, and Luke is showing us how that power is effectual, even under the most difficult circumstances.

WHAT QUALIFIED PHILIP TO DO WHAT HE DID?

Of all of those who "went around preaching the word," Luke singles out Philip and focuses the readers' attention on his ministry in the city of Samaria. He describes Philip's ministry as being charismatic in character—evidenced by effective Christ-centered proclamation (v. 5, cf. v. 12), miraculous signs, the exorcism of demons, and the healing of paralytics (vv. 6-7). As a result of this Spirit-anointed ministry, many came to know Christ, were baptized in water, and there was "much rejoicing in the city" (v. 8). The question then arises, what qualified Philip for this ministry? From where did he receive such power and authority? After all, he was not one of the twelve apostles. For Luke the answer is clear: Philip had been empowered by the Holy Spirit.

Luke artfully sets up the story of Philip's ministry in Samaria (as well as Stephen's ministry in Jerusalem) by earlier relating the episode of the seven deacons in 6:1-7. He purposively points out that

Philip, Stephen, and the other five were all men "of good reputation, full of the Spirit and wisdom" (v. 3). By implication, Philip, like Stephen, was also "full of grace and power" (v. 8). It was because he was full of the Spirit that he was able to minister with such power in Samaria. The ministry of Philip is yet another example of Spirit-empowered missional witness in Acts.

WHY DID THE APOSTLES SEND PETER AND JOHN TO SAMARIA?

Why, upon hearing about the revival in Samaria, did the apostles send Peter and John to Samaria? Luke answers our question for us: They sent them "that they [the new Samaritan believers] might receive the Holy Spirit. For He had not yet fallen upon any of them . . ." (vv. 15-16). Although many Samaritans were being saved, healed, and delivered from demonic bondage, there was a vital missing ingredient in the Samaritan revival: none were being filled with the Spirit—and this fact greatly concerned the apostles. It was such a critical issue in their minds that they dispatched the two most prominent of their group, Peter and John, to attend to the situation.

The issue at hand was continued witness. The Samaritans had received the gospel, they had experienced the miracle working power of God, they had been baptized in water, and they had experienced the joy of knowing Christ. And yet, as great as these blessings were (and we in no way want to underemphasize any of them), in Luke's estimation, they were not enough. Those who receive the gospel must do more than revel in their new-found joy; they must become effective proclaimers of that same gospel to others. In accordance with Jesus' plan, the gospel was first preached in Jerusalem. It had now penetrated the regions of Judea and Samaria—but it must not stop there. It must go from there to the ends of the earth. If the Samaritans were to become full participants in Christ's mission, they, too, had to be empowered by the Spirit, just as were the disciples on the Day of Pentecost.

Menzies agrees with the assessment that Luke viewed the gift of the Spirit received by the Samaritans as the same gift as was received by the 120 at Pentecost. He states that it was "a prophetic endowment granted to the converted which enabled them to participate effectively in the mission of the church."[6] He writes further:

> It is abundantly clear from Luke's choice of language in Acts 8:15-19 that he considered the pneumatic gift received by the Samaritans to be identical to the Pentecostal gift. The terms descriptive of the Samaritan experience are also associated with Pentecost: . . . [*lambanein pneuma hagion*] ('to receive', 2:38; 8:15, 17, 19, cf. 1:8); . . . [*epipiptein to pneuma to hagion*] ('to come upon', 8:16; 11:15).[7]

The apostles sent Peter and John to Samaria because they believed that the church there must be more than just a fellowship of blessed believers (as are too many Pentecostal and charismatic churches today), it must be a prophetic witnessing community, just like the church in Jerusalem. The new Samaritan believers, therefore, needed the same empowering experience. J. Rodman Williams writes about the Samaritan Outpouring:

> The result [of the Samaritans receiving the Spirit] was that the people not only entered into salvation through Philip's ministry, but they also became a witnessing community through the ministry of Peter and John. Since Jesus had said to His disciples, "You shall be my witnesses in Jerusalem and in all Judea and Samaria and to the ends of the earth," His reference to Samaria could well signify not only a people to

---

6   Robert P. Menzies, *Empowered for Witness: The Spirit in Luke-Acts* (Sheffield, Eng: Sheffield Academic Press, 2001), 211.
7   Ibid.

whom witness is to be made but also by whom it is to be continued.[8]

We conclude that the Samaritan's reception of the Holy Spirit was in accordance with the Lukan pattern: It was a gift of the Spirit subsequent to salvation for the purpose of empowerment for witness in and beyond the borders of Samaria, and "even to the remotest part of the earth" (1:8). Shelton agrees: "It is safe to assume that here among the Samaritans, as elsewhere in Luke-Acts, the activity of the Holy Spirit reflects inspired witness of the power of God."[9]

WHY DID PETER AND JOHN LAY HANDS ON THE SAMARITAN BELIEVERS?

Verse 17 says, "Then they [Peter and John] began laying their hands on them, and they were receiving the Holy Spirit." But why? Why did the two apostles lay hands on the Samaritan believers on this occasion? Some, like Bruce, have suggested that they laid hands on them because "some special evidence may have been necessary to assure the Samaritans, so accustomed to being despised as outsiders by the people of Jerusalem, that they were fully incorporated into the new community of the people of God."[10] While it is without question that the Samaritans were encouraged by the apostles' acceptance of them into the community of believers, this explanation does not adequately explain the reason why hands were laid on them.

---

8   J. Rodman Williams, *Renewal Theology: Systematic Theology from a Charismatic Perspective, in Three Volumes in One*, vol. 2, *Salvation, the Holy Spirit and Christian Living* (Grand Rapids, MI: Zondervan Publishing House, 1990), 249.

9   James B. Shelton, *Mighty in Word and Deed: The Role of the Holy Spirit in Luke-Acts* (Peabody, Massachusetts: Hendrickson Publishers, 1991), 130.

10   F. F. Bruce, *The Book of The Acts*, rev. ed. (Grand Rapids, MI: William B. Eerdmans Publishing Co., 1988), 170.

Others have suggested that the laying on of hands is a necessary element in people's receiving the Holy Spirit. This conclusion, however, cannot be supported. Of the seven key outpourings discussed in Acts, hands are applied in only three (8:17; 9:17; 19:6), while in four they are not (2:4; 4:31; 10:44; 13:2). We must conclude, therefore, that laying on of hands, though it is sometimes used in conjunction with receiving the Spirit, is not an essential element in the same.

The practice of laying on of hands is, however, used clearly in Acts for two purposes: for healing the sick, as in the case of Paul and the father of Publius (9:12, 17; 28:8), and for commissioning to service, as in the case of the seven deacons (6:6), and in the case of Barnabas and Saul as they began their first missionary journey (13:3). Commissioning is also strongly implied in the cases of Paul (9:12-19, cf. 22:14-15; 26:16-18) and the Ephesians (19:6, cf. v. 10). These two uses of laying on of hands—i.e., healing and commissioning—seem, therefore, to be the main uses of the practice in Luke's understanding. With these facts in mind, Menzies draws the following conclusion concerning Peter's and John's laying of hands on the Samaritans:

> Since the rite is clearly not related to healing in 8:17 and 19:6, it is not unreasonable to assume that in these instances it forms a part of a commissioning ceremony. I therefore suggest that Peter and John incorporate the Samaritans, not into the church, but into the missionary enterprise of the church.[11]

So we ask again, Why were hands laid on the Samaritan believers when they received the Spirit? The answer is twofold: The first reason was to assist them in receiving the Spirit. The text is clear: Peter and John prayed for them "that they might receive the Holy Spirit" (v. 15). Secondly, the two apostles laid hands on them in order

---

11   Menzies, 212.

to commission them for missional service. It was not enough that the gospel had gone *to* Samaria; it must also go *from* Samaria to the ends of the earth, as Jesus had indicated. Samaria must become a new base for missionary activity. Stronstad writes, "The gift of the Spirit to the believers at Samaria demonstrates that all, even a despised group like the Samaritans, are to engage in the missionary task. For this common responsibility they receive the same equipment—the vocational gift of the Spirit."[12] Menzies adds, "Thus the Samaritans are commissioned and empowered for the missionary task which lay before them. A prophetic community has been formed. A new center of missionary activity has been established."[13]

Someone may ask why Philip did not pray with these new believers to receive the Spirit. After all, he was certainly qualified, since he himself was "full of the Spirit" (6:3). Some have suggested that only the apostles could lay hands on others to receive the Spirit. This, however, cannot be true since Ananias, a mere disciple, laid hands on Paul when he received the Spirit (9:10, 17). Why, then, did Philip not lead the Samaritans into the Pentecostal experience? We can only wonder. We are, however, prompted to ask a similar question: Why do thousands of Pentecostal pastors around the world fail to lead their church members into Spirit baptism? Again, we can only wonder.

It was once said to a particular preacher who had led many into the experience of Spirit-baptism, "You have the *gift* of praying with people to receive the Holy Spirit." He replied, "No I don't have the gift of praying with people to receive the Holy Spirit. I read of no such gift in the Scriptures. I do, however, have the *goal* of seeing people filled with the Spirit." Possibly Philip simply did not have the goal. Whatever the reason, the apostles quickly moved to remedy the unacceptable situation.

---

12   Roger Stronstad, *The Charismatic Theology of St. Luke* (Peabody, MS: Hendrickson Publishers, 1984), 65.
13   Menzies, 212.

WHAT RESULTED?

A WITNESSING COMMUNITY

As a result of the Samaritans' reception of the Spirit, a Spirit-anointed witnessing community was established that continued to advance the gospel in and beyond the region of Samaria. In 9:31 Luke summarizes,

> So the church throughout all Judea and Galilee and Samaria enjoyed peace, being built up; and going on in the fear of the Lord and in the comfort of the Holy Spirit, *it continued to increase.* (italics added).

Note how Luke says that the church "continued to increase" throughout all of Judea, Galilee, and Samaria. Soon after the outpouring of the Spirit in Samaria, we read of the church as having been established in Damascus (9:1). A short time later we discover that the church had ranged as far as Phoenicia, Cyprus, and Antioch (11:19-21). If we look closely at the text, we do indeed discover Luke's empowerment—witness motif being advanced. Although the theme is presented more subtly than in other cases, it is nevertheless present, a fact that a number of commentators have observed. For instance, F. F. Bruce, citing G. W. H. Lampe, comments on the "Samaritan Pentecost":

> Luke presents the Samaritan mission as the first important advance of the Christian mission. The record of the Samaritan "Pentecost" implies that a new nucleus of the expanding community has been established so that the

gospel could now 'radiate outwards from this new centre of the Spirit's mission."[14]

RECIPROCAL BLESSING

There are two other indications of Spirit-empowered witness resulting from the Samaritan outpouring: First, there seems to be a sort of "reciprocal effect" on Peter and John. Luke notes that, after the two apostles had prayed for the Samaritans to receive the Spirit, they stayed on for a while in Samaria and "solemnly testified" and spoke "the word of the Lord" (8:25). Throughout Acts both phrases indicate the proclamation of the gospel, primarily to the lost (2:40; 10:42: 12:24; 13:44, 48-49; 15:8, 35-36; 16:32; 19:10; 20:24). The implication is that Peter and John joined with Philip and the newly Spirit-filled Samaritan believers in a time of evangelistic outreach. Then, on their way back to Jerusalem, Peter and John preached the gospel "to many villages of the Samaritans" (8:25). It thus appears that the apostles themselves received a reciprocal blessing when praying for the Samaritans to receive the Spirit.

As anyone who has ever prayed with others to receive the Spirit knows, the one ministering in the Spirit often receives benefit equal to the one receiving ministry. In order to pray with others to be filled with the Spirit, one must himself or herself first be refilled with the Spirit—and so it may have been for Peter and John. As a result, they themselves received a renewed passion to preach the gospel. Though we read nothing of their preaching the gospel on the way to Samaria, after praying with the believers there to receive the Spirit, they preached the gospel "to many villages of the Samaritans" (v. 25).

A second reciprocal benefit received by the apostles was a greater understanding of the mission of God, and a renewed passion to engage in that mission. This is the first time in Acts we read of any

---

14   G. W. H. Lampe, *The Seal of the Spirit* (London, Eng: Longmans, Green, 1951), 70; quoted in Bruce, 170.

of the apostles preaching the gospel to anyone other than Jews. It appears as if Peter and John learned a valuable lesson from Philip the deacon. They learned that they were to freely declare the gospel without prejudice to all people. This is a lesson the Spirit of God would have to re-teach Peter a couple of years later (10:9-16, 28). Remember, it was John who, on a previous visit to the region, wanted to call fire down from heaven to consume the Samaritans (Luke 9:54). Seeing the Spirit poured out on the Samaritans--and receiving a fresh touch of the Holy Spirit themselves--helped the apostles to see the Samaritan people with new, more redemptive, eyes.

Not only did the apostles receive a reciprocal blessing from the Samaritan Outpouring, Philip too must have received a fresh touch of the Holy Spirit on his life. He again heard the voice of the Lord, this time spoken by an angel, saying, "Get up and go south to the road that descends from Jerusalem to Gaza" (v. 26). There on a desert road Philip encountered an Ethiopian man riding in a chariot. This black African is the first "pure Gentile" to receive the gospel in the book of Acts. Robert C. Tannehill describes Philip's encounter with the Ethiopian as an "anticipatory scene," and the Ethiopian as representing "those who are at the end of the earth . . ."[15] He writes, "Ethiopia was on the edge of the known world. This scene anticipates the power of the gospel to reach 'the end of the earth' (1:8)."[16]

Again, Luke pictures Philip as moving under the Spirit's direction: "Then the Spirit said to Philip, 'Go up and join the chariot'" (v. 29). Providentially, Philip finds the Ethiopian reading from a scroll of Isaiah. This is indeed a divine appointment! Even more amazingly, he is reading from Isaiah 53, which prophetically speaks of Jesus' passion and vicarious death. Prompted by the Spirit, Philip seizes the opportunity: "Then Philip opened his mouth, and beginning from this Scripture he preached Jesus to him" (v. 35). The

---

15   Robert C. Tannehill, *The Narrative Unity of Luke-Acts: A Literary Interpretation*, vol. 2, *The Acts of the Apostles* (Philadelphia: Fortress Press, 1994), 108.
16   Ibid., 107.

Ethiopian believed and was baptized. Philip is then "snatched away" by the Spirit of God.

Bruce points out that there is a variant reading of verse 39. This reading, known as the Western Text, is found in several manuscripts of the church fathers. It reads "the Spirit of the Lord fell upon the eunuch, and the angel of the Lord caught Philip away." According to Bruce,

> The Western text, however, makes the angel of the Lord snatch Philip away, while the *Spirit* of the Lord falls on the Ethiopian. . . . the effect of the longer reading is to make it clear that the Ethiopian's baptism was followed by the gift of the Spirit. Even with the shorter reading it is a reasonable inference that he did receive the Spirit . . .[17]

Howard Ervin, supporting this view, adds, "The context itself suggests that the Ethiopian's immediate reaction to the effusion of the divine Spirit was vocal, for 'the eunuch . . . went on his way rejoicing.'"[18]

A RECOGNIZABLE SIGN

Another immediate effect of the Samaritans' reception of the Holy Spirit was some sort of visible manifestation of the Spirit. This is evident since "Simon saw that the Spirit was bestowed through the laying on of the apostles' hands" (v 18). As others have pointed out, the manifestation that he saw must have been an impressive sign since Simon, who was a powerful sorcerer, was so impressed that he wanted to purchase the ability to pray with others to receive the Spirit—and by implication, the accompanying manifestation.

We can only speculate as to the exact nature of the sign. Classical Pentecostals have opted for speaking in tongues. This is a

---

17   Bruce, 178.
18   Howard M. Ervin, *Spirit Baptism: A Biblical Investigation* (Peabody, MS: Hendrickson Publishers, Inc., 1987), 75.

reasonable inference, since tongues speech is the only sign explicitly stated in Acts as occurring at Spirit baptism, and it is clearly mentioned in three other instances (2:4; 10:47; 19:6). As Menzies has pointed out, it would follow from Luke's pattern that the Samaritan sign was Spirit-inspired speech, concluding that "implicit within the narrative is the assumption that the Samaritans, upon reception of the Spirit, began to prophesy and speak in tongues as on the day of Pentecost (8:16-18; cf. 2:4-13; 10:45-46; 19: 6)."[19]

So What?

We now ask our final question for this chapter. What modern-day lessons can we learn from the Samaritan Outpouring?

LESSONS LEARNED FROM PHILIP'S MINISTRY

From Philip's ministry we learn three lessons: First, we learn about the importance of one's being filled with the Spirit in order to maximize his or her effectiveness in ministry. Although Philip was not himself an apostle, he had a powerful Spirit-empowered evangelistic ministry. We too can expect to maximize our effectiveness in ministry if we are filled with, and remain full of, the Holy Spirit.

Further, we learn from Philip the importance of proclaiming Christ. Luke says that "Philip went down to the city of Samaria and began proclaiming Christ to them." And later on, when he met the Ethiopian on the desert road, he "preached Jesus to him" (8:35). It was the power of the gospel (Rom. 1:16) coupled with the power of the Spirit (Acts 1:8) that brought the amazing results in both cases.

Finally, from Philip's ministry we learn something about the evangelistic power of signs and wonders. Luke says that the "crowds with one accord were giving attention to what was said by Philip, as they heard and saw the signs which he was performing" (8:6). Today

---

19   Menzies, 211.

the church is coming into a greater realization of the need for missionaries to minister in the power and anointing of the Holy Spirit with signs following if the resistant peoples of the world are to be reached with the gospel.

A LESSON LEARNED FROM THE APOSTLE'S ACTION

Not only do we learn lessons concerning evangelism from the ministry of Philip, we also learn an important lesson concerning church planting from the action of the apostles. Luke says that when the apostles in Jerusalem heard about the work in Samaria, they immediately dispatched Peter and John to go to Samaria to pray with the new believers "that they might receive the Holy Spirit" (8:15). Those who receive Christ must then be empowered by the Spirit so that they can be enabled to effectively proclaim Him to others. We thus learn an important lesson: When planting new churches, it is not enough that we simply preach Christ; neither is it enough to work miracles or even to establish a local congregation of believers; we must intentionally plant Spirit-empowered missional churches capable of reproducing themselves and planting other Spirit-empowered missional churches. We will discuss this issue more in Chapter 10.

FURTHER SPIRIT-EMPOWERED MINISTRY IN THE REGION (8:25-40)

Before we close this chapter and move to the next, let's take a moment to look briefly at some other acts of Spirit-empowered ministry in Judea, Samaria and the surrounding regions.

PHILIP'S SPIRIT-EMPOWERED MINISTRY IN THE COASTAL REGIONS

The story of Philip's witness to the Ethiopian eunuch ends with his being "snatched away" from Gaza to be found in the town of Azotus, about twenty miles (thirty-two kilometers) to the north. From there he sets out on an evangelistic tour northward "to all the cities until he came to Caesarea" (v. 40). As he traveled, Luke says, "he kept preaching the gospel." This he certainly did, according to his usual *modus operandi*, in the power of the Spirit.

PETER'S SPIRIT-EMPOWERED MINISTRY IN THE REGION

Luke also tells of Peter's itinerant ministry in the regions of Judea, Samaria, and Galilee (9:31-43). Luke cites two specific examples of that ministry: The first, the healing of a paralytic by the name of Aeneas, took place in the Judean village of Lydda about thirty miles northwest of Jerusalem (9:32-35). By including this story in Acts, Luke informs his readers that Peter continued to minister in the Spirit's power. Since Luke has already told the reader that the apostles' healing ministry was done in the power of the Holy Spirit (2:43, cf. 2:4; 3:6; 4:31-33), we can assume that this miracle was done in that same power. A second example of Peter's itinerant ministry in the region is the story of the raising of Tabitha, which took place in the coastal town of Joppa (9:36-43).

Although both the healing of Aeneas and the raising of Tabitha were miracles performed on believers, each serves as a powerful witness to their respective communities. As a result of Aeneas' healing, "all who lived in Lydda and Sharon saw him, and they turned to the Lord" (v. 35). When Tabitha was raised "it became known all over Joppa, and many believed in the Lord" (v. 42). Again, Luke portrays Spirit-empowered ministry in word and deed as producing dramatic evangelistic results.

A SUMMARY OF
MINISTRY IN JUDEA AND SAMARIA

The evangelistic outreach of the church into Judea and Samaria can be defined as ministry conducted in the power of the Spirit. In its entirety, it is representative of Luke's *empowerment-witness motif*. This Spirit-empowered ministry involved divine guidance, angelic intervention, visions, demonstrations of miracle working power, praying with others to receive the Spirit, and bold anointed proclamation of the gospel. It resulted in a great harvest of souls. The driving impetus behind this entire ministry was the repeated outpouring of the Spirit on the church.

CONCLUSION

Luke included the story of Peter and John's visit to Samaria, and the subsequent outpouring of the Spirit there, to demonstrate the apostles' ongoing concern that believers in new "church plants" were also empowered by the Spirit. As a result of the Samaritan Outpouring, the gospel continued to spread throughout Judea and Samaria, reaching northward into Galilee (9:31), Phoenicia (11:19), Damascus (9:2), and Antioch (11:19), and westward into Cyprus and Cyrene (11:20).

Thus far in our study we have discussed three key outpourings of the Spirit in the book of Acts. We have seen how each resulted in powerful Spirit-anointed missional witness. In the next chapter we will be looking at the fourth key outpouring of the Spirit in the book of Acts, the Damascene Outpouring. Although on this occasion only one person received the Holy Spirit, the significance of the event is undeniable, for the one filled with the Spirit was Saul of Tarsus (later to become Paul, the apostle). As with the other outpourings, the Damascene Outpouring will result in powerful Spirit-anointed witness.

CHAPTER 7

THE
DAMASCENE
OUTPOURING

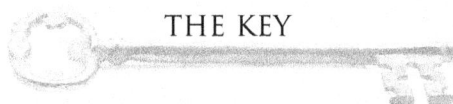

THE KEY

ACTS 1:8

But you will receive power when the Holy Spirit has come upon you;
and you shall be My witnesses . . . even to the remotest part of the earth.

THE DAMASCENE OUTPOURING

ACTS 9:17-18

So Ananias departed and entered the house, and after laying his
hands on him said, "Brother Saul, the Lord Jesus, who appeared to
you on the road by which you were coming, has sent me so that you
may regain your sight and be filled with the Holy Spirit."
And immediately there fell from his eyes something like scales,
and he regained his sight, and he got up and was baptized . . .

Thus far in our study we have examined three key outpourings of the Holy Spirit in Acts. Two took place in Jerusalem and another in Samaria. We have demonstrated how each outpouring resulted in powerful missional witness, and how each advanced Luke's missio-pneumatological intent in writing Acts. In this chapter we will discuss a fourth key outpouring of the Spirit, the Damascene Outpouring.

This outpouring, along with the one preceding and the one following it, occurs during a "transitional period" in Acts between the Jewish and Gentile missions (see Fig. 7.1, below). These three outpourings serve to prepare the church for its upcoming Gentile mission. They are as follows:

- The Samaritan Outpouring (8:14-18)

- The Damascene Outpouring (9:15-19)

- The Caesarean Outpouring (10:44-46).

These outpourings are followed by two others, which also relate to the Gentile mission. They, however, serve to propel the church onward to "the remotest part of the earth." They are as follows:

- The Antiochian "Outpouring" (13:1-4)

- The Ephesian Outpouring (19:1-7).

We will discuss each of these outpourings in detail in this book. For now, however, it is important that we understand how each fits into the overall missional structure of Acts.

As you will remember, in Chapter 3 we described Acts 1:8 as the interpretative key to the book of Acts. This important verse, standing at the beginning of Luke's narrative, serves two strategic purposes: It first lays out a *paradigmatic pattern* that functions as the guiding motif for the entire book. This pattern is found in the first half of the verse: "But you will receive power when the Holy Spirit has come upon you; and you shall be My witnesses . . ." In this study we are calling this pattern Luke's *empowerment–witness motif.*

Secondly, the verse functions as a *programmatic outline* for the book of Acts. This programmatic outline is found in the second half of the verse: ". . . in Jerusalem, and in all Judea and Samaria, and even to the remotest part of the earth." These three designations (i.e., Jerusalem; Judea and Samaria; and the remotest part of the earth) suggest three divisions of the book which can be outlined as follows:

"Jerusalem"	Acts 1:12-8:1a	The Jewish mission
"Judea and Samaria"	Acts 8:1b-12:25	The transition from the Jewish to the Gentile mission
"Remotest part of the earth"	Acts 13:1-28:31	The Gentile mission

Figure 7.1 helps us to understand these relationships:

SEVEN KEY OUTPOURINGS
AS THEY RELATE TO THE JEWISH AND GENTILE MISSIONS
(FIGURE 7.1)

Introduc-tory 1:1-11	The Jewish Mission *Jerusalem*	Transitional Period *Judea and Samaria* (Extending to Galilee, Cyprus, Cyrene, Antioch)	The Gentile Mission *The Remotest Part of the Earth*
	1:12-8:1a Fulfilling the Jewish Mission	**8:1b-12:25** Preparation for the Gentile Mission	**13:1-28:31** Carrying out the Gentile Mission
Acts 1:8 "You will receive power... you will be my witnesses...	1 Pentecost 2 The Second Jerusalem Outpouring	3 The Samaritan Outpouring 4 The Damascene Outpouring 5 The Caesarean Outpouring	6 The Antiochian "Outpouring" 7 The Ephesian Outpouring

The Samaritan Outpouring, discussed in the last chapter, represented the church's first tentative venture into cross-cultural missions. It was the first mission outside of greater Jerusalem and Judea and to a non-purely-Jewish people group. What happened in Samaria was the first challenge to the sectarian attitudes and cultural biases of many Jewish Christians living in Jerusalem. It showed them that, not only will God accept into His family those who are culturally different from themselves, He will also fill them with His Spirit and use them to fulfill His mission in the earth. This chapter will look at the second of these three "transitional" outpourings in Acts, the Damascene Outpouring, noting how it helped to prepare the church for its upcoming Gentile mission, and how it advanced Luke's missio-pneumatological intent in writing the book.

THE DAMASCENE OUTPOURING

The Damascene Outpouring occurred around A.D. 32, about four years after the initial outpouring of the Spirit on the Day of Pentecost. This outpouring is unique in Acts in that only one man is filled with the Spirit, a man by the name of Saul of Tarsus, later to become the apostle Paul.

Luke first introduces Saul of Tarsus as an arch enemy of the church. In a parenthetical aside during the account of Stephen's martyrdom, Luke notes how Saul, by tending to the robes of those who were stoning Stephen to death, lent his implicit support to the act (7:58). He soon became a ringleader in the Jerusalem persecution that broke out after Stephen's stoning. Luke says that he was "ravaging the church, entering house after house, and dragging off men and women, he would put them in prison" (8:3). Paul later testified, "I persecuted this Way to the death, binding and putting both men and women into prison, . . . In one synagogue after another I used to imprison and beat those who believed in [Christ]" (22:4, 19). On another occasion Paul testified, "I thought to myself that I had to do many things hostile to the name of Jesus of Nazareth. . . .

when they were being put to death I cast my vote against them"
(26:9-10). He further laments, "I tried to force them to blaspheme;
and being furiously enraged at them, I kept pursuing them even to
foreign cities" (v. 11).

While on his way to one such foreign city, Syrian Damascus,
the direction of Saul's life was forever altered. Years later he testified,
"[I] started off for Damascus in order to bring even those who were
there to Jerusalem as prisoners to be punished" (22:5). Had he
received reports from Damascus that the scattered believers were
having success there? Could Damascus have been experiencing a
revival similar to the one in Samaria? The text does not say.
Whatever the case, Saul was destined to have two powerful
encounters with God—one with the risen Christ and the other with
the outpoured Spirit—and his life was to be forever changed. The
arch persecutor of the church was to become its ardent promoter. As
we did with the first three outpourings of the Spirit, we will ask three
questions about this one.

WHAT HAPPENED?

Saul and his band of zealots had been on the road for several
days. They had traveled northeastward from Jerusalem, across Judea
and into southern Syria. The chief priest had granted Saul permission
to go to Damascus, arrest the fleeing Christians, and bring them back
to Jerusalem in chains for trial and punishment. At midday the band
drew near to their destination. As they approached the city, a
brilliant light suddenly shone around them. Overcome by fear, they
fell to the ground. In the Hebrew dialect a commanding voice spoke
from the midst of the light: "Saul, Saul, why are you persecuting me?"
Bewildered, Saul answered, "Who are you, Lord?" Jesus replied, "I
am Jesus who you are persecuting." The Voice gave him instructions:
He was to go into the city of Damascus, and there he would be told
what to do. Later on in Acts, Paul revealed that Jesus spoke another
word to him at this time:

... for this purpose I have appeared to you, to appoint you a minister and a witness not only to the things which you have seen, but also to the things in which I will appear to you rescuing you from the Jewish people and from the Gentiles, to whom I am sending you, to open their eyes so that they might turn from darkness to light and from the dominion of Satan to God, that they may receive forgiveness of sins and an inheritance among those who have been sanctified by faith in me (26:16).

When Saul finally arose from the ground, he could no longer see. His traveling companions led him by the hand into the city to the house of a man by the name of Judas, who lived on a street called Straight. For three days Saul remained in the house blinded. Much of his time was spent in prayer. During this time he had a second vision. In this vision he saw a man named Ananias coming to him, laying hands on him and healing him of his blindness.

SAUL'S CONVERSION

Here a question presents itself: Was Saul a Christian at this time? Was he converted on the Damascus road, or did his conversion take place, as some say, three days later when Ananias laid hands on him and he was filled with the Spirit? Or, was he converted at some time between these two events? Some, since they interpret Spirit-baptism as conversion-initiation, say that Saul could not have been converted before Ananias laid hands on him and he received the Spirit.[1] Their theology will not allow it.

The facts, however, lead to the conclusion that Saul was, indeed, converted on the Damascus road. We say this for three

---

1   i.e., James D. G. Dunn, *Baptism in the Holy Spirit: A Re-examination of the New Testament Teaching on the Gift of the Spirit in Relation to Pentecostalism Today* (Philadelphia, PA: The Westminister Press, 1970); John R. W. Stott, *Baptism and Fulness of the Holy Spirit* (Downers Grove, IL: Inter-Varsity Press, 1964).

reasons: First, Paul called Jesus "Lord" (v. 5), and he himself taught that "no one can say, 'Jesus is Lord,' except by the Holy Spirit" (1 Cor. 12:3). Secondly, he obeyed Jesus and submitted to His will (vv. 6-9). One proof that a person has been truly born again is submission to the will of God (John 14:15). Jesus commanded Saul to go into the city of Damascus to receive further instructions. Though he was blind, Saul submitted himself totally to the will of his newfound Lord, following His instructions to the letter. Finally, Ananias called him "Brother Saul" (v. 17; cf. Acts 22:13). Ananias obviously realized that Saul had become a member of the community of true believers, the church. James B. Shelton writes, "Ananias did not proclaim Jesus as Lord to Paul; the risen Jesus himself did— before Paul arrived at Damascus (9:3-8). Paul was already in a state of prayer *before* Ananias arrived (v. 11). A strong case could be made for Paul's conversion on the road to Damascus instead of in the city of Damascus."[2] Howard M. Ervin states further,

> From the preceding context, it is clear that Ananias knew who Saul was and why he had come to Damascus—to persecute the believers there. He would never, therefore, have entered Saul's presence and addressed him as "Brother Saul," unless he had been assured in advance that Saul was, in very truth, a "Brother" in Christ. Saul must, therefore, have become a Christian, in the fullest sense of the word, before Ananias came to him.[3]

In actuality Saul had five significant spiritual experiences at this time: He was converted; he was healed of blindness; he was empowered by the Spirit; he was commissioned to missionary

2   James B. Shelton, *Mighty in Word and Deed: The Role of the Holy Spirit in Luke-Acts.* (Peabody, MA: Hendrickson Publishers, Inc., 1991), 131.
3   Howard M. Ervin, *Spirit Baptism, a Biblical Investigation* (Peabody, MA: Hendrickson Publishers, Inc., 1987), 76.

service; and he was baptized in water. We have already discussed his
first experience; let's now look at the other four.

SAUL'S HEALING

As He did to Saul, Jesus also appeared in a vision to Ananias.
In the vision He instructed Ananias to go to the house of Judas and
pray for Saul. At first Ananias was afraid, since he had heard about
Saul's brutal treatment of believers in Jerusalem. The Lord, however,
pressed the issue. "Go," He said, "for he is a chosen instrument of
Mine, to bear My name before Gentiles and kings and the sons of
Israel; . . ." (v. 15). Obeying, Ananias went to the appointed place.
Entering into the house, he found Saul, just as he had seen in his
vision. Speaking to him, Ananias said, "Brother Saul, the Lord Jesus,
who appeared to you on the road by the way which you were coming,
has sent me so that you may regain your sight and be filled with the
Holy Spirit" (v. 17).

As stated above, Saul's first spiritual experience was his
conversion to Christ. His second occurred when Ananias laid hands
on him, for "immediately there fell from his eyes something like
scales, and he regained his sight" (9:18). This miracle must have been
a great encouragement to Saul. It was a physical demonstration of the
inner transformation that had just taken place in his life. For years
his life had been "full of darkness" but now it was "wholly
illuminated" by the light of Christ (cf. Luke 11:34-36). The miracle
was also symbolic of Saul's future missionary ministry, which was "to
open their [both the Jews and the Gentiles] eyes so that they may
turn from darkness to light and from the dominion of Satan to
God . . ." (Acts 26:18).

SAUL'S EMPOWERING

God also sent Ananias to Saul to pray with him that he might
be "filled with the Holy Spirit" (v. 17). Although Luke does not
explicitly state that Saul was filled with the Spirit at the moment

Ananias laid hands on him, the obvious implication is that he was. This is also indicated by Saul's bold and persuasive ministry that immediately followed this experience. (I will discuss this more in the paragraphs below.) Commenting on this passage French L. Arrington writes,

> Luke's primary concern was with God's call and the empowering of Saul for his apostolic ministry. So Paul's experience was consistent with the purpose of the outpouring of the Spirit on the disciples at Pentecost and at Samaria. They too, were equipped to bear the name of their Lord.[4]

There is no mention of any charismatic phenomenon accompanying Saul's Spirit baptism, such as speaking in tongues, as in other accounts. Paul in another place does, however, affirm that he did indeed speak in tongues, an experience which he ascribes to the Holy Spirit (1 Cor. 12:10-11; 14:13-18). As others have pointed out, Paul had to have begun speaking in tongues at some point in time. It is, therefore, not unreasonable to assume that he began on the occasion of his Spirit baptism as did other believers in Acts (2:4; 10:46; 19:6). The key point that Luke is attempting to emphasize here, however, is that Saul was empowered for witness, which he demonstrates in the verses following (vv. 20, 22, 27).

SAUL'S COMMISSIONING

Saul was not only healed and empowered by the Spirit when Ananias laid hands on him, he was also commissioned to missionary ministry. As discussed in the last chapter, in Acts the laying on of hands often signifies commissioning to ministry (Acts 6:6; 13:3). Given the context of Ananias' laying hands on Saul, it is probable

---

4   French L. Arrington, *The Acts of the Apostles: An Introduction and Commentary* (Peabody, MA: Hendrickson Publishers, Inc., 1988), 100.

that this incident also represented an act of commissioning. Note what the Lord said to Ananias when he sent him to lay hands on Saul: ". . . he is a chosen instrument of Mine, to bear My name before the Gentiles and kings and the sons of Israel . . ." (v. 15); and note the Lord's words to Saul when He appeared to him on the Damascus road: ". . . for this purpose I have appeared to you, to appoint you a minister and a witness . . . rescuing you from the Jewish people and from the Gentiles, to whom I am sending you, . . ." (26:16-17, cf. 22:14-15). In that context Ananias lays hands on Saul of Tarsus— who was soon to become Paul, the apostle—commissioning him to missionary service.

SAUL'S BAPTISM IN WATER

Finally, Saul was baptized in water. Luke says simply, ". . . he got up and was baptized" (v. 18). Some have suggested that this statement refers, not to Saul's baptism in water, but to his baptism in the Holy Spirit. A plausible case can be made for this explanation (cf., 1:5; 11:16). It is more likely, however, that the statement is referring to Saul's baptism in water, since later in Acts, when testifying before the Jews about his conversion, he mentions his water baptism (22:16). It is possible, nevertheless, based on Peter's statement in 2:38, that he could have been baptized in the Spirit in conjunction with his baptism in water.

WHAT RESULTED?

We come now to our second question about the Damascene Outpouring. What were the results of Saul's being filled with the Spirit? The results were powerful immediate and ongoing witness. These witnessing results can be divided into three groups: immediate results, intermediate results, and long term results, as follows:

IMMEDIATE RESULTS

The immediate result of Saul's being filled with the Spirit was bold Spirit-empowered witness. After his Spirit baptism (vv. 17-19)—in fact, in the very next verse—Luke writes, "And immediately he began to proclaim Jesus in the synagogues, saying, 'He is the Son of God.'" (v. 20). Two verses later, Luke emphasizes Saul's increasingly more powerful witness in Damascus: "But Saul kept increasing in strength and confounding the Jews who lived at Damascus by proving that this Jesus is the Christ" (v. 22). Arrington notes, "His increase in power speaks of the dynamic ongoing work of the Spirit. Such spiritual power is basic to the pentecostal experience (1:8)."[5] As with the three previous outpourings, Luke's *empowerment-witness motif* is clearly evidenced. This account, like the others, closely parallels 4:31: "they were all filled with the Holy Spirit and began to speak the word of God with boldness."

INTERMEDIATE RESULTS

Not only does Luke indicate that there were immediate results of Saul's being filled with the Spirit, he also indicates that there were intermediate results. Like the immediate results, the intermediate results are witness. Luke continues his witness theme in verses 27-28:

> But Barnabas took hold of him and brought him to the apostles and described to them how . . . he had spoken out boldly in the name of Jesus. And he was with them, moving about freely in Jerusalem, speaking out boldly in the name of the Lord (9:27-28).

In a casual reading of this account, it appears that only a short time has passed (days, rather than months or years) between Saul's being filled with the Spirit in Damascus and his subsequent

---

5   Ibid.

witness in Jerusalem; however, in actuality, three full years pass
between the two incidents. We discover this by reading Paul's letter
to the Galatians:

> But when God, who had set me apart even from my mother's
> womb and called me through His grace, was pleased to reveal
> His Son in me so that I might preach Him among the
> Gentiles, I did not immediately consult with flesh and blood,
> nor did I go up to Jerusalem to those who were apostles
> before me; but I went away to Arabia, and returned once
> more to Damascus. Then three years later I went up to
> Jerusalem . . . (1:15-18).

Some suggest that Paul's Arabic sojourn occurred between
verse 25, when Saul was let down in a basket to flee Damascus (cf. 2
Cor 11:32), and verse 26, when he arrived in Jerusalem. It is more
likely, however, that his Arabian experience took place between
verses 22 and 23. According to this view, it was during this time
("when many days had elapsed') that Paul preached the gospel in
Arabia. F. F. Bruce, comparing the Acts and the Galatians passages,
comments:

> It is commonly supposed that Paul's sojourn in Arabia had
> the nature of a religious retreat: that he sought solitude in the
> desert . . . in order to commune with God and think out all
> the implications of his new life, without disturbance. But the
> context in which he tells of his going to Arabia, immediately
> after receiving his commission to proclaim Christ among the
> Gentiles, suggests that he went there to preach the gospel.[6]

At the end of these days, Luke notes, "the Jews plotted together to do
away with him" (v. 23). Arrington speculates, "This plot against his
life could have been the consequence of missionary activity in

---

6   F. F. Bruce, *The Book of the Acts,* rev. ed. (Grand Rapids, MI: William B.
Eerdmans Publishing Co., 1988), 191-192.

Arabia."[7] After returning to Damascus, Saul has to escape for his life, and from there he goes to Jerusalem. In Jerusalem, Luke characteristically notes, he is seen "speaking out boldly in the name of the Lord" (v. 28).

As stated above, according to the Lukan narrative, it appears that all of these witnessing activities of Saul (vv. 20, 22, 27-29) take place almost one after the other, when in actuality they occurred over a three year period. Could Luke have deliberately truncated these accounts in order to more closely connect Paul's powerful witness to his Spirit baptism in verses 17-18? This is a possibility. Whatever Luke's motive, his ordering of events again serves to emphasize his *empowerment–witness motif.*

LONG-TERM RESULTS

Luke also records long-term results of Saul's being filled with the Spirit. These long-term results are recorded in chapters 13-28 of Acts and include Paul's three missionary journeys as well as his voyage to Rome. Luke prefaces Paul's missionary ministry with the account of his Spirit baptism because, in Luke's mind, it is essential that his readers know that Paul was filled with the Spirit, and that his entire missionary ministry was done in the Spirit's power.[8]

Throughout Acts, Luke portrays Paul's ministry as being charismatic in content and character. Paul preaches with power (13:16ff; 14:3, 21), receives divine revelation (13:9-11; 14:9; 27:9-10), heals the sick (14:10; 28:8-9), performs signs and wonders (14:3; 15:12), casts out demons (16:18), is guided by the Spirit (16:6-10; 19:21; 20:22-23), has visions (16:9-10; 18:9; 22:17-21; 23:11; 27:23-25), exhibits supernatural courage (14:20), prays for others to receive

---

7   Arrington, 100.

8   Just as were the ministries of Jesus (Luke 3:22-23; 4:1, 14, 18-19; 5:17; 6:19; Acts 10:38), Peter (Acts 2:14; 3:6; 4:8; 5:3ff, 15-16; 8:14-17), John (5:25; 8:14-17), the apostles (2:43; 5:12; 5:33), the early believers (4:31; 8:4), Stephen (6:8-10; 7:55), Philip (8:5-13, 26, 29, 39-40), and Ananias (9:10-18).

the Spirit (19:6), and works extraordinary miracles (19:11-13). Arrington compares the charismatic ministries of Peter and Paul:

> In Acts, Luke parallels Paul's charismatic experience with that of Peter. Both Peter and Paul received the gift of the Spirit for service (2:4; 4:8; 4:31; 9:17; 13:9, 52). The most important factor in their success was that they were moved and directed by the Holy Spirit (10:19-20; 13:1-2; 16:6-7; 21:4, 10-11) . . . Consistent with his purpose, Luke teaches that when Paul was filled with the Spirit he received a charismatic anointing rather than a conversion experience. Such anointing precedes and affects mission. Like Peter, Paul's special anointing had tremendous significance for his new vocation in life.[9]

Another result of Paul's being filled with the Spirit (although Luke does not mention this) is the fact that he penned thirteen books of the New Testament, more than any other New Testament writer. Without controversy, his being filled with the Spirit was an essential factor in his writing of New Testament scripture (1 Cor. 2:10-16; 1 Thess. 3:13; 2 Tim. 3:16; 2 Pet. 1:21).

Luke concludes his accounts of the Samaritan and Damascene outpourings with a summary statement: "So the church throughout all Judea and Galilee and Samaria enjoyed peace, being built up; and going on in the fear of the Lord and in the comfort of the Holy Spirit, it continued to increase" (9:31). True to his primary intent Luke notes how these outpourings resulted in ever-widening witness in the region.

SO WHAT?

What applications can we make concerning the Damascene Outpouring in regard to our lives and ministries today? Previous

---

9   Arrington, 100.

applications apply here, like the necessity of being filled with the Spirit before venturing forth into evangelistic or missionary work. Such an action would be tantamount to a soldier sallying forth into battle without his weapon or a construction worker going to the jobsite without his tools. Thus, any theology that de-emphasizes an empowering experience with the Spirit subsequent to the new birth can only do disservice to the cause of world missions and weaken the worldwide evangelistic efforts of the church. There are three additional lessons we can be learn from the Damascene Outpouring.

THE IMPORTANCE OF ONE

First, we should never downplay the importance of just one person being filled with the Spirit. In Damascus, on this occasion, only one man was filled. But what a powerful difference his filling made in the history and progress of church! And what a difference one Spirit-empowered person can make in advancing the cause of Christ today. We should never be discouraged when only one or a few are filled with the Spirit when we minister. We should rather rejoice and continue to preach the message of Pentecost and faithfully pray with those seeking the Spirit's empowering—no matter how great or how small the number.

ANYONE CAN BE USED

A second lesson we can learn is that any Spirit-filled person—no matter how insignificant that person might appear to be in the greater scheme of things—can be used by God to lead others into the baptism in the Holy Spirit. This vital ministry is not to be regarded as the sole purview of "apostles" or other high-profile Christian leaders. God used Ananias to pray with Paul, and today anyone willing to listen to the voice of the Spirit and to move in obedience and faith can be used in the same way.

KNOW THE PURPOSE

A final lesson we can learn from the Damascene Outpouring is that it is essential for those being filled with the Spirit to know the purpose of their infilling. Both Jesus and Ananias revealed to Saul the purpose of his being filled—empowerment for mission (Acts 9:15-17; 22:10-16; 26:14-18). This knowledge certainly had a great effect on his response to being filled, which was immediate powerful witness. Many today are truly filled with the Spirit but without a proper understanding of why God filled them. This state of affairs often results in either disillusionment with the gift, or in various forms of fanaticism and misuse. It is important, therefore, that believers not only be led into the experience, but that they are also taught the meaning and purpose of the experience.

Conclusion

In the Damascene outpouring, as in the three before it, we can see Luke continuing to develop his *empowerment–witness motif* first presented in Acts 1:8. Saul was filled with the Spirit, not to affect his new birth, but that he might "carry [the Lord's] name before the Gentiles and their kings and before the people of Israel." His filling resulted in immediate witness for "at once he began to preach in the synagogues that Jesus is the Son of God" (Acts 9:20). Ultimately he was to become the great apostle to the Gentiles. This theme will dominate chapters 13-28 of Acts. In the next chapter we will investigate the fifth key outpouring of the Spirit in the book of Acts, the Caesarean Outpouring, where Luke continues to pursue his missio-pneumatic theme.

CHAPTER 8

THE
CAESAREAN
OUTPOURING

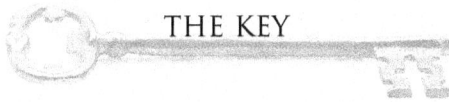

THE KEY

ACTS 1:8

*But you will receive power when the Holy Spirit has come upon you;
and you shall be My witnesses . . . even to the remotest part of the earth.*

THE CAESAREAN OUTPOURING

ACTS 10:44-46

*While Peter was still speaking these words, the Holy Spirit fell upon
all those who were listening to the message. All the circumcised believers
who came with Peter were amazed, because the gift of the Holy Spirit
had been poured out on the Gentiles also, for they were hearing
them speaking with tongues and exalting God.*

Just before His return to heaven, Jesus promised His disciples He would send the Holy Spirit to empower them for the work ahead (Luke 24:49). As a result, they would become His witnesses in Jerusalem, Judea, Samaria, and to the ends of the earth (Acts 1:8). He first fulfilled that promise on the Day of Pentecost when He poured out His Spirit on the waiting disciples in Jerusalem (2:4). Upon receiving the Spirit, the church in Jerusalem became a powerful witnessing community (2:14, 47). Spirit-baptized disciples immediately began to proclaim the gospel in Pentecostal power to their city and the surrounding areas. The church grew exponentially, and soon thousands of new converts peopled its ranks (2:41; 47; 4:4).

As the weeks passed, and as a result of the church being scattered by persecution (8:1; 11:19), Spirit-empowered believers proclaimed Christ and made converts in such distant places as Samaria, Gaza, Damascus, Phoenicia, Cyprus, Cyrene, and Antioch (8:5, 26; 9:2; 11:19-20). However, to this point, their witness was almost exclusively to Jews, with the notable exception of Philip's ministry in Samaria. The Samaritans, however, were at least partly Jewish.

The Christians in Jerusalem were true followers of Christ, and they had truly been empowered by the Spirit. Yet they still struggled with the "Gentile question." How could those who were ritually unclean be accepted by God? How could uncircumcised Gentiles, who ate nonkosher foods, and who defiled themselves by participating in pagan practices, become the children of Jehovah? Could they really become true followers of the Messiah without first becoming good Jews? And yet, had not Jesus Himself commanded them to take the gospel to the nations? Had He not said that they would be His witnesses, not only in Jerusalem, Judea, and Samaria, but to the "remotest parts of the earth?" How were they to reconcile these thorny issues?

God was soon to provide an answer to their questions, and He would do it in an almost unthinkable way: He would pour out His Spirit on uncircumcised Gentiles, just as he had poured Him out on the Jews on the Day of Pentecost. He, Himself would cleanse, indwell, and make them part of His family. Even more, He would empower them to be His witnesses to the nations.

THE CAESAREAN OUTPOURING

We come to the fifth outpouring of the Holy Spirit in Acts, the Caesarean Outpouring. (It is, at the same time, the third and last outpouring that occurred during the transition period between the Jewish and Gentile missions.)[1] As we have already seen in Chapters 6 and 7, two previous outpourings during this transition period had far-reaching implications in preparing the emerging church for its upcoming Gentile mission. The first was in Samaria. Philip's ministry there was the church's first venture away from a purely Jewish witness, and the subsequent ministry of Peter and John in Samaria was the apostles' first post-Pentecost ministry outside of Jerusalem and Judea. By giving the Spirit to the Samaritans, God demonstrated to the Jewish Christians that even a despised people such as they could become participants in His mission to the nations.

Like the Samaritan Outpouring, the Damascene Outpouring also had far-reaching implications for the church's upcoming Gentile mission in that it served as the beginning point in Paul's missionary career. It was there that, soon after his conversion, Paul was empowered and commissioned to be the "apostle to the Gentiles."

Now, as with the two outpourings before it, the Caesarean Outpouring would help to prepare the church for missionary outreach to the nations. This outpouring is often referred to as the "Gentile Pentecost," since it was the first outpouring of the Spirit on a purely Gentile people.

The Caesarean Outpouring occurred in Caesarea, a magnificent Roman-built seaport city about 50 miles (80 kilometers) northwest of Jerusalem. The date of the outpouring was about A.D.

---

1   See Figure 7.1, page 115.

35, seven years after the initial outpouring of the Spirit on the Day of Pentecost.[2] On this occasion the Spirit was poured out on the household of a Roman centurion by the name of Cornelius. Luke describes Cornelius as "a devout man and one who feared God with all his household, and gave many alms to the Jewish people and prayed to God continually" (10:2). Nevertheless, although Cornelius was a sincere worshiper of the God of Israel, in the Jewish mind he remained a Gentile and a foreigner. As before, in looking at the momentous events that transpired in Caesarea, we will ask our three guiding questions: "What happened?", "What resulted?", and "So what?"

WHAT HAPPENED?

The Caesarean Outpouring—including the circumstances leading up to it—is one of the clearest examples in the book of Acts of the Holy Spirit functioning in His role as Superintendent of the Harvest. In this story Luke presents the Spirit as the One who is actively directing the missionary work of the church. A clear emphasis of the entire episode is the conspicuous working of the Holy Spirit on both ends of the situation to arrange a divine appointment between Peter and Cornelius. Through a coordinated series of divine interventions (vv. 3, 10-16, 19) and providential circumstances (vv. 9, 17-18), the Spirit of God brings together Peter, the Jewish apostle, and Cornelius, the Gentile centurion.

The Spirit works in two primary ways to bring about this pivotal event: He first works through visions. One is given to Cornelius (vv. 3-6) and another to Peter (9-16). He also speaks directly to Peter, telling them what to do (vv. 18-19). Afterward, in a meeting with the brethren in Jerusalem, Peter defends his actions in Caesarea by testifying that it was the Holy Spirit who directed him to the work (11:12).

---

2   See Figure 6.2, page 90.

Upon arriving at the home of Cornelius, Peter preached a powerful Spirit-inspired message. Before he was able to conclude his message, however, "the Holy Spirit fell upon all those who were listening" (v. 44). The "all" in this verse appears to include both the Gentile hosts and the Jewish visitors. The six Jewish Christians who accompanied Peter from Joppa were amazed that "the gift of the Holy Spirit had been poured out on the Gentiles *also*" (v. 45, italics added). The "also" indicates that their amazement was not that they themselves had been refilled with the Spirit, but that God had also filled uncircumcised Gentiles with His Spirit. They knew this "for they were hearing them speaking with tongues and exalting God" (v. 46).

Upon hearing them speak with tongues, Peter observed that these Caesarean Gentiles "received the Holy Spirit just as we have," that is, just as they had received Him on the Day of Pentecost. In his later report to the apostles and brethren in Jerusalem, Peter explained to them how "the Holy Spirit fell upon them, just as He did upon us at the beginning" (11:14). He is again referring to the Day of Pentecost. Just as the Holy Spirit was given to the 120 in Jerusalem to empower them for missional witness according to Jesus' promise in 1:8, He is now given to the Gentiles for the same purpose.

Luke's intention of presenting the outpouring of the Spirit on the Caesarean Gentiles as an empowering experience, rather than as a conversion-initiation experience, is evidenced by how carefully he uses Peter's sermon to set the stage for the dramatic outpouring (vv. 34-43). An examination of Peter's message reveals three main themes:

The first is Peter's new understanding of God's desire for the Gentiles to be unconditionally welcomed into the family of God (vv. 34-35). This new understanding was first revealed to Peter in his rooftop vision in Joppa (vv. 9-16). The second theme is the gospel. Peter proclaims the Lordship of Christ (v. 36), speaks of His life, death, and resurrection (vv. 37-40), declares that He is the judge of the living and the dead (v. 42), and then calls his hearers to faith in

Him (v. 43). The third theme emphasized by Peter is Spirit-empowered vocational witness, which he mentions five times in his sermon, as follows:

1. Jesus' Spirit-empowered ministry. Peter's first reference to Spirit-empowered witness is found in 10:38, where he describes Jesus' ministry as follows: "You know of Jesus of Nazareth, how God anointed Him with the Holy Spirit and with power, and how He went about doing good and healing all who were oppressed by the devil, for God was with Him." Jesus' was a vocational anointing, that is, He was anointed by the Spirit to accomplish a God-appointed task. This passage echoes Jesus words in Luke 4:18, where Jesus announced, "The Spirit of the Lord is upon me, because He anointed me to preach the gospel . . . to set free those who are oppressed . . ." By implication, Luke is saying that the anointing the Caesarean Gentiles were to receive would also be vocational. Its purpose, like that of Jesus, was empowerment for service.

2. The apostles' role as witnesses. Next, Peter reminds his hearers of his and the other apostles' role as witnesses: "We are witnesses of all the things He did . . ." (v. 39). This statement references Luke 24:48 and Acts 1:8, where Jesus told His disciples they would be His witnesses once they had been empowered by the Holy Spirit.

3. Witnesses of His resurrection. Peter then tells how God raised Jesus from the dead, and how He appeared to "witnesses who were chosen beforehand by God" (vv. 40-41). The apostle thus informs his hearers that Jesus' followers are called to be witnesses of His resurrection (Luke 24:46-48; Acts 1:22). This statement reminds us of how, earlier in Acts, after the Second Jerusalem Outpouring, the apostles were "with great power . . . giving testimony to the resurrection of the Lord Jesus" (4:33). Once the Spirit is poured out on the Caesarean Gentiles, they too will become witnesses to Christ's resurrection.

4. The command to witness. Next, Peter tells how Jesus had "ordered [those who had witnessed His resurrection] to preach to the

people, and solemnly to testify that this is the One who has been appointed by God as Judge of the living and the dead" (v. 42).

5. The prophets bear witness. Finally, Peter describes Jesus as the One of whom "all the prophets bear witness" (v. 43).

So, in the last seven verses of Peter's sermon of only nine verses, there are no less than five direct references to witness. It is at this moment—in the context of Peter's description of the church's Spirit-anointed witness—that the Spirit is poured out on the mixed, Jewish-Gentile, congregation: "While Peter was still speaking *these words*, the Holy Spirit fell upon all those who were listening to the message" (v. 44, italics added). Note the phrase "these words." To what words is Luke referring? He is referring to the words Peter was speaking at the moment, words about Spirit-inspired vocational witness. It was at that precise moment that God poured out His Spirit on the people. The implication is obvious: God poured out His Spirit on the Gentiles for the same reason He poured out the Spirit on the Jewish believers at Pentecost, that they might receive power to be His witnesses (1:8).

This interpretation of this passage is strengthened by Peter's explanation of the event to the apostles and brethren in Jerusalem. He describes the scene like this:

> And as I began to speak, the Holy Spirit fell upon them just as He did upon us at the beginning. And I remembered the word of the Lord, how He used to say, "John baptized with water, but you will be baptized with the Holy Spirit." Therefore if God gave to them the same gift as He gave to us also after believing in the Lord Jesus Christ, who was I that I could stand in God's way? (11:15-17).

Note how Peter testified that the Spirit fell on the Gentiles "just as He did upon us at the beginning" (v. 15). The Caesareans' infilling with the Holy Spirit was in the same manner, and for the same purpose, as was the infilling of the 120 on the Day of Pentecost. They could therefore expect the same results—empowerment for witness. Peter also quoted Jesus' words: "You will be baptized in the Holy Spirit" (v. 16). This is an obvious reference to 1:4-8 where Jesus linked the Spirit baptism to global witness. Then Peter added, "God gave to them the same gift as He gave to us" (v. 17). The same gift was given for the same purpose—empowerment for mission.

WHAT RESULTED?

What were the results of the outpouring of the Spirit on the Gentile believers in Caesarea? There were at least three, all with strong missiological implications.

IMMEDIATE SPIRIT-ANOINTED WITNESS

First, in accordance with Luke's *empowerment–witness motif,* the Gentile's reception of the Spirit at Caesarea resulted in immediate Spirit-anointed proclamation. Verses 45-46 read: "All the circumcised believers who came with Peter were amazed, because the gift of the Holy Spirit had been poured out on the Gentiles also. For they were hearing them speaking with tongues and exalting God." The phrase, "exalting God," is commonly viewed as describing Spirit-inspired praise directed to God. Such an interpretation, however, stems from a cursory reading, rather than from a careful exegesis of the text. When taken in its missiological context, the phrase is more likely describing Spirit-anointed proclamation, rather than God-directed praise.

In considering this verse, we should remember that God can be exalted in two ways: He can be exalted by our directing praise *to Him.* He can also be exalted by our declaring His greatness *to others.* Peter said that we should "declare the praises" of God (2 Pet. 2:9).[3] Either way, God is exalted. The question, then, is, which way did

---

[3] Other passages that speak of declaring God's praises include Ps. 9:14; 35:28; 51:15; 71:8; 96:2; 102:21; 106:2; 145:4; Isa 42:12; 43:21. Luke could have had such passages in mind when he penned Acts 2:11 and 10:46?

these newly Spirit-baptized believers in Caesarea exalt God in this instance?

Of special interest in this regard is the word *megaloono*, which is translated "exalted". The word and its derivatives are used only eight times in the Greek New Testament. Luke employs it five times, Paul twice, and Matthew once. Let's look briefly at Luke's four other uses of the word:

1. Luke 1:46-47

"And Mary said: 'My soul exalts (*megaloonei*) the Lord, and my spirit has rejoiced in God my Savior . . .'" A careful reading of Mary's Magnificat (vv. 46-55) reveals just how she "exalted" the Lord. Her words are proclamational, occurring in the third person and directed at other people, rather than praise, which is spoken in the second person and directed to God. In Mary's song she speaks of God, using His name or titles four times and the third person pronouns "He," "Him," or "His" thirteen times. Mary, thus, exalts the Lord, not by directing praise to Him, but by declaring His greatness to others.

2. Luke 1:58

"Her [Elizabeth's] neighbors and her relatives heard that the Lord had displayed (*emegaloonen*) His great mercy toward her and they were rejoicing with her." The ASV translates this verse, "And her neighbors and her kinsfolk heard that the Lord had *magnified* His mercy towards her . . ." (italics added). Again, as in the last passage, the message of God's mercy is directed, not toward God, but to a person. God *magnified* His own name in the sight of the people by showing his great mercy to Elizabeth.

3. Acts 5:13

"But none of the rest dared to associate with them; however, the people held them in high esteem (*emegaloonen*)." This esteem that the people held for the Christian community was, no doubt, expressed in complimentary words to others about the Christians, rather than praise directed to them.

4.   Acts 19:17

"This became known to all, both Jews and Greeks, who lived in Ephesus; and fear fell upon them all and the name of the Lord Jesus was being magnified (*emegalooneto*)." It is unlikely that these unbelieving Jews and pagans living in Ephesus magnified the name of the Lord Jesus by directing their praise to Him. They more likely magnified His name by speaking to one another about His mighty power over demons.

It is noteworthy that in none of the four instances cited above is the word *megaloono* used as praise directed toward God. In three instances it is praise words about God spoken by people to other people. In the fourth it is God magnifying His own mercy towards an individual, which also results in witness.

Therefore, since in every other case where Luke uses the word, or one of its derivatives, he uses it in the sense of speaking praise words *about* someone (either God or man) rather than *to* someone, it is reasonable to conclude that *megaloono* in 10:46 could also be describing the disciples' proclamation of God's greatness to others. This is the most plausible meaning, especially when we apply Luke's hermeneutical key, found in Acts 1:8. F. F. Bruce concurs with this interpretation:

> The descent of the Spirit on those Gentiles was outwardly manifested in much the same way as it had been when the original disciples received the Spirit at Pentecost: they spoke with tongues and proclaimed the mighty works of God.[4]

---

4   F. F. Bruce, *The Book of the Acts* rev. ed. (Grand Rapids, MI: William B. Eerdmans, 1988), 217. In an attendant footnote he adds, "Magnifying God" (μεγαλυνόντων τόν θεόν) in v. 46 is synonymous with "declaring the mighty words of God" (λαλούντων . . . τὰ μεγαλεῖα τοῦ θεοῦ) in 2:11."

Further, when we compare this incident with what happened on the Day of Pentecost, and what would later happen in Ephesus, a clear pattern emerges. At Pentecost the disciples were filled with the Spirit and spoke in tongues (2:4). Immediately afterwards, Peter stood up and "prophesied," declaring the good news to the on-looking crowd by direct inspiration of the Spirit.[5] Following the same pattern, when Paul laid hands on the twelve disciples at Ephesus "they began speaking with tongues and prophesying" (19:6). Certainly their prophesying involved more than speaking prophetic utterances over one another. More likely, they did as Peter did at Pentecost. After they had spoken in tongues, they prophesied by proclaiming the gospel to the people of Ephesus as they were being inspired by the Spirit. (We will discuss this more in Chapter 10.)

What happened at Pentecost and Ephesus also happened in Caesarea. The Gentile believers were filled with the Spirit and, as a result, they spoke in tongues and exalted God by declaring the glory of His Son to all who would listen. This interpretation of the text is in line with Luke's *empowerment–witness motif*, introduced in 1:8.

A WITNESS TO THE CHURCH IN JERUSALEM

Not only did the outpouring of the Spirit on the Gentiles in Caesarea result in immediate Spirit-inspired witness to the people of Caesarea, it also served as a powerful witness to the church in Jerusalem. It demonstrated to the Jewish believers there that the Gentiles were also included in God's provision of salvation. The door of faith was opened to Gentiles as well as Jews. The outpouring of the Spirit on the Gentiles also spoke another important message to the Jerusalem church: Not only were Gentiles to be included in the family of God, they were also to be included as full participants in the mission of God. This two-fold provision was demonstrated by their conversion to Christ and by their empowerment by the Spirit for

---

5   See comments on Peter's Pentecostal prophecy in Chapter 4.

missional witness. Peter pressed this argument in his report to the leaders of the Jerusalem church (11:15-18) and later at the Jerusalem Council (15:6-9).

A NEW CENTER OF MISSIONARY WITNESS

Finally, the Caesarean Outpouring resulted in the founding of a new center of missionary witness. Just as the outpourings of the Spirit in Jerusalem and Samaria (and later in Ephesus) resulted in the establishment of a base of missionary outreach, the same thing occurred in Caesarea (18:22, 21:8).

THE CHURCH IN ROME

Before we conclude our discussion on the results of the Caesarean Outpouring, there is another possible missiological result, although Luke does not cite it. It is possible that this outpouring of the Spirit contributed to the founding of the church in Rome. Paul wrote a letter to the church there, but he did not found the church. The question then arises, "Who did found it?" There are at least two plausible answers to this question: First, the church in Rome was possibly started by some of the "visitors from Rome" present on the Day of Pentecost (2:10). It is conceivable that some of these visitors could have been converted and filled with the Spirit on the Day of Pentecost and then, once they had returned home to Rome, began to preach the gospel and founded the church there.

Another possibility is that Cornelius, who was a Roman centurion with the "Italian cohort" (10:1), was involved in starting the Roman church. Once his tour of duty ended in Judea, it is possible that he returned to Rome, and being full of the Spirit as he was, he would have certainly preached the gospel there, and possibly helped found the Roman church. Whether this is the case or not, by opening wide the door to the full participation of Gentiles in the mission of God, the Caesarean Outpouring, like the Samaritan and

Damascene Outpourings before, helped to set the stage for the church's witness "to the remotest part of the earth."

SO WHAT?

Now we ask our final question about the Caesarea Outpouring. What practical lessons can we learn from the outpouring of the Spirit on the Gentile believers in Caesarea? As before, we are reminded of the necessity of our empowerment by the Spirit in order to be effective witnesses for Christ. Because Peter was full of the Spirit, God was able to speak to him on the rooftop and guide him to the household of Cornelius. For the same reason, he was able to preach with power and insight. Surely his anointed preaching contributed to the Spirit-imbued atmosphere which prepared the Caesareans to receive the Spirit. In addition, we can learn three other lessons from the Caesarean Outpouring.

A LESSON ON PREPARATION

First, we learn that, when we go to preach the gospel, we can depend on the Spirit to guide us on the way. If we, like Peter, will prepare out hearts through prayer, and remain open to the Spirit's voice, we can expect that He, as Superintendent of the Harvest, will direct our paths. It was during Peter's time of prayer that God gave him a vision that changed his attitude toward the Gentiles. It was also during this time that the Holy Spirit spoke to him, instructing him to receive the three visitors, and then accompany them back to Caesarea. If we, like Peter, will be filled with the Spirit, and if we will invest time in prayer to God, and if we will remain sensitive to the moving of His Spirit, we too can expect God to supernaturally direct us in ministries.

A LESSON ON CONFIDENCE

A second lesson we can learn from this story is that we can trust God to work on both sides of a Spirit-directed ministry encounter. When God directs us into a ministry encounter, we can confidently obey Him, knowing that He is also working on the other end, preparing the way for our ministry. As God was directing Peter to preach the gospel to Cornelius and his household, He was also preparing Cornelius' heart, and the hearts of his companions, to receive Peter's message. It is a great encouragement to know that God is at work arranging divine appointments for those who will prayerfully partner with Him. When God directs us into a ministry situation, we can be assured that He has gone before us, and that He is already at work preparing the soil for the sowing of the seed.

A LESSON ON INCLUSION

A final lesson we can learn from the Caesarean Outpouring is that all people everywhere have the potential to become full participants in the *missio Dei*. Not only can all people receive the gospel and be saved. They can also participate in God's mission, and can themselves become powerful proclaimers of the gospel to the ends of the earth. God poured out His Spirit on the Gentiles in Caesarea so that they too might be empowered for mission. He will do the same for anyone who today will humbly ask Him for the Spirit (Luke 11:9-13).

Further, the Caesareans' receiving of the Spirit served as an important lesson to the Jews—many of whom felt they were to be God's exclusive standard bearers. They learned that all people, even Gentiles, could participate in God's mission. All can participate precisely because all bear His image (Gen. 1:26-27) and all can be empowered by His Spirit (Acts 1:8; 2:17, 39). If this is so, it should inspire us to boldly proclaim the message of Pentecost to all. We should work to see that everyone who is born of the Spirit is also empowered by the Spirit and taught about their privilege and responsibility to be His witnesses to the nations.

CONCLUSION

Thus far in our study we have examined five of the seven key outpourings of the Holy Spirit in Acts. In each instance we have seen that Luke's consistent purpose in including each was to advance his missio-pneumatological intent in writing Acts. The first two outpourings empowered the church for witness in Jerusalem, and prepared it for further outreach into Judea and Samaria. The third (Samaria) empowered the church to reach deeper into Judea, Samaria, Galilee and beyond. It also began the process of readying the church for witness to the "remotest part of the earth." The outpouring in Damascus resulted in immediate witness in Damascus and the surrounding area. Like the Samaritan Outpouring, it also served to ready the church for witness to the nations by giving to the church Paul, the apostle to the Gentiles. The fifth outpouring, the Caesarean Outpouring, opened the door of Christian fellowship to the Gentiles and demonstrated that they too could be full participants in the *missio Dei.*

In the next chapter we will look at the sixth key outpouring of the Spirit in Acts, the Antiochian Outpouring. This outpouring of the Spirit will officially launch the church on its mission to the "regions beyond" (2 Cor. 10:16).

CHAPTER 9

THE
ANTIOCHIAN
"OUTPOURING"

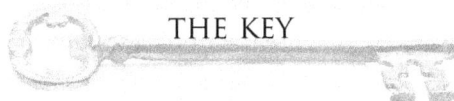

THE KEY

ACTS 1:8

But you will receive power when the Holy Spirit has come upon you; and you shall be My witnesses ... even to the remotest part of the earth.

THE ANTIOCHIAN "OUTPOURING"

ACTS 13:1-4

Now there were at Antioch, in the church that was there, prophets and teachers: Barnabas, and Simeon whom they called Niger, and Lucius of Cyrene, and Manaen who had been brought up with Herod the tetrarch, and Saul. While they were ministering to the Lord and fasting, the Holy Spirit said, "Set apart for Me Barnabas and Saul for the work to which I have called them." Then, when they had fasted and prayed and laid their hands on them, they sent them away. So, being sent out by the Holy Spirit, they went down to Seleucia and from there they sailed to Cyprus ...

An Antiochian "Outpouring"

In this chapter we will investigate the sixth key outpouring of the Spirit in Acts, the Antiochian "Outpouring." It is also the first of two outpourings occurring during the period of the "Gentile Mission."[1] This event launches the church into full-blown intentional missions "to the remotest part of the earth" (1:8). As a result of the continued activity of the Spirit in the church in Antioch, it was to become the second major center of Christian missions after Jerusalem, and the cradle of Gentile Christianity. Paul's three missionary tours began in Antioch (13:1-4, 15:36, 18:23) and the first two ended there (15:30, 18:22).

You will notice that in this instance the word "outpouring" has been put in quotation marks. This is because what happened in Antioch could more properly be called a "move" or an "action" of the Holy Spirit, rather than an outpouring. For purposes of continuity, however, we have chosen to use the word "outpouring" (albeit in quotation marks). It should be quickly noted, however, that this move of the Spirit in Acts 13:1-4, of necessity, presupposes one or more mighty outpourings of the Holy Spirit on the Antiochian church. Only a church that had been endued with the presence and power of the Spirit could have operated in the manner we see this church operating. It is also significant that in Antioch, some seventeen years after the first outpouring of the Holy Spirit on the Day of Pentecost, the Spirit is still powerfully at work in the church, empowering and superintending its mission.

The church in Antioch was truly an international church, with a dynamic mix of Jewish and Gentile believers. Located as it was in a cosmopolitan Roman city (Antioch was the capital of the Roman province of Syria), and open as it was to Gentile inclusion, it is likely that the church quickly became significantly Gentile in makeup. It

---

1   See Figure 7.1

was in Antioch that the followers of Christ were first called
Christians (11:26).

The church was started by Christian refugees who were
scattered during the persecution that arose in Jerusalem after the
stoning of Stephen (11:19-21). The first wave of Jewish Christian
immigrants to arrive in the city reached out to Jews only. The second
wave, however, from Cyprus and Cyrene, preached Christ to the
Hellenists (Greeks) also. The title Hellenists often refers to Greek-
speaking Jews and proselytes. The context of Acts 13, however, seems
to infer that the Hellenists there also included Syrians and Romans.
This view is supported by the fact that in 19:10 Luke contrasts Jews
with Greeks (*Helleenas*), meaning Gentiles, when speaking of the
people of Asia.[2] Be that as it may, this new missions strategy resulted
in many Gentiles coming to know the Lord.

Lucius of Cyrene, one of the prophet/teachers mentioned in
verse one, was possibly one of the group from Cyprus and Cyrene
"who came to Antioch and began speaking to the Greeks also,
preaching the Lord Jesus" (11:20). Also, in Acts 6 one of the seven
Spirit-filled men chosen as "deacons" was a proselyte from Antioch
by the name of Nicolas (v. 5). It is fascinating to think that he could
have been one of the refugees fleeing from Jerusalem who helped to
found the church in Antioch.

James D. G. Dunn describes the Antiochian church as "the
springboard of the most important [missionary] expansion of
all. . . ." He then interestingly adds, ". . . yet Luke does not so much as
mention the Spirit in connection with Antioch (except in his
description of Barnabas)."[3] To the first statement we can say a hardy,
"Amen!" To the second, we can only wonder if he is reading the same

---

2   Paul also uses the word "Greek" to speak generically of Gentiles (Rom. 1:16; 2:9-
10; 10:12; Gal. 3:28; Col. 3:11).
3   James D. G. Dunn, *Baptism in the Holy Spirit: A Re-examination of the New
Testament Teaching on the Gift of the Spirit in Relation to Pentecostalism Today*
(Philadelphia, PA: Westminister Press, 1970), 62.

Bible we are reading.[4] Commenting on the missionary zeal of the
church in Antioch, Stanley Horton notes, "Up to this point the
gospel was carried to new places by those who were scattered abroad.
But there were none who gave themselves specifically to the work of
going to new places to start and organize new assemblies."[5] It was at
this point, however, that the church began to intentionally send
missionaries to the Gentile nations. T. C. Smith comments, "In a
sense, this may be said to mark the launching of Christian world
missions."[6] And it all began, as we will see, with a dynamic move of
the Holy Spirit in the Antiochian church. Let's now ask our first
question concerning the Antiochian "Outpouring".

WHAT HAPPENED?

The church in Antioch was a congregation filled with the
presence and power of the Holy Spirit. This is evident from Luke's
description of the church. He points out that there were "prophets
and teachers" in the church (13:1). Both, according to Luke, speak by
inspiration of the Spirit (Luke 5:17; Acts 2:17-18, 4:2, 5:21, 25, 28,
11:28, 13:9-12; 21:10). Gatherings of the church were filled with
worship, prayer, fasting, and prophetic utterances.

It was during one of these gatherings that the presence of the
Lord was especially evident. As the people were "ministering to the
Lord and fasting," the Holy Spirit spoke. Whether this word came
through a tongue and interpretation, a prophecy, or some other
means, we are not told. What we do know is that it was received by
the church as a clear word from the Lord. The Lord's message to the
church was, "Set apart for Me Barnabas and Saul for the work to

---

4   I am sure that Dunn must be referring to Acts 11:19-30 in the above quote;
however, it still seems remarkable that he could have completely overlooked 11:27-28
and 13:1-4.
5   Stanley M. Horton, *The Book of Acts: The Wind of the Spirit* (Springfield, MO:
Gospel Publishing House, 1996), 155.
6   Allen, Clifton J., ed., *The Broadman Bible Commentary,* Vol. 10, *Acts—
1 Corinthians,* by T. C. Smith (Nashville, TN: The Broadman Press, 1970), 80.

which I have called them." Here again, as in other places in Acts, we see the Spirit functioning as the Superintendent of the Harvest. Evidently the Spirit had already confirmed to Barnabas, Saul, and the church that these two men were to be missionaries to the Gentiles on the island of Cyprus and in the Roman provinces Pisidia and Galatia. Through this prophetic word, the Lord was saying that the time had come to begin this mission.

Even though the prophecy came with great strength and clarity, the church still fasted and prayed over it. Were they testing the prophecy? Were they seeking confirmation from the Lord? We are not told. However, we must remember that "prophecies are not self-authenticating but must be tested"[7] (1 Cor. 14:29). A prophecy of such import cannot be handled in a careless or cavalier manner. It demands serious evaluation, and if found authentic, wholehearted response.

Once the spiritual leaders of the Antiochian church were satisfied that this word had indeed come from the Lord, they commissioned the two missionaries, laying hands on them and sending them on their way. Barnabas and Saul went out, however, not only with the blessing of the church, but also with the blessing of God, for they were also "sent out by the Holy Spirit" (v. 4). French L. Arrington notes, "The work of Barnabas and Saul originates with God—not with plans devised by humans—and is undertaken in obedience to the voice of the Spirit."[8] Robert C. Tannehill has observed that the commissioning scene found in this passage is part of a larger pattern of Luke's. He writes,

> The beginnings of the mission of Jesus and the apostles are preceded by reference to prayer (Luke 3:21; Acts 1:14), which

---

7   Clark H. Pinnock, *Flame of Love: A Theology of the Holy Spirit* (Downers Grove, IL: Inter-Varsity Press, 1996), 134.

8   French L. Arrington, "Acts of the Apostles," in *The Full Life Bible Commentary to the New Testament,* eds. French L. Arrington and Roger Stronstad (Grand Rapids, MI: Zondervan Publishing House, 1999), 598.

provides opportunity for action of the Spirit (Luke 3:22; Acts 2:1-4), and the Spirit leads directly to mission (Luke 4:14, 18; Acts 2:5-41), . . . The mission journey of Paul and Barnabas, like the missions of Jesus and the apostles, is born out of the searching and alertness of prayer and is empowered by the Spirit.[9]

John R. W. Stott asks, "Would it not be true to say both that the Spirit sent them out, by instructing the church to do so, and that the church sent them out, having been directed by the Spirit to do so?"[10]

What qualified the two missionaries sent out from Antioch, at least in Luke's opinion? In Luke-Acts, Luke emphasizes two primary qualifications for ministry: a divine call and the fullness of the Spirit. Both are indicated in this passage:

> Now there were at Antioch, in the church that was there, prophets and teachers: Barnabas . . . and Saul. . . . While they were ministering to the Lord and fasting, the Holy Spirit said, "Set apart for Me Barnabas and Saul for the work to which I *have called them*" (italics added).

The two men's experience with the Spirit is indicated in the designation "prophets and teachers," both of which, in Luke's understanding, required the fullness of the Spirit, as mentioned above. Their divine call is indicated by the Holy Spirit's speaking of "the work to which I have called them."

Further evidences of Barnabas' and Saul's anointing and call can also be found. Paul's qualifications have already been discussed in Chapter 7. Suffice it to say here that he was called and filled with the Spirit soon after he was converted on the Damascus road, and throughout his entire ministry that same calling and touch of the

---

9   Robert C. Tannehill, *The Narrative Unity of Luke-Acts: A Literary Interpretation*, vol. 2, *The Acts of the Apostles* (Philadelphia, PA: Fortress Press, 1994), 161.
10   John R. W. Stott, *The Message of Acts: The Spirit, the Church and the World* (Leichester, Eng: Inter-Varsity Press, 1990), 217-218.

Spirit remained with him (9:15-17, 13:9, 16:18, 17:16, 19:6, 15, 21).
Roger Stronstad comments:

> Paul's experience of the Spirit began when he was filled with
> the Spirit to empower him to witness about Jesus to the
> Gentiles (9:15-17). Luke's portrait of the charismatic
> dimension of Paul's life concludes some twenty-five or more
> years later with his report that, as Paul journeys to Jerusalem,
> the Holy Spirit solemnly testifies (i.e., witnesses) to him
> about his impending bonds and afflictions (20:23).[11]

Barnabas was also a man full of the Spirit. When we think of
Barnabas, we often think of his kind and generous spirit. It was, after
all, this spirit that earned him the name Barnabas, meaning "son of
encouragement" (4:36). What is less known is that Luke describes
Barnabas, not only as a "good man," but as a man who was "full of
the Holy Spirit and faith" (11:24). It was these qualities and
endowments, along with his divine calling, that enabled him to be an
effective evangelist (11:24), teacher (11:26, 13:1, 15:35), preacher
(15:35), prophet (13:1), worker of miracles (15:12), and apostle
(14:14).

WHAT RESULTED?

What was the result of this move of the Holy Spirit in the
Antiochian church? True to his missio-pneumatological intent in
writing Acts, Luke promptly ties this action of the Spirit with witness.
The immediate result was the launching of Paul and Barnabas into
their first missionary tour (13:2, 4). Soon upon their arrival at Cyprus
Spirit-empowered witness commenced. They immediately began "to
proclaim the word of God" (v. 7). The missionaries' ministry during
the entire tour was empowered and gifted by the Holy Spirit. Paul

---

11   Roger Stronstad, *The Prophethood of All Believers* (Irving TX: ICI University
Press, 1997), 90-91.

and Barnabas preached the gospel with power and effectiveness (13:5, 16-41, 44-47; 14:1, 3, 9-17, 21-22, 25). They discerned the work of Satan, the hand of the Lord, and the faith of a crippled man (13:9-10; 14:9). They also performed healings, signs, and wonders (14:3, 9-10), established churches, and appointed elders to lead the churches (14:23). Two summary-type statements characterize their first missionary tour:

- "And the word of the Lord was being spread throughout the whole region" (13:49).

- "And the disciples were continually filled with joy and with the Holy Spirit" (13:52).

The second statement indicates that the two missionaries did not only concern themselves with leading people to Christ, but also into the Spirit-filled life.

As mentioned above, the same power and presence of the Spirit that characterized Paul's first missionary tour characterized his entire ministry. Stronstad notes how each of Paul's three missionary tours began with an action of the Spirit[12] (what might be called a "*pneuma* event"):

- His first tour began with a prophetic move of the Spirit in the city of Antioch (13:1-4).

- His second tour began with a series of revelations, including a vision, which guided Paul and his missionary band westward into Europe (16:6-10).

- His third tour began with an outpouring of the Spirit on twelve disciples in the city of Ephesus (Acts 19:1-7).

Stronstad comments: "The programmic function of these references to the Holy Spirit at the beginning of each missionary tour is Luke's

---

12   Ibid., 92-93.

way of demonstrating that Paul, from first to last, does the work of a charismatic apostle and prophet."[13]

According to Stronstad, these three *pneuma* events further serve as "programmic narratives" for the missionary tours which follow them. Just as each tour begins with a demonstration of the Spirit's presence or power, it is anticipated that the subsequent events of that tour will also be conducted in the power of the Spirit. Stronstad notes how this narrative pattern is part of a larger pattern developed by Luke throughout all of Luke-Acts. For instance, the ministry of Jesus began with a programmatic narrative in which Luke tells about Jesus' experience of the Spirit (Luke 3:22; 4:1, 14, 18). In the same manner, the disciples' ministry began with a programmatic narrative describing their experience with the Holy Spirit (Acts 1:5, 8; 2:4, 33). As in Paul's case, these programmatic *pneuma* events at the beginning of the ministries of Jesus and His disciples demonstrate that their entire ministries would be characterized by the presence and power of the Holy Spirit.

As in the five outpourings which preceded it, the Antiochian "Outpouring" resulted in Spirit-empowered witness. It is yet another example of how, throughout Acts, Luke consistently re-emphasizes his *empowerment–witness motif* introduced in 1:8. This fact supports the assertion that Luke wrote Acts with the primary intent of calling the church of his day—and the church of all time—back to its Pentecostal and missionary roots. In narrative form Luke is saying, "This is how the church should look and act until Jesus returns."

SO WHAT?

The church in Antioch was, indeed, a special church. Out of the many that had been planted in Judea, Samaria, Galilee, Phoenicia, Cyprus, Cyrene, Syria, and other places, this church shone the brightest. It became the congregation God used to launch the church

---

13   Ibid., 93.

into intentional missions to "the remotest part of the earth." What made this church so special, and what two important lessons can we learn from it for our churches today?

THE IMPORTANCE OF CONTEXT

We learn from the church in Antioch the importance of context in creating a truly missionary church. Luke begins his description of the church in Antioch by saying, "Now there were at Antioch, in the church that was there, prophets and teachers: . . ." He seems to be saying that in the church there was a free flow of both Spirit and truth. Although both prophets and teachers deal in both commodities, the prophet is more closely associated with the transmission of Spirit, while the teacher is more closely associated with the transmission of truth. Both ministries are needed in any church—local or national—desiring to be used significantly in fulfilling the *missio Dei*. Note further how the church in Antioch gave itself to "ministering to the Lord," prayer, and fasting. It was in this Spirit-charged atmosphere that the teachers taught and the prophets prophesied.

The pastor or church leader wanting to lead his church into substantive participation in missions must address the issue of context within the church. The following questions must be asked: Is there a manifest presence of the Spirit in the church services? Is the word of the Lord, especially those portions dealing with the mission of the church, clearly and forcefully taught? Are the prophets given the freedom to speak and exercise their giftings? Clark Pinnock writes, "It is wrong for churches to suppress this gift [of prophecy]. The community that silences its prophets is in danger of becoming a Spirit-less place."[14]

If we work to create in our congregations a missional context—that is, an atmosphere filled with teaching about the

---

14   Pinnock, 134.

mission of God—and if we encourage the free flow of the Spirit in our churches, He will inevitably direct us toward world harvest. After all, He is the Spirit of Missions and the Superintendent of the Harvest. Pinnock speaks further of the importance of prophecy in the church. After citing 1 Corinthians 14, he comments on the Antiochian church:

> The picture Paul paints for us is that of a people waiting on God and listening to the Spirit. The potential can be glimpsed in the fact that world missions began by means of prophecy. The church in Antioch was fasting, praying and listening to its prophets when the call came to commission Paul and Barnabas as missionaries (Acts 13:1-4)."[15]

A proper context is essential in creating a missional people, a people whose minds and hearts are focused on harvest both at home and abroad.

SENSITIVITY TO THE SPIRIT

We further learn from the Antiochian church about the necessity of being sensitive to the voice of the Spirit. Missions is, above all else, a work of the Holy Spirit. In the final analysis it is He who does the strategizing, the calling, and the sending of missionaries into the field. Stott has written,

> There is no evidence that Barnabas and Saul "volunteered" for missionary service; they were "sent" by the Spirit through the church. Still today it is the responsibility of every local church (especially of its leaders) to be sensitive to the Holy Spirit, in order to discover whom he may be gifting and calling.[16]

---

15   Ibid.
16   Stott, 218.

To have a truly missional church, we must remain ever open to the voice of the Spirit, whether it comes through a prophet or through an inner prompting. And, when the Spirit speaks, we must be quick to obey.

OTHER SPIRIT-ANOINTED ACTS DURING PAUL'S MISSIONARY TOURS

Before closing this chapter, let's look briefly at some other significant Spirit-anointed missional ministry that occurred during Paul's second and third missionary tours.

THE JERUSALEM COUNCIL (15:1-29)

Soon after their first tour, Paul and Barnabas were called upon to participate in a church council in Jerusalem. It was at this council that the church officially determined not to require Gentiles to become Jewish proselytes, necessitating circumcision, before they were accepted into full membership in the church. As this was a highly significant event in the missionary history of the church, Luke includes it in his account. The church's decision would determine whether the church would be a mere Jewish sub-sect or the global force that Christ had intended. We can be forever thankful that the council decided on the latter.

Looming largely in this account is the central role played by the Holy Spirit. Peter appealed to the outpouring of the Spirit in Caesarea as evidence that the Gentiles should be included in the church without circumcision (15:7-11). Paul and Barnabas told of how the Spirit of God had worked through them to perform signs and wonders among the Gentiles (15:12). This work was presented as another evidence that God had accepted the Gentiles with no preconditions other than faith in Christ. The final decision of the council came as a "word of wisdom" given through James (15:13-29). This is indicated by his assertion that the council's decision had originated with "the Holy Ghost and us" (v. 28). Theirs was a decision too important to be left to human wisdom alone. God graciously intervened, giving them wisdom through His Spirit.[17]

OTHER *PNEUMA* EVENTS

Other significant *pneuma* events during Paul's second missionary tour include an occasion when the "Spirit of Jesus" directed Paul and his missionary companions westward into Europe through a series of divine revelations, including the Macedonian Vision (16:6-10). Spirit anointed ministry during this tour also included inspired preaching and teaching, exorcisms (16:16ff), signs and wonders (1 Cor. 2:1-5; 2 Cor. 12:12; 2 Cor. 10:4; 1 Thessalonias 1:5-6), and visions (18:9-10). During Paul's third tour he prayed with men to receive the Holy Spirit (19:9), worked "extraordinary miracles" (19:11-12), and was publicly acknowledged by demon spirits (19:13-19). These and many other examples of Spirit-anointed ministry indicate that from first to last, beginning with his conversion, empowering, and commissioning in Damascus (9:15-18), until his final ministry in Rome (28:25), Paul ministered in the power and anointing of the Spirit.

Conclusion

In the Antiochian Outpouring, as in the five outpourings of the Spirit that preceded it, Luke advances his missio-pneumatic intent in writing Acts. Once again the outpouring of the Spirit on the church resulted in Spirit-empowered charismatic ministry. In the

---

17   As John V. York notes, James' "word" was not an impression received without reference to his prior knowledge of Scripture. Rather, the Spirit, through the charism, gave James the supernatural ability to correctly interpret the meaning of Amos 9:11-12. He notes, "It is especially significant that the Jerusalem council did not settle a doctrinal dispute on the basis of testimony, not even the united testimony of Peter and Paul. Rather, James appealed to Amos 9:11-12 to settle it, not as a proof text but as a text representative of a wide body of relevant Old Testament texts" (*Missions in the Age of the Spirit*, 58).

next chapter we will look at the seventh and final outpouring of the Spirit in Acts. We are calling it the Ephesian Outpouring. As before, we will see how an outpouring of the Spirit resulted in powerful missional witness. Further, we will see how pneumatic empowering played a central role in Paul's missions strategy, and how it should play a central role in our missionary strategies today.

PART THREE

The PAULINE PERSPECTIVE *on* EMPOWERMENT *for* MISSIONS

- CHAPTER 10 -

THE

EPHESIAN

OUTPOURING

|REACHING ASIA MINOR: A STRATEGIC CASE STUDY|

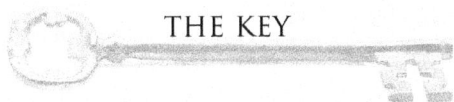

THE KEY

ACTS 1:8

*But you will receive power when the Holy Spirit has come upon you;
and you shall be My witnesses . . . even to the remotest part of the earth.*

THE EPHESIAN OUTPOURING

ACTS 19:1-7

*It happened that while Apollos was at Corinth, Paul passed through the
upper country and came to Ephesus, and found some disciples. He said to
them, "Did you receive the Holy Spirit when you believed?" And they said to
him, "No, we have not even heard whether there is a Holy Spirit." And he*

said, "Into what then were you baptized?" And they said, "Into John's baptism." Paul said, "John baptized with the baptism of repentance, telling the people to believe in Him who was coming after him, that is, in Jesus." When they heard this, they were baptized in the name of the Lord Jesus. And when Paul had laid his hands upon them, the Holy Spirit came on them, and they began speaking with tongues and prophesying. There were in all about twelve men.

On October 1, 1999, about 4,000 Christians from more than fifty countries gathered in Ephesus (Selcuk), Turkey, for an international missions event billed as "Celebration Ephesus." This event was conceived and led by C. Peter Wagner, Third Wave author and president of Global Harvest Ministries. According to Wagner, the aim of the celebration, and the prayer tours that preceded it, was to "take another step in pushing back the same forces of darkness that are again, like in the days of Paul, preventing millions from hearing the gospel and getting saved."[1]

The intercessors and worshipers gathered for the event held in the amphitheater in Ephesus were intent on breaking the power of a major demonic stronghold. In Acts 19, Luke describes Ephesus as the center of worship of the Roman goddess Diana (also known to the Greeks as Artemis). According to Wagner, Diana of the Ephesians is the same demonic entity as the "queen of heaven" mentioned in Jeremiah chapters 7 and 44.[2] She is, according to his understanding, "a demonic principal of very high rank . . . responsible for sending more people to hell than any other idol." Wagner stated, "Recent spiritual mapping has revealed that one of

---

1   Dixon, Thomas. "'Celebration Ephesus' in Historic Turkish Ruins Celebrates Major Spiritual Breakthrough," *Charisma NOW* Website, available <http://www.charismanow.com/a.php? ArticleID= 2185> (September 8, 2004).
2   You can read more about Wagner's views in his book *Confronting the Queen of Heaven* (Colorado Springs, CO: Wagner Publications, 1999).

the Queen of Heaven's major strongholds, if not the principal one, is located in ancient Ephesus, Turkey."[3]

The celebration was a four-hour worship, praise, and prayer service. It included, according to one report, a team of over one hundred "visual worshipers with dance and banners" and "a lineup of international Christian leaders" who offered prayers.[4] In an e-mail announcement prior to the event, a Wagner associate wrote, "Chuck Pierce, Ted Haggard and Dr. Wagner will lead '24 elders and 4 living creatures' in prayers and Scripture readings," and "Larry Brown will lead 120 shofar players in sounding the trumpets."[5] One participant tells how, on their way to the event, her busload of pilgrims "visited the seven cities of Revelation, praying and placing pieces of paper with Scriptures in cracks in idol statues along the way." Another said, "Turkey is about to explode with the Holy Spirit." Wagner concluded the celebration by stating, "There is no doubt in my mind that our goal was achieved."

Celebration Ephesus was an effort by some to implement a mission strategy based on a particular understanding of Scripture. This missions strategy involves, among other things, spiritual mapping, strategic-level prayer warfare, and on-site prayer. It is one of many strategies being promoted in missions circles today. In fact, across the spectrum, the strategy is a much discussed issue in missions. And rightly so, for the task of missions, whether conducted on a global or local level, requires prayerful effective strategizing if our limited resources are to be used to maximum effect.

This chapter will examine the missionary strategy of the apostle Paul. It was a strategy aimed at reaching a major city (Ephesus) and an entire region (Asia Minor, now western Turkey)

---

3   Stan Guthrie, quoting an email announcement sent out prior to Celebration Ephesus in *Missions in the Third Millennium: 21 Key Trends for the 21ˢᵗ Century* (Waynesboro, GA: Paternoster Press, 2000), 77.

4   *Joel News* Website, 5 October 1999, available <http:// www.joelnews.org/news-en/jn294.htm#eph1> (September 8, 2004).

5   Ibid.

with the message of gospel. It is noteworthy that this is the same city and region targeted by Wagner and his associates in their Celebration Ephesus campaign. As we will discover, however, Paul's strategy was very different from that of Global Harvest Ministries, and much more effective.

In the Ephesian account (Acts 19:1-20), Luke presents the clearest and most comprehensive example of the strategy Paul used in his missionary work. Although the literary context of this passage is obviously Lukan, the methodology is clearly Pauline. Writing as a divinely inspired historian, Luke accurately records Paul's missionary activities in Ephesus. Writing as a theologian and missiologist, he outlines, in narrative form, Paul's—and, I believe, his own— missionary strategy. As we will discover later, this strategy has three key components, the first of which involves the pneumatic empowering of the missionary and the church he is seeking to plant. Let's now look at how this strategy was applied to the planting of the church in Ephesus and in all the Roman province of Asia Minor.

THE EPHESIAN OUTPOURING

Paul's ministry in Ephesus holds a special place in Luke's plan for writing Acts. It represents the book's last record of Paul's evangelistic ministry, and the only detailed account of church planting efforts during his third missionary tour. Robert Menzies calls Paul's work in Ephesus "the chief achievement of [his] missionary career."[6] Robert Tannehill refers to it as "the climax of Paul's missionary work."[7] Commenting on Paul's ministry in Ephesus, he says, "Ephesus is not just another stop in a series. It is Paul's last major place of new mission work; indeed, it is the sole

---

6   Robert P. Menzies, *Empowered for Witness: The Spirit in Luke-Acts* (Sheffield, Eng: Sheffield Academic Press, 2001), 220.
7   Robert C. Tannehill, *The Narrative Unity of Luke-Acts: A Literary Interpretation*, vol. 2, *The Acts of the Apostles* (Philadelphia, PA: Fortress Press, 1994), 236.

center of mission noted in the last stage of Paul's work . . ."[8]
According to Tannehill, this fact is confirmed in Paul's address to the
Ephesian elders (20:18-35), which, he says, "suggests that this
description of Paul's work at Ephesus is also meant as a lasting model
for the church after Paul's departure."[9]

In this "lasting model for the church," Luke, in narrative
form, sums up and applies the concepts he introduced in the
previous six outpourings. The Ephesian Outpouring, and the events
accompanying it, succinctly recap Paul's missionary strategy, a
strategy he successfully employed throughout the Roman empire. In
this chapter we will attempt to identify and analyze that strategy. It is
a strategy we are calling the "Strategy of the Spirit."

WHAT HAPPENED?

As with his first two missionary tours, Paul's third tour
started in Antioch, Syria (18:22-23). It began with a pastoral visit to
the churches of southern Galatia and Phrygia (v. 23). Paul then
journeyed westward through the mountainous regions of Phrygia
until he came to Ephesus, the capital city of the Roman province of
Asia. Arriving in Ephesus, he found a local congregation of believers
already in existence—although it appears it was a small, inactive
group. How this church was started we do not know. What we do
know, however, is that Paul had previously visited Ephesus, where he
taught briefly in the local synagogue. When he departed, he promised
the people that he would return to them "if God wills" (18:19-21).
Priscilla and Aquila (18:18-19), and later Apollos (18:24-27), also
ministered to "the brethren" in Ephesus before Paul's arrival.

Paul arrived in Ephesus with a well-formulated plan in mind.
His goal was to plant the church, not only in Ephesus, but
throughout all of Asia Minor. We know this from verse 10, which

---

8   Ibid., 231.
9   Ibid., 236.

says that at the end of just two years "all who lived in Asia heard the word of the Lord, both Jews and Greeks." This amazing accomplishment was the culmination of a deliberate and sustained application of Paul's missionary strategy.

Soon after arriving in the city Paul met twelve men to whom Luke refers as "disciples." They were likely members of the struggling Ephesian church and possibly the same individuals who were referred to as "the brethren" in 18:27. We can assume that they were disciples of Christ since, without exception, when Luke uses the word disciple with no qualifying adjective, he always means a disciple of Christ.[10]

Paul immediately asked these men a thought-provoking question: "Did you receive the Holy Spirit when you believed?" This particular wording of Paul's question is found in most modern English versions of the Bible. It is an accurate rendering of the Greek text. It is, however, only one of two possible translations. Another acceptable rendering is the one employed by the King James Version: "Have ye received the Holy Ghost since ye believed?" Although its diction is dated, the KJV translation is an accurate and acceptable translation of the Greek text. Some Greek scholars maintain that it is the more plausible of the two.[11] How the text is translated can be influenced by the translators' theological presuppositions. Be that as it may, however the question is worded, it presupposes that the Holy Spirit, in the Lukan sense of empowerment for mission, is not, as a matter of course, received at conversion.

---

10   Ref., Luke 9:16, 18, 9:54; 10:23; 16:1; 17:22; 18:15; 19:29, 19:37; 20:45; 22:39, 22:45; Acts 6:1, 2, 7; 9:10, 19, 26, 38; 11:26, 29; 13:52; 14:20, 22, 28; 15:10; 16:1; 18:23, 27; 19:1, 9, 30; 20:1, 30; 21:4, 16. For a complete discussion on whether the twelve Ephesians were disciples of Christ or John the Baptist see Anthony D. Palma, *The Holy Spirit: A Pentecostal Perspective* (Springfield, MO: Gospel Publishing House, 2001), 125-130.

11   Palma, 125-130; Stanley M. Horton, *The Book of Acts: The Wind of the Spirit* (Springfield, MO: Gospel Publishing House, 1996), 221; French L. Arrington, *The Acts of the Apostles: An Introduction and Commentary* (Peabody, MA: Hendrickson Publishers, 1988), 191-192.

The immediacy and abruptness of Paul's leading question demonstrates the importance he placed on the issue. He had come to Ephesus with a master plan for reaching the Roman province with the gospel. His first task was to ensure that the Ephesian believers were empowered by the Spirit as were the Jerusalem believers on the Day of Pentecost. The words of Jesus to His disciples before the Day of Pentecost ("Stay in the city until you are clothed with power from on high") could have been in Paul's mind when he queried the twelve. Paul was not inquiring into their saving faith in Christ, but into their reception of the Spirit as an empowering experience after conversion. Shelton concurs: "Paul initially raised the question about the Holy Spirit because he was primarily interested in empowerment."[12] The men's answer revealed to Paul that they lacked both an understanding of the Pentecostal gift and an empowering experience with the Spirit of God. Paul immediately moved to remedy this unacceptable situation. He first re-baptized the twelve in the name of the Lord Jesus.[13] He then laid hands on them and "the Holy Spirit came on them, and they began speaking with tongues and prophesying" (v. 6). According to Arrington,

> Just as the outpouring of the Spirit at Jerusalem and Samaria, the Ephesian Pentecost marked not a conversion experience but an enduement with the power of the Spirit for spreading the gospel. The whole context of Acts teaches this, and rather than initiatory or soteriological, the immediate context of the Ephesian Pentecost is clearly charismatic: "When Paul laid

---

12   James B. Shelton, *Mighty in Word and Deed: The Role of the Holy Spirit in Luke-Acts* (Peabody, MA: Hendrickson Publishers, 1991), 134.

13   Why Paul rebaptized these men while Priscilla and Aquila did not rebaptize Apollos, who seems to have been in the same spiritual circumstance, is difficult to determine. Arrington attempts to resolve this dilemma by citing 18:25 where Apollos is said to be "fervent in s(S)pirit." According to Arrington, this phrase indicates that Apollos had been "extraordinarily endowed by the Spirit." He reasons: since he had been filled with the Spirit, and the Ephesians had not, Priscilla and Aquila did not require rebaptism while Paul did. In Arrington, *The Acts of the Apostles,*188-189, including footnotes.

his hand on them, the Holy Spirit came upon them; and they spoke in tongues and prophesied . . ."[14]

Luke's use of the phrase "the Holy Spirit *came upon* them" to describe the Ephesians' reception of the Spirit helps us to understand how he intends for his readers to view their experience. He uses the same words spoken by Jesus in 1:8: "You will receive power when the Holy Spirit has *come upon* you." The implication is clear: the purpose of the Holy Spirit's coming upon the Ephesian disciples was empowerment for witness as Jesus had promised.

Also, the fact that Paul laid his hands on these men when they were filled with the Spirit is not without significance. As discussed in Chapters 6 and 7, the laying on of hands in the Book of Acts is often performed as an act of commissioning to service. Here, as in Samaria and Damascus, the purpose seems to be twofold: the first was to facilitate the seeker's receiving the Spirit; the second was to effect their commissioning to missional service. Menzies says, ". . . the association of the gift with the laying on of hands suggests that, according to Luke, the prophetic gift enabled the Ephesians to participate effectively in the mission of the church."[15] Commenting on the Ephesian Outpouring he says that "as a result of their encounter with Paul, they became his fellow-workers in the mission of the church."[16]

Once the twelve had been empowered by the Spirit, Paul immediately moved to implement the second component of his missionary strategy—witness: "And he entered the synagogue [presumably with the twelve newly Spirit-baptized disciples in tow][17] and continued speaking out boldly for three months, reasoning and

---

14   Ibid., 193.
15   Robert P. Menzies, *Empowered for Mission: The Spirit in Luke-Acts* (Sheffield, Eng: Sheffield Academic Press, 2001), 224.
16   Ibid., 221.
17   The twelve disciples being with him is indicated by the statement in the following verse that in departing from the synagogue he "took away the disciples" with him.

persuading them about the kingdom of God" (19:8). While in the synagogue, Paul "preached about the kingdom of God." You will remember that we discussed in Chapter 2 the kingdom of God as one of the five key missio-pneumatological themes found in Acts. The central message of the kingdom of God is the message of its King, Jesus (cf. 17:7). By saying that Paul spoke concerning the kingdom of God, Luke was, in effect, saying he proclaimed the gospel of Christ. Earlier in Acts, Luke spoke of Philip "preaching the good news about the kingdom of God *and the name of Jesus Christ*" (8:12, emphasis added). He will later speak of Paul "testifying about the kingdom of God *and trying to persuade them concerning Jesus*" (28:23, emphasis added), and of his "preaching the kingdom of God *and teaching concerning the Lord Jesus Christ*" (28:31, emphasis added). Arrington insightfully notes that Paul's boldness in proclaiming the kingdom is "a characteristic indication that he is inspired by the Spirit (9:27)."[18]

Upon departing from the synagogue, Paul initiates the third key component of his missionary strategy—mobilization. He does this by establishing an institution for training and sending workers into the field. Verses 9 and 10 say that Paul "withdrew from them and took away the disciples, reasoning daily in the school of Tyrannus. This took place for two years, so that all who lived in Asia heard the word of the Lord, both Jews and Greeks." We will discuss this pillar of Paul's strategy in more detail later in this chapter.

WHAT RESULTED?

The Ephesians disciples' reception of the Spirit had both immediate and longer-term results, as follows:

---

18   French L. Arrington, "Acts of the Apostles" in *The Full Life Bible Commentary to the New Testament,* eds. French L. Arrington and Roger Stronstad (Grand Rapids, MI: Zondervan Publishing House, 1999), 638.

IMMEDIATE RESULTS

The immediate result of the Spirit's fall upon the twelve disciples was Spirit-anointed witness, for "they began speaking with tongues and prophesying" (v. 6). This outcome almost exactly parallels what happened at Pentecost and Caesarea. In all three instances those who were filled with the Spirit spoke with tongues, and in all three instances they bore prophetic witness to the gospel. On the Day of Pentecost the 120 were filled with the Spirit and spoke in tongues. Peter then stood, and under the same inspiration of the Spirit, powerfully declared the gospel of Christ. The same thing happened here at Ephesus when the twelve disciples spoke in tongues and prophesied. Their prophesying is not to be construed as some introverted or narcissistic activity where they simply blessed one another and themselves. It is inconceivable in the context of Luke's missio-pneumatological intent in writing Acts that they turned and spoke "personal prophecies" over one another. This incident is rather to be understood in light of Luke's interpretative key for the entire book, Acts 1:8: "You will receive power when the Holy Spirit has come upon you, and you will be my witnesses . . ." Citing G. W. H. Lampe, Bruce notes:

> . . . Paul's coming to Ephesus marks "another decisive moment in the missionary history." Ephesus was to be a new center for the Gentile mission—the next in importance after Antioch. . . . By this exceptional procedure, then, they were integrated into the church's missionary program.[19]

Paul's witness in Ephesus included not only proclamation but also a demonstration of kingdom power through signs, wonders, and power encounters (vv. 11-19). In Luke's understanding, such

---

19   G. W. H. Lampe, *The Seal of the Spirit* (London, Eng: Longmans, Green, 1951), 76; quoted in F. F. Bruce, *The Book of the Acts,* rev. ed. (Grand Rapids, MI: William B. Eerdmans Publishing Co., 1988), 365.

demonstrations of God's power are a result of one's being empowered by the Spirit, and serve as an integral part of bearing witness to the gospel. They demonstrate the power and proximity of the kingdom (Luke 9:2, 11; 10:9, 11:20) and the love and compassion of Christ (Luke 7:13).

LONGER-TERM RESULTS

There were also some longer-term results of the outpouring of the Spirit on the church in Ephesus. When combined with the other two pillars of Paul's missionary strategy—witness and mobilization—the outpouring of the Spirit in Ephesus ultimately resulted in "all who lived in Asia [hearing] the word of the Lord, both Jews and Greeks" (v. 10). This was an amazing feat, especially when one considers the fact that these first century believers had none of the modern communication technologies we have today. Even the printing press would not be invented for fourteen hundred years! Luke reemphasizes his *empowerment–witness motif* by concluding the episodic series with a summary statement: "So the word of the Lord grew mightily and prevailed" (v. 20).

The consequences of the Ephesian Outpouring went far beyond mere proclamation. The seven churches mentioned in Revelation 2 and 3 were probably indigenous churches planted at this time. Bruce writes, "The province was intensively evangelized, and remained one of the leading centers of Christianity for many centuries."[20] In Paul's epistle to the Colossians we discover that one of Paul's colleagues in Ephesus, a man by the name of Epaphras, participated in the planting of churches in Colossae, Laodicea, and Heirapolis (1:7-8, 2:1-4, 4:12-13).[21] We cannot help but wonder if he was one of the original twelve Ephesian disciples.

---

20   Ibid., 366.
21   Ibid.

PAUL'S MISSIONARY STRATEGY

Let us now look more closely at the missionary "Strategy of the Spirit" Paul employed in reaching Asia with the gospel of Christ. In doing this we will also attempt to create a strategic model for missionary practice today. In the Ephesian episode we have observed three key "pillars" in Paul's strategy for reaching Ephesus and Asia Minor. Let's now look at each in more detail.

PILLAR ONE: EMPOWERING

The first pillar of Paul's "Strategy of the Spirit" is empowering. This empowering must begin with the cross-cultural missionary himself. Paul thus arrived in Ephesus full of the Spirit. This fact is evident from the nature of his ministry there: he preached with boldness (cf. 4:21), prayed with others to receive the Spirit (19:6), and worked "extraordinary miracles" (v. 11). Paul was not content, however, with only himself being full of the Spirit; his first order of business upon arriving in Ephesus was to ensure that the church in that city was also full of the Spirit. He was thus prompted to ask of the twelve disciples, "Did you receive the Holy Spirit when you believed?" (v. 2). This same concern evidently persisted throughout Paul's entire time in Ephesus. He must have continued to labor to see that those who were constantly being brought into the community of faith were also being empowered by the Spirit. It is also likely that Paul instilled in his disciples this same passion to see their converts filled with the Spirit.

We observe, then, two essential aspects of the first pillar of Paul's missionary strategy: (1) the empowering of the cross-cultural missionary, and (2) the equally important empowering of workers in the church being planted (see Fig. 10.1). This two-fold empowering thuslaid the spiritual foundation for the church in Ephesus to become a center of mission activity to reach out to the remainder of the province.

THE NEW TESTATAMENT "STRATEGY OF THE SPIRIT"
ACTS 19:1-20 (FIGURE 10.1)

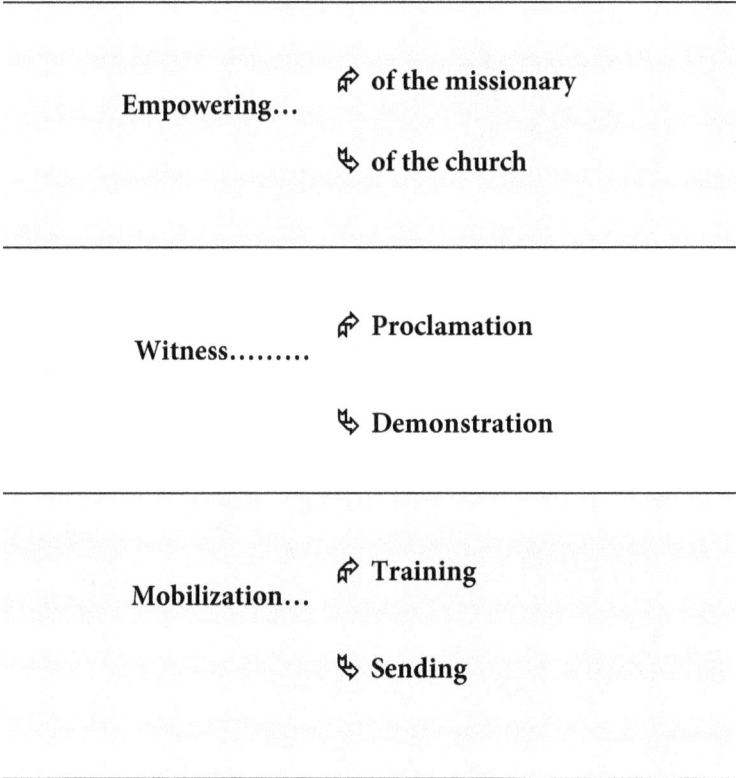

Empowering...
⤷ of the missionary

⤷ of the church

Witness.........
⤷ Proclamation

⤷ Demonstration

Mobilization...
⤷ Training

⤷ Sending

Even today, the first component of any effective missionary strategy must be the spiritual empowering of both the missionary and the church being planted. The church must become a center of Spirit-empowered missions activity. It must have within itself the dynamic spiritual vitality and clear missionary vision to impact its surrounding areas with the gospel. Roland Allen has astutely observed that "there is no particular virtue in attacking a centre or establishing a church in an important place unless the church established in the important place is a church possessed of sufficient life to be a source of light to the whole country round."[22]

PILLAR TWO: WITNESS

The second pillar of Paul's missionary strategy was witness. Paul bore witness to the gospel through powerful preaching of the kingdom of God. This preaching began in the synagogue in Ephesus. Luke tells us that Paul "entered the synagogue and continued speaking out boldly for three months, reasoning and persuading them about the kingdom of God" (v. 8). His ministry is reminiscent of the ministries of Jesus and the apostles in Jerusalem, who daily taught and preached in the temple (Luke 19:47; Acts 5:42). Paul's teaching concerning the kingdom of God also reminds us of Jesus' post-resurrection ministry when for forty days He spoke "of the things concerning the kingdom of God" (Acts 1:3). As we discussed in Chapter 2, two of Jesus' primary kingdom themes during this time were the global mission of the church (Matt. 28:18-20; Mark 16:15-16; Luke 24:46-48; John 20:21; Acts 1:8) and the need for the empowering of the Spirit to accomplish that mission (Matt. 28:20; Mark 16:17-18; Luke 24:49; John 20:22; Acts 1:8). Paul certainly must also have emphasized these kingdom themes in his teaching ministry in Ephesus.

While in Ephesus, Paul also taught "publicly and from house to house, solemnly testifying to both Jews and Greeks of repentance toward God and faith in our Lord Jesus Christ" (20:20-21). As we have already mentioned, Paul's oral witness was accompanied by powerful demonstrations of kingdom power through signs following (vv. 11-20). This second pillar of Paul's strategy of the Spirit, like the first, has two components: (1) the proclamation of the gospel and (2) a demonstration of its power through accompanying signs (Fig.

---

22   Roland Allen, *Missionary Methods: St. Paul's or Ours* (Grand Rapids, MI: William B. Eerdmans Publishing, Co., 1962), 12.

10:1). No doubt the witness of Paul's newly Spirit-filled colleagues included the same two aspects.

PILLAR THREE: MOBILIZATION

The third pillar of Paul's missionary "Strategy of the Spirit" was mobilization. Once the church had been empowered by the Spirit, and as the gospel was being preached, Paul began mobilizing the church for regional missions. This mobilization is indicated in verse 10: "This took place for two years, so that all who lived in Asia heard the word of the Lord, both Jews and Greeks." Without leaving Ephesus, Paul reached the entire province of Asia with the gospel in just two short years. This could only have been accomplished by effectively mobilizing the believers in Ephesus. Paul did this in two ways: First, he trained workers and church planters in the rented school of Tyrannus. There seems to be a clear cause-and-effect relationship between Paul's leadership training and the fact that in the space of only two years everyone living in Asia heard the word of the Lord. The school's curriculum must have included a strong practical emphasis on church planting and evangelism, and the atmosphere of the school must have been saturated with the presence of the Spirit.

Paul's training procedure also seems to have included on-the-job mentoring. As mentioned earlier, this is hinted at in verses 8 and 9 where Paul included the newly Spirit- baptized disciples in his evangelistic ministry. This mentoring relationship is further evidenced by the way he remained in close company with the disciples in Ephesus (v. 9; 20:1). He presumably mentored his students in his missionary methods. Paul later wrote Timothy in the same city (Ephesus) instructing him, "The things which you have heard from me in the presence of many witnesses, entrust these to faithful men who will be able to teach others also" (2 Tim. 2:2).

Once the believers had been trained—or possibly while they were yet being trained—Paul sent them into every corner of the province to preach the gospel and plant Spirit-filled churches.

Doubtlessly, they employed the same missionary strategy as their mentor. The application of this strategy resulted in a spontaneous multiplication of churches throughout the entire region. It is also evident that Paul's strategy included reaching people from all ethnic and cultural backgrounds, for Luke says the gospel was presented to "both Jews and Greeks."

A New Testament "Strategy of the Spirit"

Paul's strategy for Ephesus and Asia Minor was part of a larger New Testament "Strategy of the Spirit." The strategy was not original with Paul. He was simply "working the plan." This same threefold pattern of witness can be clearly observed in the Father's missionary strategy for Jesus, and also in Jesus' missionary strategy for the church He founded. Let's look briefly at each of these strategies.

THE FATHER'S MISSIONARY STRATEGY FOR JESUS

The Heavenly Father sent His Son to earth with a well-defined missionary strategy. Jesus would come in the Father's name (Luke 13:35; 19:38; John 5:43). Before He began His ministry, however, He would need to be empowered by the Spirit (Luke 3:22). Jesus received this empowering for ministry at His baptism: ". . . while He was praying, heaven was opened, and the Holy Spirit descended upon Him in bodily form like a dove" (Luke 3:21-22). In the very next verse, Luke continues, "Now Jesus Himself began His ministry . . ." (NKJV). Jesus did not begin His ministry until He was first anointed by the Spirit. His ministry was thus defined by the power and presence of the Holy Spirit (Luke 4:1, 14, 16-19, Acts 10:38). He further preached the gospel with "authority and power" (Luke 4:18-19, 36), and performed miracles by the power of the Spirit (Luke 5:17; 6:19). In the process, He called (Luke 6:13-16), empowered (Luke 3:15-16; Acts 2:33), trained, and mobilized His followers to do the same (John 20:22; Acts 1:8).

JESUS' MISSIONARY STRATEGY FOR THE CHURCH

In sending His church into the world Jesus applied the same missionary "strategy of the Spirit" that the Father had used in sending Him to earth, including proclamation, mobilization, and empowering. He *proclaimed* the gospel in the power of the Spirit with signs following (Luke 4:18-19; 9:6). He *mobilized* His disciples by training them and sending them out to preach the good news, and He *empowered* them by pouring His Spirit out on them, thus equipping them for the task (Acts 2:33).

The night of His resurrection, Jesus announced to His disciples, "As the Father has sent me, I also send you" (John 20:21). Just as He had been commissioned by the Father and empowered by the Spirit before He began His missionary work, so were His disciples to be commissioned and empowered before beginning theirs. Just before He ascended into heaven Jesus promised His disciples, "You shall receive power when the Holy Spirit has come upon you, and you shall be my witnesses . . ." (Acts 1:8). They were not to attempt the task of world evangelism until they had first received "power from on high" (Luke 24:49, cf. Acts 1:4-5).

Thus, when Paul came into Ephesus, he was simply applying the strategy first employed by God the Father in sending His Son into the world, and then used by Jesus in sending His church to the nations. He employed the same plan of empowering, witness, and mobilization.

In all three of the above New Testament examples of missionary work, spiritual empowering had to take place before the work was attempted. Jesus first had to be empowered before He began His missionary ministry. He then commanded His disciples to be empowered before they began theirs. And now Paul, following the pattern set down by Jesus, immediately concerned himself with the empowering of the Ephesian disciples before he attempted to mobilize the church to reach Ephesus and Asia Minor with the gospel.

SO WHAT?

What lessons can we learn from the Ephesian Outpouring? As with the other six key outpourings in Acts, the Ephesian Outpouring has several for today's church. Let's look at some of those lessons.

SPIRIT-EMPOWERED MISSIONARIES

From Paul's ministry in Ephesus we learn that missionaries and other church leaders must never presume to do the work of God in their own human strength or ingenuity. On the contrary, as the apostle Paul did in Ephesus, they must minister in the power and anointing of the Holy Spirit. This divine enablement comes, according to the Lukan model, when one is filled with the Spirit of God. It remains as one daily walks in the Spirit.

SPIRIT-EMPOWERED CHURCHES

We learn further that any new church plant, if it is going to become a center of effective missional outreach, must have within itself the vitality and spiritual dynamic necessary to achieve that goal. Therefore, as with the apostle Paul in Ephesus, a missionary's first order of business is to see that the church is empowered by the Holy Spirit. This aim can be achieved by ensuring that those who are led to Christ are also led into Spirit baptism and taught how to live a Spirit-filled life. In addition, the new converts must be thoroughly trained in the biblical theology of missions and effective missionary practice.

A SPIRIT-INSPIRED STRATEGY

Another important lesson we can learn from the Ephesian Outpouring is the importance of employing a biblically-based, Spirit-guided strategy in doing the work of missions. In Ephesus, Paul was guided by just such a strategy. It was a strategy based on divine precedent, rather than human ingenuity, and on Spirit-inspired rather than humanly-conceived goals. Paul aimed at scattering Spirit-empowered missional congregations throughout all of Asia Minor. Each of these congregations would have within itself the vision and spiritual vigor it needed to plant other visionary Spirit-empowered churches. In this way churches would be multiplied throughout all of Asia Minor and the gospel would be proclaimed in power to all who lived there—both Jews and Gentiles.

Today we must move with the selfsame divinely-imparted wisdom and purposefulness. Certainly we must strive to "get people saved." However, we must realize that evangelism, as necessary as it is, is not in itself sufficient. We must plant Spirit-empowered missional churches—churches where these new believers are filled with the Spirit, discipled in the ways of Christ, trained to effectively advance the kingdom of God, and then mobilized and sent out to do the same in places near and far.

INTENTIONALITY IN MISSIONS

Further, in all that we do we must move with deliberate *intentionality*. Too much missions activity is done without clear purpose. Too much is assumed. We cannot assume that people will come simply because we open the doors of a new church. We cannot assume that people are being born again just because we are leading them in the "sinners' prayer." We cannot assume that believers are being truly empowered by the Spirit simply because they exhibit some outward physical manifestation. We cannot take it for granted that the church we are planting will be Spirit-empowered just because it belongs to a Pentecostal or charismatic fellowship of churches. We cannot assume that the new church plant will have missionary vision and zeal, simply because it is planted by a missionary or church planter with such qualities. On the contrary, we must have a clear idea of what we want to accomplish, and we must know how we will go about accomplishing our aim.

Intentionality must mark every decision and every move we make. We must personally seek God's face with the intention of being filled (or refilled) with the Spirit. We must preach the gospel with the intention of seeing the lost repent and be truly born again. We must pray with believers with the intention that they become empowered by the Spirit of God. We must plant churches with the intention that they evolve into Spirit-empowered missional churches. And all along, we must intentionally pass on our vision and strategy to the leaders God raises up in the churches. We must then mobilize the church with the focused intention of reaching our city, country, region, and the nations with the gospel. This is how Paul reached all of Asia with the gospel in the space of only two years, and it is what we must do today.

BIBLICALLY-BASED STRATEGY

The missions strategies we employ must always be based on sound biblical exegesis and clear New Testament precedent. For example, compare Paul's strategy for reaching Ephesus and Asia Minor with the strategy of Global Harvest Ministries (GHM) in their "Celebration Ephesus" campaign mentioned at the beginning of this chapter. The primary strategies used by GHM were spiritual mapping, strategic warfare prayer, on-site prayer meetings, and "celebration," including worship, banner waving, praise dancing, and shofar blowing. But how does this strategy stack up with Paul's?

The GHM emphasis on prayer is certainly to be welcomed and commended. All missionary work must be undergirded and sustained by prayer. And we agree that there are certainly seeds of theological truth on which some of their methodologies are founded. It appears, however, that Wagner and others have built a theological cathedral out of a wheelbarrow of exegetical bricks, with much of their theology being built on extra-biblical, rather than biblical, sources. In the process, they have taken a few scattered, sometimes obscure, biblical passages and have woven them into a theological system, and ultimately a missions strategy, which has no clear New Testament precedent.[23]

The Celebration Ephesus strategy for reaching Ephesus and Turkey is a strategy that would likely have confounded the apostle Paul. It is a strategy that neither he, nor Jesus, nor any of the other New Testament apostles and evangelists, ever employed in Scripture. The issue here goes far beyond the rightness or wrongness of the individual methodologies employed by GHM. The most significant issues are the crucial methodologies they tragically exclude from their strategy. Where in their strategy is the clear and sustained preaching of the cross? Where are the cross-cultural missionaries who are willing to learn the language, identify with the culture of their host country, and, if need be, lay down their lives for the people of that land and the sake of the gospel? To think that a series of one or two-week prayer tours concluded by a four-hour praise and worship service—including a smattering of strategic warfare prayer— is going to change the direction of a nation is, in my opinion, naive. Where in the GHM strategy is Paul's emphasis on the empowering presence of the Spirit? Where are the training and mobilization of workers and the systematic planting of Spirit-empowered missional churches? These essential elements of an effective missions strategy are simply not there.

We therefore conclude that, compared with Paul's missionary strategy, the strategy of GHM—and for that matter, any strategy that excludes the central elements of the New Testament "Strategy of the Spirit"—falls short of what is needed to get the job done. Such strategies pose the danger of giving their participants the illusion that they are doing the work of missions when they are, in actuality, being distracted from the real missions tasks of preaching Christ in the power of the Spirit and establishing Spirit-empowered

---

23   For an example of Wagner's method see Chapter 21, "Invading Diana's Territory," from his book *The Acts of the Holy Spirit*, pp. 466-483. See also Chapter 18, "To Europe with Power," pp. 385-413.

indigenous missional churches. Viable strategies do more than give
an impression of success. They bring about real, sustainable success.
Success must be judged on more than subjective feelings like, "There
is no doubt in my mind that our goal was achieved." The gospel must
go forth in Pentecostal power. Spirit-filled churches must be planted,
and those same churches must be mobilized and dispatched for
further outreach.

THE PROMISE STILL APPLIES

We learn a final lesson from the Ephesian Outpouring. The
events of Acts 19 happened some 25 years after Pentecost, and
hundreds of miles from Jerusalem, where the Spirit was first poured
out. On the Day of Pentecost Peter proclaimed that the promise of
the Spirit was for "all who are far off, as many as the Lord our God
will call to Himself" (2:39). Ephesus was one of those "far off" places.
It was far off in at least three ways: chronologically, geographically,
and culturally. Ephesus thus stands as a symbol of the "far off" places
where we live and minister today. Because of what happened in
Ephesus, we can be sure that the promises of Acts 1:8 and 2:38-39
still apply to us. The same experience and the same power for witness
are available to us today.

CONCLUSION

In conclusion, let's quickly review some of the things we
have discussed thus far in this book. In Part 1 of our study we
discussed the hermeneutical issues involved in interpreting Acts. We
then stated that Acts 1:8 serves as the interpretative key to the book.
In this verse Luke established a paradigmatic model for Spirit-
empowered missions. It is, we believe, a model that applies to the
church of every age and locale. That model is found in the first half of
the verse: "But you will receive power when the Holy Spirit has come
upon you; and you shall be My witnesses . . ." In the same verse Luke
also constructs a programmatic outline for the missionary expansion

of the first century church as recorded in the book of Acts. This outline is found in the second half of the verse: ". . . in Jerusalem, and in all Judea and Samaria, and even to the remotest part of the earth."

In Part 2 we have examined six of the seven key outpourings of the Spirit in the book of Acts. In doing this we have demonstrated how each contributes to Luke's missio-pneumatological intent in writing the book. The first outpouring took place on the Day of Pentecost and resulted in immediate powerful witness in the city of Jerusalem (2:14, 43) and a great ingathering of souls (2:41, 47). The Second Jerusalem Outpouring occurred a few weeks after the first, and like the first, also resulted in powerful witness as the disciples "began to speak the word of God with boldness" (4:31, cf. v. 33).

The third outpouring of the Spirit took place in Samaria, about three years after the Day of Pentecost (8:17). This outpouring demonstrated the apostles' concern that every new church plant would become a center of Spirit-empowered missional witness. The outpouring of the Spirit in Samaria ensured that the gospel would continue to spread throughout all of Judea, Samaria, Galilee (9:31), and then to the nations (1:8). Since this was the first outpouring of the Spirit on non-pure-blooded Jews, it represented a significant step in readying the church to take the gospel to the ends of the earth.

The fourth outpouring of the Spirit occurred in Damascus (9:17-18). This outpouring occasioned the empowering and commissioning of Saul of Tarsus (Paul) as missionary to the Gentiles. Like the others, the Damascene Outpouring resulted in powerful witness (9:20, 22, 27-28; chaps. 13-28), again demonstrating Luke's *empowerment–witness motif.* With the empowering of Paul another important step was taken in readying the church for witness to the ends of the earth.

A fifth key outpouring of the Spirit took place in Caesarea, where the Spirit was poured out on the Gentile household of Cornelius (10:44-46). As with the previous four outpourings, the Caesarean Outpouring resulted in witness. When the Spirit fell on the Caesareans, they spoke with tongues and magnified God by proclaiming His greatness to others. This outpouring demonstrated to the Jewish Christians in Jerusalem that Gentiles were to be fully included in the family of God. It also demonstrated that they could become full participants in the mission of God by being empowered by the Spirit like the disciples at Pentecost.

A sixth "outpouring" of the Spirit took place in the Syrian city of Antioch (13:1-2). True to Luke's missio-pneumatic intent in writing Acts, this move of the Spirit also resulted in witness: Paul and Barnabas were sent out on their first missionary journey (vv. 3-4). This event marked the beginning of intentional missionary outreach to the Gentile nations of the world.

Finally, in this lesson, we examined the seventh and final key outpouring of the Spirit in Acts, the Ephesian Outpouring (19:1-7). We have demonstrated that, as with the preceding six outpourings, the Ephesian Outpouring also resulted in missional witness. We have also seen how Paul's missionary work in Ephesus can serve as an enduring model for missionary strategy. In the next chapter we will switch gears a bit and examine how Paul viewed the role of the Holy Spirit in missions in his own writings.

CHAPTER 11

EMPOWERMENT
for WITNESS *in the*
PAULINE EPISTLES

In Acts, Luke presents Paul as a Spirit-endowed charismatic missionary. In the performance of his ministry, he receives the Holy Spirit (9:17-18), preaches with power (9:20-22; 17:22-31; 19:26), receives divine revelation and supernatural guidance (13:9-11; 16:6-10), sees visions (16:9-11; 18:19; 26:19; 27:23-24), heals the sick (14:8-10; 28:8-9), performs signs and wonders (14:3; 15:12), casts out demons (16:16-19; 19:12), prays with others to receive the Holy Spirit (19:6), and works extraordinary miracles (19:11). From beginning to end he discharges his ministry in the power of—and under the direction of—the Spirit of God.

In this chapter we will turn briefly from what Luke says about Paul's ministry to investigate what Paul himself says about his own ministry. We will discover that in his epistles he depicts his apostolic ministry in much the same light as does Luke in Acts. He describes it as one that is empowered by the Spirit and charismatic in character and content. Our investigation of Paul's description of his own Spirit-empowered ministry will center on three select passages from his epistles. We will discuss them in the order in which Paul

wrote them. The three passages are 1 Thessalonians 1:5-8,
1 Corinthians 2:1-5, and Romans 15:18-21.

THESSALONICA: MINISTERING IN POWER AND IN THE HOLY SPIRIT

1 THESSALONIANS 1:5-8

*For our gospel did not come to you in word only, but also in power and in
the Holy Spirit and with full conviction; just as you know what kind of men
we proved to be among you for your sake. You also became imitators of us
and of the Lord, having received the word in much tribulation with the joy
of the Holy Spirit, so that you became an example to all the believers in
Macedonia and in Achaia. For the word of the Lord has sounded forth from
you, not only in Macedonia and Achaia, but also in every place your faith
toward God has gone forth, so that we have no need to say anything.*

This passage in 1 Thessalonians is Paul's first mention of
Spirit-empowered ministry in his epistles. He writes the believers in
Thessalonica reminding how he had ministered among them "in
power and in the Holy Spirit and with full conviction." He further
reminds them of their glad reception of the word he had preached to
them. They had received it "with the joy of the Holy Spirit." As a
result of their reception of the word and the Spirit, they became
witnesses to all the believers in Macedonia and Achaia. Not only that,
but the "word of the Lord sounded forth" from them into
Macedonia, Achaia, and many other places.

The story of the beginning of the church at Thessalonica is
found in Acts 17:1-9. Note that in this account Luke makes no clear
mention of Paul's performance of any miraculous signs during his

time there.[1] Does Luke's omission therefore mean that Paul did not minister in the Spirit's power in Thessalonica (the classic argument from silence)? Not at all, for in our text Paul describes his ministry in the city as being done in the Spirit's power. In this passage he characterizes his ministry in Thessalonica in four ways: "in word," "in power," "in the Holy Spirit," and "with full conviction." Let's look more closely at each of these four descriptions of Paul's missionary ministry among the Thessalonians.

MINISTRY IN WORD

First, Paul reminds the Thessalonians that his ministry came to them "in word," that is, he preached the gospel to them. Paul often refers to the gospel he preached as "the word" (i.e., Rom. 10:8; 1 Cor. 15:2; Col. 1:5, 25-26). Wherever he ministered, his primary commitment was to declare the life-changing message of Jesus' death and resurrection (i.e., Acts 13:28-37, cf. Rom. 15:1-6), and to call his hearers to repentance and faith in the living Christ (Acts 13:38; 20:21). His ministry in Thessalonica was no exception. In the synagogue he reasoned with the Jews for three Sabbaths "explaining and giving evidence that the Christ had to suffer and rise again from the dead . . ." (Acts 17:3). As a result, a large number of Thessalonians believed and "turned to God from idols to serve a living and true God" (1 Thess. 1:9).

MINISTRY IN POWER

Paul also describes his missionary ministry in Thessalonica as being done "in power." In Paul's estimation, the gospel is not only to be powerfully proclaimed, it is to be convincingly demonstrated

---

1   The only possible exception is found in verses 2 and 3, where Luke says that Paul "reasoned with them from the Scriptures, explaining and giving evidence [NKJV: 'demonstrating'] that the Christ should suffer and rise from the dead . . ." The phrase "giving evidence" could possibly refer to certain manifestations of the Spirit that occurred during Paul's ministry in Thessalonica.

with miraculous signs following. This he consistently did in such places as Salamis (Acts 13:4-12), Iconium (14:3), Lystra (14: 8-10), Philippi (16:18), Ephesus (19:6, 11), and also in Thessalonica, as this verse indicates.

MINISTRY IN THE SPIRIT

Next, Paul identifies the source of his spiritual power when he says that his ministry in Thessalonica was performed "in the Holy Spirit." Whether he was proclaiming the gospel or demonstrating its power through signs and wonders, he did all in the power of the Spirit. He understood that his competency was from God, and that only ministry done in the Spirit's power was truly effectual for, in his own words, "the letter kills, but the Spirit gives life" (2 Cor. 3:5-6).

MINISTRY WITH FULL CONVICTION

Finally, Paul characterized his ministry as being done "with full conviction." He was totally convinced of and committed to his message, his mission, and his method. Concerning his message, he wrote, "For I am not ashamed of the gospel, for it is the power of God for salvation to everyone who believes . . ." (Rom. 1:16). Concerning his mission he wrote, ". . . inasmuch as I am an apostle to the Gentiles, I magnify my ministry" (Rom. 11:13, NKJV). Concerning his method, he testified that his ministry was performed "in power and in the Holy Spirit" (1 Thess. 1:5).

JOYOUS RECEIVERS—ZEALOUS PROCLAIMERS

As a result of receiving the word and the Spirit, the Thessalonians became both joyous receivers and zealous proclaimers of Christ. Although they had received the gospel "in much tribulation," they had, at the same time, received it "with the joy of the Holy Spirit" (v. 6). The second phrase implies that the believers in Thessalonica were filled with the Spirit under Paul's ministry. This fact is also evidenced by what the Thessalonians did with the gospel once they had received it. They became its zealous proclaimers: "For the word of the Lord has sounded forth from you, not only in Macedonia and Achaia, but also in every place your faith toward God has gone forth . . ." (v. 8).

Thus, as a result of their receiving the word and the Spirit, the Thessalonians became effective witnesses of the gospel. As in Jerusalem, Samaria, and Antioch, their Spirit infilling caused the church in Thessalonica to become a center of evangelistic and missionary outreach to the region. Paul reminds them that the word of the Lord had sounded forth from them in the regions of Macedonia and Achaia. It is almost as if he is echoing Luke's empowerment—witness motif found in Acts 1:8.

CORINTH: A DEMONSTRATION
OF THE SPIRIT AND POWER

1 CORINTHIANS 2:1-5

And when I came to you, brethren, I did not come with superiority of speech or of wisdom, proclaiming to you the testimony of God. For I determined to know nothing among you except Jesus Christ, and Him crucified. I was with you in weakness and in fear and in much trembling, and my message and my preaching were not in persuasive words of wisdom, but in demonstration of the Spirit and of power, so that your faith would not rest on the wisdom of men, but on the power of God.

In this passage Paul reminds the Corinthians of his missionary ministry among them. As with his ministry in Thessalonica, his ministry in Corinth centered on the proclamation of the gospel, and it was marked by a "demonstration of the Spirit and power" (1 Cor. 2:4).

SPIRIT-EMPOWERED MINISTRY

Paul's ministry in Corinth is described in Acts 18:1-21. It occurred near the end of his second missionary tour. Again, as in

Thessalonica, Luke makes no mention of any outward manifestations of the Spirit's power. And as before, we must not allow Luke's silence on the subject to lead to the conclusion that Paul worked no miraculous signs while in Corinth, for here in our selected text he describes his ministry in Corinth as a demonstration of the Spirit's power. Later, in 2 Corinthians, he reminds the believers there that "the signs of a true apostle were performed among you with all perseverance, by signs and wonders and miracles" (12:12).

Before arriving in Corinth Paul made a conscious choice of how he would present the gospel. This choice is indicated by his words, "for I determined" (1 Cor. 2:2). He states that he determined his ministry in Corinth would include two key elements: a clear proclamation of the gospel and an open demonstration of its power. He would preach nothing but "Jesus Christ, and Him crucified" (v. 2), and he would rely "not in persuasive words of wisdom, but in demonstration of the Spirit and of power" (v. 4). His avowed motive for adopting this strategy was "so that [the Corinthian's] faith would not rest on the wisdom of men but on the power of God" (v. 5). One wonders what could have prompted Paul to make such a resolution. Some have suggested that it could have been as a result of his poor showing in Athens, where he sought to use human wisdom and superiority of speech (Acts 17:32-34).[2]

SPIRIT-DIRECTED INTENTIONALITY

Through Paul's words in this passage ("for I determined") we are again reminded of the importance of Spirit-directed intentionality in missions, as discussed in Chapter 10. Like Paul, the wise church planter will do well to proceed to the work with such purposefulness. He will consciously and deliberately plant Spirit-

---

2   William Barclay, *The Letters to the Corinthians*, rev. ed., (Louisville, KY: Westminister John Knox Press, 1975), 23-24; A. Scott Moreau, Gary R. Corwin, and Gary B. McGee, *Introducing World Missions: A Biblical, Historical, and Practical Survey* (Grand Rapids: Baker Academic, 2004), 58-59.

empowered, missions-oriented, churches. If the work is to prosper, and the number of churches multiplies in a region, each new church must possess the spiritual and philosophical dynamic necessary to sustain and advance the work. Such a dynamic will only happen if the emerging churches are endowed with the presence and power of the Spirit and if they have a proper understanding of their missional *raison d'être.*

Paul thus arrived at Corinth with a well-formulated strategy: He would preach Christ crucified, he would expect Him to confirm the word with signs following, and he would do all in the power of the Spirit.

His strategy was evidently successful, for Luke tells us that "many of the Corinthians who heard him believed and were baptized" (Acts 18:8, NIV). A large powerful charismatic church was established in Corinth (1 Cor. 1:6). No doubt Paul's Spirit-empowered ministry in Corinth served as a model for other Spirit-empowered ministry in the church and in the area. As other believers were filled with the Spirit and gifted for ministry, Paul's ministry was multiplied. Although the Corinthian church got "off track" at some point in its understanding and use of spiritual gifts, and required correction, there is no denying that Paul's strategy resulted in a strong, thriving church.

Like Paul, we too must make calculated determinations concerning our ministries. One important decision is to keep the message of Christ and Him crucified at the center of all our preaching and teaching. Another is to do all in the power of the Spirit and to expect Christ to confirm His word with signs following. Finally, we must make it our determined aim to plant Spirit-empowered missional churches capable of replicating themselves in the surrounding region and ultimately in all of the world.

Rome: Fully Proclaiming the Gospel of Christ

ROMANS 15:18-21

For I will not presume to speak of anything except what Christ has accomplished through me, resulting in the obedience of the Gentiles by word and deed, in the power of signs and wonders, in the power of the Spirit; so that from Jerusalem and round about as far as Illyricum I have fully preached the gospel of Christ. And thus I aspired to preach the gospel, not where Christ was already named, so that I would not build on another man's foundation; but as it is written, "They who had no news of him shall see, And they who have not heard shall understand."

Paul wrote his epistle to the Romans in anticipation of an upcoming visit to their city (Rom. 1:10). His visit to Rome was to be an extended stopover on a missionary journey even further westward into Spain (15:28). Paul presumably felt that Rome would make an excellent springboard for missionary operations in Iberia, just as Antioch had been for reaching into Asia and eastern Europe. He, therefore, wrote the believers in Rome to solicit their support for this anticipated missionary campaign (15:23-24). He hoped to prepare them for his upcoming visit by informing them of his missionary plans and by making them aware of the purpose and manner of his missionary ministry.

In 15:18-21 Paul explains to the Christians in Rome how he went about his missionary task. These verses represent his most comprehensive explanation of his missionary strategy. This strategy, as we have already discovered, relied heavily on the presence and power of the Holy Spirit. Let's look more closely at how Paul describes his missionary strategy in these verses.

FOCUSING ON THE UNREACHED

Paul clearly understood his calling and mission. In this passage he reminds the Romans that God had called him to be "a

minister of Christ Jesus to the Gentiles" (v. 16). This statement is
reminiscent of the Jesus' words to Ananias when He sent him to pray
with Paul to receive the Holy Spirit: "Go, for he is a chosen
instrument of Mine, to bear My name before the Gentiles . . ." (Acts
9:15).

Paul also knew God had called him to preach the gospel
"where Christ was not known" (v. 20, NIV). He thus considered
himself a foundation layer. His eyes were steadfastly fixed on the
"regions beyond" (2 Cor. 10:16). In support of this fact, he quoted
from Isaiah: "'They who had no news of Him shall see, And they who
have not heard shall understand'" (v. 21; cf. Isa. 52:15). It was
because of this high calling that Paul was now setting his sights on
Spain. With these things in mind he wrote the Romans to explain to
them how he had, in the past, gone about fulfilling his missionary
calling, and by implication, how he intended to do it in the future.

PROCLAIMING AND DEMONSTRATING

At the center of Paul's strategy to reach the Gentiles was his
commitment to proclaim the gospel of Christ. He tells the Romans, ".
. . from Jerusalem and round about as far as Illyricum I have fully
preached the gospel of Christ" (v. 19). For Paul the story of Christ's
death, burial, and resurrection was the center of the gospel message
(1 Cor. 15:1-6), and it was this message of the victorious Christ that
he boldly proclaimed throughout the Roman Empire. The book of
Romans is itself an extended explanation of that message. The
message of Christ's death and resurrection also formed the heart of
the apostolic *kerygma* as recorded in his sermons in Acts (9:20, 22;
13:26-33; 14:15; 17:2-3, 17-18). Today, the message of "Jesus Christ,
and Him crucified," must remain the centerpiece of our missionary
ministries.

When Paul said that he had "fully preached the gospel of
Christ," he was not, however, speaking exclusively of content. Nor
was he claiming that he had proclaimed the gospel in every locality,
or to every person. He was saying that he had included every

necessary element and action required for the gospel to be presented in its powerful totality. When Paul says that he *fully* preached the gospel he is making specific reference to how he had done it "by word and deed" (Rom. 15:18). And since in this passage Paul clearly defines "deed" as "the power of signs and wonders," he is implying that the gospel has not been fully preached until its truth has been clearly proclaimed and its power has been convincingly demonstrated.

The phrase Paul uses here ("by word and deed") is also a favorite of Luke's.[3] Luke uses the same phrase to describe the anointed ministries of Moses ("a man of power in words and deeds," Acts 7:22), of Jesus ("a prophet mighty in deed and word," Luke 24:19), and of Jesus again ("all that Jesus began to do and teach," Acts 1:1). This multiple use of the phrase by Paul and Luke seems to lend strength to the view that each knew and understood the teachings of the other, and that the pneumatologies of both, though unique, were complementary.

This passage reminds us of Luke's description of Paul's ministry in Ephesus (Acts 19:1-20), as we discussed in the last chapter. There, in addition to "reasoning and persuading them about the kingdom of God" (v. 8) and preaching Jesus (v. 13), he was also used by God to perform "extraordinary miracles," including healing the sick and casting out demons (vv. 11-12). Paul's description of his missionary strategy here in Romans thus accords well with Luke's description of the way he implemented that same strategy in Ephesus.

THE SOURCE OF PAUL'S POWER

What was the source of Paul's power? What enabled him to preach and teach so effectively, and to minister so powerfully in "word and deed, in the power of signs and wonders"? He answers the

---

3   Paul also uses the phrase in Col. 3:17 and 2 Thess. 2:17.

question himself: He did it all "in the power of the Spirit" (v. 19). Throughout his ministry, the Holy Spirit, whom he received when Ananias laid hands on him many years previously (Acts 9:17-18), remained the source of Paul's spiritual power. His awareness of this fact must have influenced the way Paul ministered to others.

It became his aim to see that those who received Christ should also experience the empowering presence of the Spirit, just as he had. He thus prayed with the twelve disciples in Ephesus to receive the Spirit (Acts 19:6) and later exhorted the believers there to "be filled with the Spirit" (Eph. 5:18). With this same passion in his heart, he informed the Roman Christians that, when he came to them, he would come "in the fullness of the blessing of Christ" (Rom. 15:29), that is, in the power of the Spirit of Christ.

In summary, Paul explained to the Romans that his missionary ministry was Christ-centered, Spirit-empowered, charismatic, and focused on those who had never heard the message of the gospel. His aim was to "fully preach the gospel of Christ" which for Paul meant more than just preaching *per se*. It involved both saying and doing—and doing included a demonstration of the power of the gospel through signs and miracles performed through the Spirit of God.

CONCLUSION

What then shall we conclude concerning the theologies of Paul and Luke? Some have suggested that their pneumatologies are somehow in conflict with one another, and at times one may even teach things about the person or work of the Holy Spirit with which the other would strongly disagree. Others have contended that both men's teachings on the Holy Spirit are identical, and that neither has any unique understanding or emphasis of its own. The truth, however, seems to reside somewhere in between these two poles. A thoughtful comparison of the teachings of both men reveals, as Palma and others have noted, that Luke's and Paul's pneumatologies

should be viewed as complementary rather than competitive.[4]
Menzies, while conceding that the concept of an empowering
experience of the Spirit distinct from conversion is not clearly
articulated by Paul, contends that the idea is "consistent with (and
complementary to) [Luke's] theological perspective."[5] He states
further that "Paul frequently alludes to the power of the Spirit
enabling his own ministry (Rom. 15:19; 1 Cor. 2:4; 1 Thess. 1:5). And
he also refers to special anointings that energize the ministry of
others (1 Tim. 4:14; 2 Tim. 1:6-7; cf. 1 Thess. 5:19)."[6] In that Paul and
Luke traveled many miles together as missionary colleagues, it is
likely that they often discussed these issues at length, and that each
understood the other's unique emphasis in teaching and preaching
about the role of the Spirit in the Christian life and in missionary
endeavor.[7]

Granted, Paul's theology of the Holy Spirit is broader than
Luke's somewhat narrower focus on prophetic empowerment for
missional witness. Paul more comprehensively applies the work of
the Spirit to the wider spectrum of the entire Christian life, including
the soteriological work of the Spirit in refgeneration and
sanctification. Does this truth, however, mean that Paul fails to
address the issue of empowerment for mission? This would be a false

---

4   Anthony D. Palma, *The Holy Spirit: A Pentecostal Perspective* (Springfield, MO:
Gospel Publishing House, 1989), 93. Palma writes, "Complementariness, not
competition or contradiction, usually characterizes seemingly irreconcilable differences.
What is the perspective of the particular writer? For instance, does James really
contradict Paul on the relationship between faith and works? Or are his statements
guided by his reason for writing on the matter, and so need to be interpreted in that
light? Do Paul and Luke really contradict each other on the Spirit's ministry?"
5   William W. Menzies and Robert P. Menzies, *Spirit and Power: Foundations of
Pentecostal Experience* (Grand Rapids, MI: Zondervan Publishing House, 2000), 194.
6   Ibid.
7   Luke was with Paul during part of his second missionary tour, when Paul and his
party were in Troas and Philippi (Acts 16:10-40). He was also with Paul during his
third missionary tour, when together they journeyed from Troas to Jerusalem (20:5–
21:17). He also accompanied Paul on his final visit to Jerusalem and traveled with him
on his sea voyage to Rome (27:1–28:16). In addition, Luke spent time with Paul while
he was imprisoned in Rome (Col. 4:14, cf. 4:3, 10. 18; Phile. 24, cf. 1, 9).

conclusion, as this chapter has demonstrated. Both Luke and Paul believed and taught that the infilling of the Spirit was a necessary element in evangelistic and missionary work, and that no one should attempt extensive spiritual ministry without first being empowered by the Holy Spirit. Today, if our missionary efforts are to yield maximum results, then, we too must believe and teach these vital truths.

PART FOUR

APPLICATION

- C H A P T E R   1 2 -

THE ROLE *of*
SPIRITUAL GIFTS
in MISSIONS

1 CORINTHIANS 12:7-10

*But to each one is given the manifestation of the Spirit for the common good.
For to one is given the word of wisdom through the Spirit, and to another
the word of knowledge according to the same Spirit; to another faith by the
same Spirit, and to another gifts of healing by the one Spirit, and to another
the effecting of miracles, and to another prophecy, and to another the
distinguishing of spirits, to another various kinds of tongues, and
to another the interpretation of tongues.*

We have been examining the role of spiritual empowerment
in missions. Our study, however, would not be complete without a
discussion of spiritual gifts. The late British Pentecostal scholar,
Donald Gee, once wrote, "World evangelization should involve a
demonstration of spiritual gifts in action."[1] These sage words need to
be heard and heeded by the church today as it seeks to bring about
closure to the Great Commission.

---

1   Donald Gee, "Spiritual Gifts in World Evangelization" in *Azusa Street and
Beyond: Pentecostal Missions and Church Growth in the Twentieth Century,* ed. L Grant
McClung (South Plainfield, NJ: Bridge Publishing, 1986), 63.

In many contemporary missions circles, however, there is a tendency to rely too heavily on human intellect, modern technology, or the latest leadership theory to accomplish the mission of God. Certainly, all of these have their place in missions, and each must be employed to its fullest. The key to world evangelization, however, is not to be found in any of these humanly-conceived methods. It is to be found, rather, in the power and presence of the Holy Spirit. The missionary's chief concern must remain his own spiritual vitality and the spiritual vitality of the churches he plants. Spiritual gifts are outgrowth of such inner spiritual vitality. The power received at Spirit baptism is, to a large degree, released and manifested through the operation of spiritual gifts.

In this chapter we will examine the role of spiritual gifts in missionary work. We will attempt to interface Paul's teaching concerning spiritual gifts in 1 Corinthians 12:7-10 with the manifestation of those same gifts in the book of Acts. Our discussion will focus on four issues relating to spiritual gifts in the work of missions: We will first define and categorize the gifts. We will then look into the book of Acts and observe those same gifts in action. Next, we will discuss and evaluate the missiological implications of the use (or non-use) of spiritual gifts in the work of missions. And finally, we will examine the relationship between the baptism in the Holy Spirit and the gifts.

DEFINING AND CATEGORIZING THE GIFTS

In 1 Corinthians 12:7-10 Paul lists nine gifts, or, more properly, manifestations[2] of the Holy Spirit (v. 7). This list should, of course, not be viewed as an exhaustive list of spiritual gifts, since

---

2   Actually, Paul uses the word "manifestation" (*phaneroosis*) in its singular form (just as he uses the word "fruit" in its singular form in Galatians 5:22), implying that together all of the gifts are the way the Spirit manifests, or makes His presence known, in the church.

there are at least four other gift lists in the New Testament.[3] Paul
does, however, seem to present this list as uniquely significant, and
we should, therefore, view it as such.

INTERPRETATIVE CHALLENGES

In our investigation we face significant difficulties: The first
is that, in presenting his gift lists, Paul designates but does not define
nor demonstrate the gifts in actual operation (see Fig. 12.1 below).
He simply names the gifts, evidently assuming that his original
readers would understand what he is talking about. We as twenty-
first century interpreters are thus left wondering about the exact
nature of each gift. Thankfully, however, clues can be found in their
names and in the contexts in which they appear. Clues can also be
found by observing their numerous manifestations in the gospels and
Acts.

A COMPARISON: THE GIFTS IN THE PAULINE EPISTLES AND ACTS
(FIGURE 12.1)

	PAULINE EPISTLES	ACTS
Designates:	Yes	No
Defines:	No	No
Demonstrates:	No	Yes
Context:	The church gathered for worship	The church scattered in evangelism

A second difficulty we encounter in our study of spiritual
gifts is that, while Paul designates, yet fails to define or demonstrate,
Luke demonstrates, yet fails to designate or define (Fig. 12.1). He
simply shows the gifts in action, as they were being manifested in the
missionary advance of the early church. He does not seem to feel it is

---

3   Other gift lists include 1 Corinthians 12:28-30, Ephesians 4:11, Romans 12: 6-8,
and 1 Peter 4:10-11.

necessary to designate which specific gift (or gifts) is being employed on any given occasion.

Another interpretative challenge we face is context. The context of Paul's teaching on spiritual gifts is the church gathered for worship (Fig. 12.1). In his discussion of the gifts Paul says, "What is the outcome then, brethren? *When you assemble*, each one has a psalm, has a teaching, has a revelation, has a tongue, has an interpretation. Let all things be done for edification" (14:26, emphasis added).[4] The context of the manifestation of spiritual gifts in Acts, however, is the church scattered in evangelism—the church ministering in the marketplace. These two differing contexts naturally necessitate somewhat different approaches to the ministry and manifestation of spiritual gifts.

There is yet another difficulty we encounter in our study of spiritual gifts in Acts. As we read Acts looking for the gifts in operation, we are soon struck with the fact that there is a considerable overlapping of gifts. It is, therefore, often difficult to determine precisely which gift is being manifested in a given instance. For example, it is often difficult to determine whether a gift of healing or a gift of faith is being manifested, or whether, in another instance, a word of knowledge or a discerning of spirits is being manifested. It is, however, much easier to determine the category (revelation, prophecy, or power) into which a gift falls, as we will see later on in this chapter.

With all of these challenges before us, our defining and categorizing of the gifts must be considered, at best, tentative. It is simply an attempt to better understand spiritual gifts as presented in the New Testament. We must, therefore, be careful to approach our subject with humility.

---

4   See also 1 Cor. 5:4; 11:17-18, 20, 33-34; 14:23.

THE IMPORTANCE OF THE ISSUE

And yet, with all of these challenges before us, it is still essential that we grapple with the issue. Far too often the church has ignored or minimized spiritual gifts—thus weakening its own fabric and stunting its evangelistic outreach and missionary advance. To ignore the gifts theologically is to dismiss them practically.

The practical implications of a proper understanding and utilization of spiritual gifts are far-reaching in at least two ways: First, the implications are far-reaching in the internal life of the church. Will any church that ignores spiritual gifts be able to properly build itself up in the faith? Without spiritual gifts in operation, will the practical and spiritual needs of the people be adequately met? Can a church that is satisfied to operate on human wisdom and ingenuity, rather than on divine enablement, ever be all that Christ intends it to be?

The neglect of spiritual gifts also has far-reaching implications in relation to the church's fulfillment of its global evangelistic mandate. Without the manifestation of spiritual gifts, will the church be able to effectively challenge and overcome the spiritual forces seeking to hinder its advance? Without their operation, will missionaries be able to adequately preach the gospel, and convincingly demonstrate its true nature and power? If missionaries fail to utilize spiritual gifts, and if the gifts are not imparted to the churches they plant at home and abroad, will those churches ever be able to extend a powerful Spirit-anointed witness to their own cultures and beyond? Since the manifestation of spiritual gifts is vital to the life and mission of the church, we will endeavor to come to grips with the issue.

CATEGORIES AND DEFINITIONS

Scholars have attempted to categorize Paul's list of spiritual gifts found in 1 Corinthians 12:8-10 in various ways. Some have seen possible clues in the text based on Paul's use of the Greek words *allos* (another of the same kind) and *heteros* (another of a different kind).[5] Using this method, David Lim groups the nine spiritual gifts into three "functional" categories: (1) teaching and preaching gifts, including the message of wisdom and the message of knowledge, (2) ministry gifts to the church and the world, including, faith, gifts of healings, miraculous powers, prophecy, and distinguishing between spirits, and (3) worship gifts, including, different kinds of tongues and the interpretation of tongues. Gordon Fee, using the three categories hinted at in 1 Corinthians 12:4-6, groups the gifts under the three headings of "service, miracles, and inspired utterance."[6]

While these and other groupings are helpful, we have chosen to use the three categories into which Pentecostal and charismatic teachers and scholars have traditionally grouped these nine gifts—groupings into which the gifts seem to naturally fall.[7] Although different interpreters use slightly different terminology, the three categories are essentially the same: revelatory gifts, prophetic gifts, and power gifts. The usefulness of this schema will be demonstrated later in this chapter when we examine the operation of spiritual gifts in Acts. The gifts falling under each of these three categories and their attendant gift are as indicated in Figure 12.2 below:

---

5   David Lim, *Spiritual Gifts: A Fresh Look* (Springfield, MO: Gospel Publishing House, 1999), 65.

6   Gordon D. Fee, *Paul, the Spirit, and the People of God* (Peabody, MA: Hendrickson Publishers, Inc., 1996),165.

7   Typical examples include J. W. Jepson, *What You Should Know About the Holy Spirit* (Springfield, MO: Radiant Books, 1986), 127-150; Lester Sumrall, *The Gifts and Ministries of the Holy Spirit* (New Kensington, PA: Whitaker House, 1993), 53-56; Dennis Bennett and Rita Bennett, *The Holy Spirit and You* (Plainfield, NJ: Logos International, 1971), 83; John Rea, *The Holy Spirit in the Bible: All the Major Passages About the Spirit: A Commentary* (Lake Mary, FL: Creation House, 1990), 246-247.

THE GIFTS CATEGORIZED
(FIGURE 12.2)

	REVELATORY GIFTS	PROPHETIC GIFTS	POWER GIFTS
GIFTS INCLUDED	• Word (or message) of wisdom • Word (or message) of knowledge • Distinguishing between spirits	• Prophecy • Different kinds of tongues • Interpretation of tongues	• Gifts of healings • Faith • Works of power (Gk: *energemata dunameon*)

Our working definition for spiritual gifts is as follows: *Spiritual gifts are supernatural anointings given through Spirit-filled believers by the Holy Spirit to accomplish the will of the Father.* It will be helpful to examine this definition more closely.

As *supernatural anointings*, spiritual gifts have their origin, not in the abilities of man, but in the nature of God. They come to believers as "anointings," or divine enablements. They are thus administered under the supervision of the Holy Spirit, and are released as He moves upon, and through, yielded individuals.

Note also that, according to our definition, the gifts are *given*. In other words, they are dispensed, not on the basis of merit or reward, but as simple demonstrations of God's free grace. The fact that they are given, however, does not mean that they are given as personal possessions. They are, rather, released on a case-by-case basis to meet specific needs in relation to the work of God. Hugh Jeter has insightfully noted that "we are not made vast reservoirs of the mighty power of God, but are channels through which His Spirit can flow and do His work."[8]

---

8   Hugh Jeter, *By His Stripes: A Biblical Study on Divine Healing* (Springfield, MO: Gospel Publishing House, 1977), 68.

Spiritual gifts are further released *through Spirit-filled believers*, that is, through those who have been filled with the Holy Spirit and are currently walking and living "in step with the Spirit" (Acts 2:4; Eph. 5:18; Gal.5:25, NIV). Note further that these gifts are given *by the Holy Spirit*. It is He who is the Divine Dispenser of the gifts (1 Cor.12:4-6). They, therefore, operate, not according to the will of man, but according to the will of the Spirit (1 Cor.12:11). Finally, the gifts are given *to accomplish the will of the Father*. They are released, not to fulfill the goals and desires of any person, but rather to accomplish God's will and to advance His kingdom on the earth.

Let's now attempt to define each of the nine gifts of 1 Corinthians 12:7-10. As with our general definition of spiritual gifts, we also call these definitions "working definitions" since they can in no way be considered the final word on the matter. They will, however, help us in our investigation of the gifts in action in Acts.

Revelatory gifts. The first category is revelatory gifts. These gifts can be defined simply as Spirit-conferred insight. They are given to the Christian worker by the Spirit in order that he or she might know something of the mind of God in regards to a given matter. Their purpose, like that of all of the gifts, is to build up the body of Christ and advance His kingdom in the earth. They can be defined as we have done in the table below (Fig. 12.3):

REVELATORY GIFTS DEFINED (SPIRIT-CONFERRED INSIGHT)
(FIGURE 12.3)

GIFT	WORKING DEFINITION
Word of knowledge	A Spirit-conferred revelation of a portion of God's knowledge
Word of wisdom	A Spirit-conferred revelation of a portion of God's wisdom
Distinguishing between spirits	A Spirit-conferred revelation of what spirit is being manifested or motivating an action

Prophetic gifts. The second category is prophetic gifts. These gifts can be defined as Spirit-inspired speech. They are given that the Christian worker might be able to speak the words of God into a given situation. They can be defined as follows (see Fig. 12:4):

PROPHETIC GIFTS DEFINED (SPIRIT-INSPIRED SPEECH)
(FIGURE 12.4)

GIFT	WORKING DEFINITION
Prophecy	A Spirit-inspired speaking forth of a message from God
Different kinds of tongues	A Spirit-inspired speaking forth of a message or a prayer from God in a language unknown to the speaker
Interpretation of tongues	A Spirit-inspired speaking forth of the meaning (interpretation) of a message or prayer given in tongues

Power gifts. The third category is power gifts. These gifts can be defined as Spirit-energized works. They are often miraculous in nature and are given to the Christian worker in order that he or she

might do the works of God. They are defined in the following table
(Fig. 12.5):

POWER GIFTS DEFINED (SPIRIT-ENERGIZED WORKS)
(FIGURE 12.5)

GIFT	WORKING DEFINITION
Gifts of healings..........	A Spirit-energized healing of diseases and infirmities
Faith............................	A Spirit-energized surge of faith to accomplish a God-ordained task
Works of power..........	A Spirit-energized release of power to accomplish a God-ordained task

Having categorized and defined the gifts, we now turn our
attention to how these gifts are manifested in the missionary work of
the church as presented in the book of Acts.

THE GIFTS ILLUSTRATED IN ACTS

ACTS 6:10

*But they were unable to cope with the wisdom and the
Spirit with which [Stephen] was speaking.*

ACTS 8:5-8

*Philip went down to the city of Samaria and began proclaiming Christ to
them. The crowds with one accord were giving attention to what was said by
Philip, as they heard and saw the signs which he was performing. For in the
case of many who had unclean spirits, they were coming out of them
shouting with a loud voice; and many who had been paralyzed and
lame were healed. So there was much rejoicing in that city.*

ACTS 14:8-11

At Lystra a man was sitting who had no strength in his feet, lame from his mother's womb, who had never walked. This man was listening to Paul as he spoke, who, when he had fixed his gaze on him and had seen that he had faith to be made well, said with a loud voice, "Stand upright on your feet." And he leaped up and began to walk.

Listed above are three random examples of the many instances of the spiritual gifts in operation in Acts. There are many more— at least sixty-six according to my personal count. The sheer number of such inclusions in Acts illustrates the significance of spiritual gifts in Luke's thinking, as well as their importance in the missionary work of the church. A thoughtful look into the book of Acts reveals many interesting things about how these gifts were manifested in actual practice in advancing the missionary enterprise of the early church.

REVELATORY GIFTS IN ACTS

There are at least twenty-three examples of the revelatory gifts in operation in Acts.[9] These examples of Spirit-conferred insight include the following: the Spirit revealing to Peter and Paul the readiness of individuals to receive healing—and possibly the readiness of God to heal (two occasions), the Spirit revealing to Peter the motive of someone's heart (two occasions), the Spirit giving Stephen a glimpse into heaven (one occasion), Philip, Ananias, Peter, and Paul receiving guidance from the Spirit (five occasions), the Spirit revealing to Peter the presence of visitors (one occasion), the Spirit revealing God's will to Peter and Paul (four occasions), the Spirit revealing God's intention to Paul and James (two occasions), the Spirit comforting Paul through a vision (one occasion), the Spirit

---

9   See Appendix 2 for a complete listing, with references, of the revelation gifts manifested in Acts.

revealing future events to Paul (four occasions), and the Spirit warning Paul of imminent danger (one occasion).

From this list we can see that the revelatory gifts played a key role in the missionary advance of the first-century church. Through these gifts the early missionaries were directed to the fields of God's choosing. Once there, they were guided into key ministry opportunities and power encounters. Often a word of knowledge or a discerning of spirits began a chain of events leading to the release of a power gift, and ultimately, to the successful proclamation of the gospel. At times the Spirit showed the missionaries who to pray for and when. At other times, He comforted and encouraged them through heavenly visions, or revealed His will at crucial junctures in the church's history. As the missionaries remained sensitive to the Spirit's promptings, and obeyed His directives, the kingdom of God continued to advance.

PROPHETIC GIFTS IN ACTS

As with the revelatory gifts, there are many examples of the prophetic gifts in operation in the book of Acts, sixteen according to my count.[10] These examples of Spirit-inspired speech include the following: believers speaking in tongues as the Spirit enabled them (three occasions), the Spirit inspiring missionaries to proclaim the good news with prophetic anointing (eight occasions), the Spirit inspiring prophets to predict future events (three occasions), a Spirit-inspired prophecy launching a missionary tour (one occasion), and the Spirit calling and anointing women prophets (one mention).

The prophetic gifts were thus an indispensable component of the missionary work of the New Testament church. As Spirit-inspired evangelists and missionaries declared the gospel, the hearts of their hearers were stirred and convicted. As prophets spoke to the church, it was enabled to respond effectively to both current and

---

10   See Appendix 2 for a complete listing, with references, of the prophetic gifts manifested in Acts.

future events. Divine guidance and divine motivation often came as a result of a prophetic word. At times such words hastened or guided missionaries on their way. The missionary advance of the church was thus significantly aided through the manifestation of the prophetic gifts.

POWER GIFTS IN ACTS

As with the other two categories, there are many examples of the power gifts in operation in Acts.[11] I count at least twenty-seven including the following: The Spirit empowered the apostles and other missionaries to perform signs and wonders (six mentions). Many were healed as a result of the release of gifts of healing and other power gifts, including those who were sick, the diseased, the paralyzed, the lame, the blind, the severely injured, and those suffering from fever and dysentery (ten occasions). Demons were cast out by the Spirit of God resulting in spiritual freedom and physical healing (three occasions). The dead were raised by the power of the Spirit (two occasions). And the Spirit enabled the apostles to perform and receive extraordinary miracles, including Peter's shadow healing the sick, cloths from Paul's body effecting the healing of the sick and driving out demons, and Paul being delivered from a venomous snake bite (three mentions).

In Acts power gifts were often manifested in concert with revelatory and prophetic gifts. The various gifts thus augmented and complemented one another. For example, in the story of the healing of the lame man at the Beautiful Gate, and the great harvest of souls that followed, gifts were manifested from all three categories (3:1-4:4). Through a word of knowledge (revelatory), Peter knew that it was God's time to extend healing to the lame man. Through a gift of healing (power), the man was miraculously healed. And through a manifestation of the gift of prophecy (prophetic), Peter stood and

---

11   See Appendix 2 for a complete listing, with references, of the power gifts manifested in Acts.

powerfully addressed the crowd. As a result of this tandem release of spiritual gifts, many were added to the kingdom (4:4).

We see the same multiple use of gifts in the ministry of Paul in the southern Galatian city of Lystra (14:6-18). Through a word of knowledge (revelatory), Paul discerned that a lame man in the crowd had faith to be healed. Through the gift of faith (power), he commanded the man to "Stand upright on your feet." The man leaped up and began to walk. Then Paul, as was his custom, preached a powerful, Spirit-inspired message (prophetic).

FAITH SHIFT

In these and other miracle stories in Acts, an interesting human phenomenon occurs, a phenomenon I call a "faith shift" (see Fig. 12.6, below). As a result of the onlookers seeing the power of God demonstrated, something amazing happens in their hearts. Those who were previously disinterested in—or even, at times, hostile to—the message of the gospel, suddenly become vitally interested. Upon seeing a miracle take place, their attitudes are instantly changed. They are no longer disinterested passersby, but are transformed into engaged participants in the event, ready to give the preacher a sympathetic hearing. I have seen this phenomenon occur in Africa when, in open-air meetings, the people witnessed a miracle. Signs and wonders are thus a powerful evangelistic tool available to the Spirit-empowered missionary. This is particularly true in Islamic and animistic contexts, and among other resistant and power-oriented people groups.

"FAITH SHIFT" OCCURS WHEN A MIRACLE TAKES PLACE
(FIGURE 12.6)

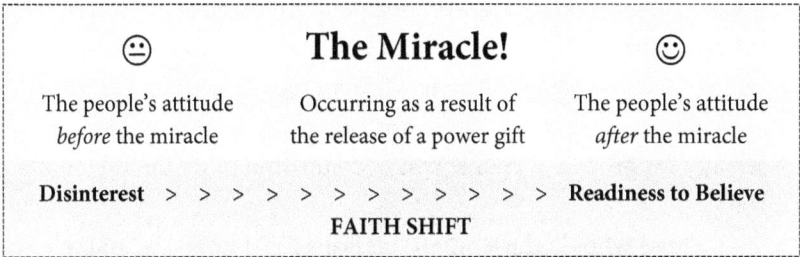

☹	**The Miracle!**	☺
The people's attitude *before* the miracle	Occurring as a result of the release of a power gift	The people's attitude *after* the miracle
Disinterest > > > > > > > > > > > > **Readiness to Believe**		
FAITH SHIFT		

MISSIOLOGICAL IMPLICATIONS

Can anyone except the most strident cessationist deny that the missionary work of the church should include the frequent manifestation of spiritual gifts? A common tendency today, however, even in Pentecostal circles, is to downplay or overlook the central role of spiritual gifts in the work of missions. According to Gee, such a tendency will result in the movement's missing "the fullest purposes of God."[12] He called on the missionary leadership of the Pentecostal church to give this issue top priority:

> The present Pentecostal Movement has girded the earth. It is still growing. Its health has largely been due to its world evangelization. The divine impetus for that has been the baptism in the Holy Spirit accompanied by spiritual gifts. What is the future for such a movement? That will depend, under God, on its spiritual leadership; and, if it is to remain loyal to its heavenly vision, that leadership will manifest spiritual gifts.[13]

---

12   Gee, 63.
13   Ibid., 64-65.

Those who focus exclusively on Paul's teaching concerning spiritual gifts (to the exclusion of Luke's) tend to view spiritual gifts in solely congregational terms. An informed reading of Acts helps bring a necessary balance to one's thinking. In this context the gifts are seen occurring in evangelism and missions. Gee warned about the tendency to mentally divorce the operation of spiritual gifts from world evangelization: "We must hold fast to rightly understanding the gifts of the Spirit as a divine equipment for the work of world evangelization. To regard them in any other way is to turn them into a specialty for groups of people that become little more than religious clubs."[14]

Those who do the work of missions must not only concern themselves with the operation of spiritual gifts in their own lives (Remember Paul's words, "covet spiritual gifts"), they must also concern themselves with teaching the churches they plant or serve about the role and operation of spiritual gifts. Gee observed that "when gifts of the Spirit are lacking, there are produced churches that are run by natural gifts just like efficient business concerns in the world . . . In the end such churches produce spiritual starvation."[15] He then issues this cogent observation concerning the use of spiritual gifts in missions: "The continuance in spiritual prosperity of the Pentecostal Revival depends upon continual consecration to worldwide missions. If our spiritual gifts cannot flourish in the wide arena of universal witness there is something wrong. Their use in evangelism is a healthy test for their validity and our use of them."[16]

BAPTISM IN THE HOLY SPIRIT AND SPIRITUAL GIFTS

In discussing the manifestation of spiritual gifts in Acts, the question naturally presents itself: What is the relationship between

---

14   Ibid., 64.
15   Ibid., 65.
16   Ibid., 66.

Spirit baptism and the manifestation of spiritual gifts? Classical Pentecostals have traditionally espoused a "gateway theology" concerning spiritual gifts, stating that the baptism in the Holy Spirit is the door, or gateway, to the reception and manifestation of spiritual gifts. A line from the "Statement of Fundamental Truths" of the Assemblies of God, U.S.A., seems to lend its support to this view. Under the heading "The Baptism in the Holy Ghost," the statement reads, "With it [Spirit baptism] comes the enduement of power for life and service, the bestowment of the gifts and their uses in the work of the ministry (Luke 24:49; Acts 1:4, 8; 1 Corinthians 12:1-31)." Later in the same document, the same idea is expressed again. Under the heading "The Church and Its Mission," it reads, "The Assemblies of God exists expressly to give continuing emphasis to this reason-for-being in the New Testament apostolic pattern by teaching and encouraging believers to be baptized in the Holy Spirit. This experience: . . . enables them to evangelize in the power of the Spirit with accompanying supernatural signs (Mark 16:15-20; Acts 4:29-31; Hebrews 2:3, 4)."

A later statement in the same section, however, somewhat modifies this one. It reads: "[The baptism in the Holy Spirit] enables [believers] to respond to *the full working of the Holy Spirit* in expression of fruit and gifts and ministries as in New Testament times for the edifying of the body of Christ (Galatians 5:22-26; 1 Corinthians 14:12; Ephesians 4:11-12; 1 Corinthians 12:28; Colossians 1:29)" (italics added). Note how the phrase "the full working of the Holy Spirit" modifies and softens the previous statement. It implies that those who have been born of the Spirit, but have not as yet been baptized in the Holy Spirit, can also be used by God in the "expression of fruit and gifts and ministries," albeit in a lesser measure.

Nevertheless, in its most dogmatic form, gateway theology contends that no believer can in any way manifest any spiritual gift until he or she has first been baptized in the Holy Spirit according to

Acts 2:4. This view, when stated in such narrow terms, cannot be sustained by Scripture, by history, or by contemporary practice.

Miraculous and prophetic gifts were manifested throughout the Bible prior to the Day of Pentecost. A list of Old Testament miracle workers includes such men as Moses, Joshua, Elijah, and Elisha. The disciples of Jesus exercised spiritual gifts in a limited and transitory way before they were baptized in the Holy Spirit on the Day of Pentecost. This included healing the sick (Luke 9:1-11), exorcizing demons (Luke 10:17), and receiving divine revelation (Matt. 16:13-17). Paul further taught that every believer can be expected to have a role in the operation of spiritual gifts in the body (1 Cor. 12:7, 11; 14:26).

In addition, throughout the history of the Christian church, believers have exercised spiritual gifts without first being baptized in the Holy Spirit evidenced by speaking in tongues. In the late nineteenth century, prior to the beginning of the Pentecostal revival in 1901, certain individuals were greatly used by God through the gift of healing. These included such notables as A. B. Simpson, Maria B. Woodworth-Etter, and John Alexander Dowie. Even Charles F. Parham, the disputed founder of the Pentecostal Movement, practiced divine healing before he was baptized in the Holy Spirit in January of 1901.

Yet another challenge to the classical gateway theology is the Third Wave movement occurring among evangelical Christians today with its emphasis on spiritual gifts. These evangelicals, while denying that the baptism in the Holy Spirit is an experience separate from conversion and accompanied by speaking in tongues, advocate the operation of spiritual gifts in their meetings. It cannot be denied that many healings and other manifestations of spiritual gifts occur among them.

What, then, should be the Pentecostal response to these challenges? Pentecostals must begin by squarely facing their traditional gateway theology concerning spiritual gifts, and by freely admitting that, in its most dogmatic form, it simply cannot be supported. To say that no Christian can be used in any way in spiritual gifts prior to Spirit baptism is simply overstating the case. After all, every Christian is indwelt by the Spirit, and many non-Pentecostals have been, and presently are being, used by God in significant ways.

Does this mean that Pentecostals should abandon their gateway theology altogether? Absolutely not. What it does mean, however, is that their understanding and articulation of this theology must be more thoughtful and nuanced. Lim attempts this when he writes that "the baptism in the Spirit is not primarily a qualifying experience but an equipping experience."[17] In other words, Spirit baptism does not qualify someone as a Christian, or even as a Christian worker, it rather equips the Christian worker for greater effectiveness in ministry. Lim continues, "[The baptism in the Holy Spirit] enables Christians to do the job more effectively. The person who is fully yielded to the Holy Spirit will find a greater dimension of ministry than could be realized without the infilling."[18] The fact that a person can be used by God before Spirit baptism does not negate the fact that he or she should continue to ardently seek the promise of Pentecostal power.

No one can deny that, once the disciples had received the Spirit on the Day of Pentecost, a virtual explosion of charismatic activity occurred. At that moment a dynamic release of spiritual power resulted, along with the most dramatic proliferation of spiritual gifts the world had ever seen. This proliferation was the direct result of the disciples' being baptized in the Holy Spirit. Jesus had promised power to witness, and that power manifested itself in, among other things, a powerful release of spiritual gifts. And none can deny that in the last century those churches who advocate Spirit baptism as a subsequent work of grace evidenced by speaking in

---

17   Lim, 64.
18   Ibid.

tongues have been the church's greatest advocates and practitioners
of spiritual gifts. According to J. B. Lawrence,

> There are no gifts apart from the Spirit. The promise of
> power is connected with the coming of the Spirit. A Spirit-
> baptized church is a gifted church. The amount of good done
> by any church never exceeds the degree in which the Spirit is
> being recognized and obeyed. The church is tragically
> ineffective, deficient, and limited in usefulness in carrying
> out the will of Christ in the world unless it is empowered and
> directed by the Holy Spirit.[19]

The baptism in the Holy Spirit is indeed the gateway to "an
enduement of power for life and service" and *a greater* "bestowment
of the gifts and their uses in the work of the ministry." When
properly understood, and scripturally received, Spirit baptism results
in a powerful release of spiritual energy in a believer's life. It opens
the floodgates of heaven, resulting in a powerful flow of the Spirit
into and out from his or her innermost being (John 7:37-39). Once a
believer has been baptized in the Spirit, he can expect that spiritual
gifts will be released in his life and ministry in a greater measure than
ever before. According to Pentecostal educator, Gordon L. Anderson,
"The baptism in the Holy Spirit is significant *additional* power for
life and ministry given by God subsequent to salvation. . . . This
experience results in *added* faith in God, *increased* power and gifts
for ministry, *increased* emotion and passion, and an *enhanced*
awareness of the experiential dimension of God's presence in the life
of the Pentecostal believer."[20]

---

19   J. B. Lawrence, *The Holy Spirit in Missions* (Atlanta, GA: The Home Missions
Board of the Southern Baptist Convention, 1947).
20   Gordon L. Anderson, "Baptism in the Holy Spirit, Initial Evidence, A New
Model" in *Enrichment Journal* Website, available
<http://enrichmentjournal.ag.org/200501/200501_071_BaptismHS
.cfm> (December 26 2004), emphasis added.

While the issue cannot be scripturally framed in terms of "all or none," every Christian must come face to face with the question, "In what measure do I want to see the gifts of the Spirit operative in my own life and ministry?" This question will inevitably bring him or her to the issue of Spirit baptism. Jesus did, after all, command His disciples to wait until they had received power from on high (Luke 24:49). Any believer wanting to be used mightily by God in the manifestation of spiritual gifts in his or her life must, therefore, take seriously the final command of Jesus to be baptized in the Holy Spirit (Acts 1:4-5).

CHAPTER 13

THREE

APPLICATIONS

As we have observed, the church birthed by Jesus and empowered by the Spirit at Pentecost quickly became a powerful force in the earth. Pentecost, and the many other outpourings of the Spirit that followed it, spawned a powerful first-century missionary movement, a movement that has never been equaled in the church's two-thousand year history. What can we learn today from the missionary practice of the New Testament church? We learn that any truly New Testament missions strategy must give top priority to the empowering role of the Spirit of God. Neither Luke nor Paul could have conceived of a missionary strategy devoid of the Spirit's empowering presence and active leadership—and neither must we.

The twenty-first century church, like its first century counterpart, must therefore look to the Spirit to empower and direct its mission. This empowering work must begin in the life of the cross-cultural missionary. No missionary, no matter how gifted or well trained, should attempt the work in his own strength. The missionaries presented by Luke in Acts are Spirit-anointed men and women, people who have been empowered to preach the gospel, receive revelations from God, prophesy under the Spirit's direction,

Empowered for Global Mission

heal the sick, work miracles, cast out demons, and pray with others to receive the Spirit. That is the kind of missionaries we need today.

Not only must the missionary be concerned with his own spiritual empowering, he must also be concerned with the empowering of the church. This was a chief concern of Jesus (Luke 24:49; Acts 1:4-8), Peter and John (Acts 8:16-17), and Paul (Acts 19:1-7, Eph. 5:18). A key goal of any missionary, therefore, must be to impart Pentecost to the church to which he or she is called to work.

To accomplish this task the missionary must place high value on Pentecostal experience. Any missionary who lacks conviction concerning the church's need for spiritual empowerment will do little to emphasize the experience of Spirit baptism. The missionary, however, who values Pentecostal experience will frequently preach and teach on the subject. He will contend for a truly Spirit-empowered missional church, knowing that only such a church will have within itself the spiritual vitality needed to penetrate resistant cultures and effectively expand and reproduce itself over a wide geographical region.

William Menzies contended that "if a biblical truth is to be promulgated, then it ought to be demonstrable in life."[1] I agree. In the work of missions, theology for theology's sake will never do. To be truly viable, any theology of missions must be given feet; it must take us some place; it must lead to effective missionary practice.

With these things in mind we will address three practical issues relating to the role of the Holy Spirit in the work of missions and in the life of the missionary: receiving Spirit baptism, ministering Spirit baptism, and ministering spiritual gifts.

---

1   William W. Menzies, "The Methodology of Pentecostal Theology: An Essay on Hermeneutics," in *Essays on Apostolic Themes: Studies in Honor of Howard M. Ervin*, ed. Paul Elbert, (Peabody, MA: Hendrickson Publishers, 1986), 13, quoted in Roger Stronstad, *Spirit, Scripture and Theology: A Pentecostal Perspective* (Baguio City, Philippines: Asia Pacific Theological Seminary Press, 1995), 29.

RECEIVING SPIRIT BAPTISM

In this study, we have often spoken of the importance of one's being baptized in the Holy Spirit in order to maximize his or her effectiveness in the work of missions. We must now ask the crucial question: How may one personally receive this empowering experience? In answering this question we will first discuss the scriptural context in which the experience is received, and then we will discuss the act of receiving the Spirit.

THE CONTEXT OF RECEIVING THE SPIRIT

When one approaches Spirit baptism, it is important that he or she understand the biblical context in which the experience is received. Scripture indicates that this context includes at least five essential elements, as follows:

1. <u>Earnest Prayer</u>. Spirit baptism is received in the context of earnest prayer. The Holy Spirit descended upon Jesus "while He was praying" (Luke 3:21). Leading up to the Day of Pentecost, the disciples were "continually devoting themselves to prayer" (Acts 1:14). Before Ananias laid his hands on Saul to receive the Spirit, the apostle-to-be spent three days in prayer to God (9:9, 11). Luke notes how Cornelius "prayed to God continually" (10:2), and how Peter also prayed in preparation for the outpouring of the Spirit at Caesarea (v. 9). Finally, it was in the context of teaching about prayer that Jesus instructed His disciples to ask their heavenly Father for the Holy Spirit (Luke 11:1-2, 9-13). Anyone desiring to be filled with the Holy Spirit should thus commit himself or herself to earnest and expectant prayer to God.

2. <u>The Mission of God</u>. The baptism in the Holy Spirit is properly received in the context of mission. Jesus wedded Spirit baptism to the mission of God in Acts 1:8: "But you will receive power when the Holy Spirit has come upon you; and you shall be My witnesses . . . even to the remotest part of the earth." When married to God's mission, the experience becomes a powerful force in the

Christian life, compelling and equipping believers to reach out to the lost both at home and around the world. However, when it is divorced from mission—as is often the case in Pentecostal and charismatic churches—the focus often turns to self gratification and personal blessing, and the mission of God is eclipsed. In this context many excesses have occurred in the name of Pentecost, and the forward movement of the church has often been hindered. Those seeking Spirit baptism should be taught that the purpose of their pursuit is spiritual power to participate in the mission of God to reach the nations with the gospel.

   3. <u>Spiritual Quest</u>. Spirit baptism is also received in the context of spiritual quest, that is, in the context of sincerely seeking after God. In His Sermon on the Mount, Jesus said, "Blessed are those who hunger and thirst for righteousness, for they will be filled" (Matt. 5:6, NIV). On another occasion, when talking about the Spirit, Jesus said, "If anyone is thirsty, let him come to Me and drink" (John 7:37).

   Spirit baptism begins with spiritual desire. It is received neither casually nor complacently. Thousands of Christians throughout the world could testify to the fact that it was when they began to ardently seek after God that they were baptized in the Holy Spirit. Anyone desiring to be filled with the Spirit should turn his or her heart toward God and earnestly seek His face.

   4. <u>Humility of Heart</u>. Further, Spirit baptism is received in the context of humility of heart and life. Jesus humbled Himself before others by being baptized in water.[2] It was then that the Spirit descended upon Him and He was anointed for ministry (Luke 3:21-22, cf. 4:18-19). In like manner, Saul of Tarsus humbled himself before Jesus and Ananias when he was filled with the Spirit (Acts 9:5, 17), as did Cornelius with Peter (Acts 10:25). Pride is a great hindrance to receiving the Holy Spirit. The person desiring to be

---

2   Jesus' humility is further shown by the fact that He was baptized "when all the people were baptized."

baptized in the Holy Spirit must be prepared to humble himself or herself before God.

5. Obedience. Additionally, the baptism in the Holy Spirit is received in the context of obedience. Peter told the Jewish leaders that God gives the Holy Spirit "to those who obey Him" (Acts 5:32). In obedience to Christ's command, the disciples waited in Jerusalem to receive the promised Spirit (Luke 24:49; Acts 1:4-5). Saul of Tarsus also obeyed the risen Christ, and though blinded and bewildered, made his way to the home of Judas to await Christ's further instructions (Acts 9:6-8). As Christians, we have been commanded to be filled with the Spirit (Acts 1:4; Eph. 5:18). We too must obey His clear command.

Jesus further commanded His church to preach the gospel to all nations. A close examination of His five statements in the Great Commission reveals that each is integrally connected to the Spirit's presence or power (Matt. 28:18-20; Mark 16:15-18; Luke 24:46-49; John 20:21-22; Acts 1:8). The implication is clear. Spirit baptism is for those whose hearts are set on taking Christ to the nations, that is, those whose hearts are prepared to obey all Jesus has commanded (Matt. 28:20). Those ready to obey Christ's command are thus prime candidates for Spirit baptism.

THE ACT OF RECEIVING THE SPIRIT

As with all of God's promises, the promise of the Holy Spirit is appropriated by faith. Paul reminded the Galatian believers that they had "receive[d] the promise of the Spirit through faith" (Gal. 3:14). Jesus said that the Holy Spirit flows from (and, by implication, into) the one "who believes" (John 7:37-38). He stated further that supernatural signs, including speaking in tongues, would follow "those who have believed" (Mark 16:17).

The single act of receiving the Spirit by faith, nevertheless, can be practically subdivided into three definite "faith steps." In my years of praying with people to be filled with the Spirit, I have found that leading them through these three steps has helped many to immediately receive the Holy Spirit. Let's look more closely at each of these three steps:

1. *Asking in Faith.* Speaking of the Holy Spirit, Jesus said, "Ask, and it will be given to you . . ." (Luke 11:9). One begins the process of receiving the Spirit by asking God for the gift. The seeker's prayer could proceed something like this:

> Jesus, You promised. You said that if I would ask, I would be given the Holy Spirit. In fact, You said that everyone who asks receives. So, I ask You right now, give me the Holy Spirit. Fill me and empower me to be Your witness.

As he prays, the seeker should believe that God is hearing his prayer and at that very moment, He is answering. He should focus his attention on what God is doing for and in him. Many have testified that it was at this point that they began to sense the Spirit's presence as He descended upon them.

2. *Receiving by Faith.* Closely akin to asking for the Spirit is the act of receiving the Spirit. Receiving in this case is a definite act of faith, occurring at a definite point in time when the gift of the Holy Spirit is fully appropriated. It can be compared to Peter's step of faith when he, at the command of Jesus, stepped from the boat and began to walk on water (Matt. 14:29).

Jesus not only instructed His disciples to ask for the Holy Spirit (Luke 11:9-13), He also told them how they were to ask: "Therefore I say to you, all things for which you pray and ask, believe that you have received them, and they will be granted you" (Mark 11:24). This general promise concerning the efficacy of faith has a clear application to receiving the Holy Spirit. The Holy Spirit is received at the moment of faith.

This faith is not to be perceived as a passive or future-oriented faith. It is rather to be understood as an active faith, located in the immediate present. Note carefully the verb tense of Jesus' exhortation. It is not stated in the future tense ("believe that you *will receive*"), but in the present perfect tense ("believe that you *have received*").[3] The act of receiving the Spirit is a bold present-tense step of faith.

The seeker may, at this point, pray with complete confidence in the promises of Christ: "I truly believe that I *have received* the Holy Spirit!" In response to his or her faith, the Holy Spirit will fill the seeker with His power and presence. If he remains sensitive to what God is doing, he will, deep within his spirit, sense the Spirit's coming.

3. *Speaking in Faith.* All that remains for the seeker to do at this point is to speak out in faith. On the Day of Pentecost the 120 disciples "were all filled with the Holy Spirit *and began to speak . . .*" (Acts 2:4, emphasis added). As they spoke, the Spirit flowed into, through, and out of them, and they "began to speak with other tongues, as the Spirit was giving them utterance." When a person is filled with the Spirit, he too should expect to speak in tongues.[4]

The words he speaks, however, will not come from his mind as in natural speech, but from deep inside, from his spirit. Speaking of the believers' experience with the Spirit, Jesus said, "He who believes in Me, as the Scripture said, 'From his innermost being will flow rivers of living water'" (John 7:38). Speaking in tongues is not an activity of the human mind but of the human spirit. It is not a cognitive but a spiritual and intuitive exercise. It proceeds from one's innermost being. Paul wrote, "For one who speaks in a tongue does not speak to men but to God; for no one understands, but in his spirit he speaks mysteries" (1 Cor. 14:2). He further stated, "For if I pray in a tongue, my spirit prays, but my mind is unfruitful" (v. 14).

When one presents himself before God to be filled with the Spirit, he should relax and open his heart fully to God. Then, in faith he should ask for the Holy Spirit, fully expecting God to answer his prayer. As he waits on God, he should sense the presence of the Spirit

---

3   The present perfect tense indicates that the action has been completed at the time of speaking.

4   See Chapter 14 for a fuller discussion on this topic.

coming upon him. Then, through a conscious act of faith, he should "believe that [he has] received." He will sense the Spirit's powerful presence deep within, filling and empowering him. By this he will know that God is indeed filling him with the Holy Spirit! He must, then, begin to *speak from the Presence*, that is, from where he senses God's presence deep within. It will not be a forced effort, but a natural flow of supernatural words. He should simply allow it to happen, and cooperate fully with the Spirit by boldly speaking out in faith. He will begin to speak words he does not understand, words that are coming from the Spirit of God.[5]

Although no two peoples' Spirit baptisms are exactly the same, certain uniform results can be anticipated by all. The first, as mentioned above, is speaking in tongues as the Spirit enables (Acts 2:4; 10:44-46; 19:6). The second result also involves Spirit-enabled speech. The person who is filled with the Spirit will be empowered and emboldened to share Christ with others (Acts 2:14, 4:31).[6] Both results should be considered normative signs of Spirit baptism, and both should be expected when one is filled with the Holy Spirit.

In addition, the newly Spirit-baptized believer can expect a heightened awareness of the Spirit's presence in his or her life. There will be a greater liberty in worship and prayer (2 Cor. 3:17; Eph. 5:18-20), and an increased flow of the Spirit, resulting in more effective ministry (John 7:37-38).

A further note: the newly Spirit-baptized believer should not make the mistake of thinking that once he has been baptized in the Spirit, he has somehow "arrived," and there is nothing more he needs

---

5   As he speaks in tongues (i.e., languages), he should be reminded of the purpose of Spirit baptism: empowered witness to the nations. He should remember that there are many peoples of the world who speak "strange" tongues and who are in desperate need of the gospel of Christ. He should realize that God is empowering him so that he can participate in God's mission of taking the gospel to the nations in Pentecostal power.

6   This proclamation can either be one-to-one (personal evangelism), as did Philip to the Ethiopian, or in a public or congregational setting (mass evangelism), as did Peter on the Day of Pentecost.

to do in order to maintain a Spirit-empowered life. Spirit baptism brings one into a relationship with the Spirit that must be continually renewed and conscientiously maintained. No matter how powerful one's initial infilling may have been, if the experience does not find further expression in a life of sincere devotion, disciplined prayer, and committed witness, the efficacy of the experience will soon fade, resulting in an eventual loss of spiritual power.

MINISTERING SPIRIT BAPTISM[7]

It is the responsibility of the cross-cultural missionary not only to be filled with the Spirit himself, but to lead others into the experience. The long-term success of his work in the field will be determined, to a large extent, by his ability to lead others into the fullness of God's Spirit. The work will prosper, plateau, or decline in direct proportion to the work of the Spirit in the lives of local believers. According to the late Pentecostal missiologist Melvin L. Hodges, "The greatest contribution that the missionary can make to the church in any country is a spiritual contribution."[8] He continues, "His ability as an administrator or organizer may be important, but it pales beside that of being a spiritual leader, able to encourage the church, bringing it into an atmosphere of revival through his teaching, praying, and the spiritual impact of his life."[9] A missionary can maximize his or her spiritual impact on the church by leading others into the dynamic experience of Spirit baptism.

---

7   For a more complete explanation of how to lead believers into Spirit baptism, see Chapter 14, "Praying with Believers to Receive the Holy Spirit," in the author's book, *Power Ministry: A Handbook for Pentecostal Preachers* (Springfield, MO: Discovery Books, 1998).

8   Melvin L. Hodges, *The Indigenous Church and the Missionary: A Sequel to the Indigenous Church* (Pasadena, CA: William Carey Library, 1978), 86.

9   Ibid.

TWO PRELIMINARY GOALS

When seekers present themselves to be filled with the Spirit, the minister is faced with two preliminary tasks: The first is to stir up expectant faith in their hearts; the second is to bring them into an accurate understanding of what they can expect to happen as they seek for the Spirit. One way he can encourage their faith is by reminding them of the promise of Jesus that "everyone who asks receives" (Luke 11:10). Another is by assuring them that, if they have been truly born again, God is ready and willing to fill them with His Spirit.

He should, then, tell the candidates exactly what he plans to do, and what they can expect to happen. This will help to alleviate any anxiety they might have, and prepare them to respond more fully to the Spirit's work in their lives. The leader could say something like this:

> First, we will pray together. Then, I will lead you in a prayer in which we will ask God to fill us with His Spirit. The Lord will hear and answer our prayer. We will sense His Spirit coming upon us. Then, I will ask you to take a step of faith with me and receive the Holy Spirit. To do this I will lead you in a second short prayer. It will go something like this: "Lord, right now, in the name of Jesus, I receive the Holy Spirit." You should at that moment, by faith, believe that God is filling you with His Spirit. You will sense His presence inside. When this happens, begin to speak, not from your mind, but from deep inside, from where you sense the Spirit's presence. You will begin to utter words in a language you have never learned. Don't be afraid, just continue to speak. God is filling you with His power and His presence. Are you ready to be filled with the Spirit? Do you have any questions?"

If any of the candidates have questions, they should be answered. If they have no questions, the group should proceed to the prayer time.

TWO PRAYERS

As is indicated in the prayer illustration above, the minister will actually lead the seekers in two prayers. The first is a prayer of petition in which they ask God to fill them with the Spirit. After the prayer, and after a period of open-hearted waiting together on God, and sensing His presence, the minister will then lead the candidates in a second prayer. This prayer will be their "step of faith" in which they receive the Spirit. This prayer provides a definite point in time when the seekers can focus their faith to receive the Holy Spirit. The leader should encourage them to sense the Spirit filling them. He should then instruct them to begin to speak, not from their minds, but from their innermost beings— from where they feel the Lord's presence inside.

Often, seekers will be immediately filled with the Spirit, and begin speaking in tongues. If some are not immediately filled, the leader can encourage them to worship the Lord for a time, sensing His presence upon them. He may want to worship with them, allowing the Lord to refill him with the Holy Spirit. This will help encourage the candidates to keep seeking until they too are filled.

If any of the candidates seems to have difficulty responding to the Lord, it is sometimes helpful to repeat the above procedure, pointing out ways in which they may more perfectly respond to the Spirit. Once any of the candidates begin to speak in tongues, they should be encouraged to continue on. The minister should remain with the seekers as long as they continue to pray.

POST-PRAYER COUNSELING

Post-prayer counseling should be given to all who have prayed to be filled with the Spirit. If any are filled, let them know that receiving the Spirit is not an end in itself; it is rather a means to a greater end. The purpose for their receiving the Spirit is that they may receive power for life and service. The minister should tell them that they can expect God to begin to use them in new and more effective ways. He will also want to instruct them as to how the Spirit-filled life may be maintained.[10] If there are any who are not filled with the Spirit, they should be encouraged to continue seeking God. Assure them that the promise of Jesus is still true: "Everyone who asks, receives" (Luke 11:10). Delay does not mean denial. Soon they too will receive the Spirit.

MINISTERING SPIRITUAL GIFTS

In chapter 12 we discussed the role of spiritual gifts in missionary work. We now ask, "How can a missionary be used by the Spirit in the release of spiritual gifts in his or her ministry?" The missionary must begin at the beginning—he or she must "be filled with the Spirit" (Acts 2:4; Eph. 5:18). Then, in order to prepare himself for a Spirit-gifted ministry, he must learn to daily walk in (or by) the Spirit (Gal 5:25). Walking in the Spirit goes well beyond one's initial infilling. It is accomplished through a life of purity, prayer, and submission to God. Walking in the Spirit also requires repeated refilling with the Spirit.

Further, the missionary must "desire earnestly spiritual gifts" (1 Cor. 14:1). The Greek word translated "desire earnestly" is *zeloute*. Paul uses it four times in 1 Corinthians 12-14, three of which speak of desire for spiritual gifts, as follows:[11]

- 12:31: "But earnestly desire (*zeloute*) the greater gifts."

- 14:1: "Desire earnestly (*zeloute*) spiritual gifts."

- 14:39 "Desire earnestly (*zeloute*) to prophesy."

---

10   Chapter 5, "Maintaining the Spirit-filled Life," in the author's book *Life in the Spirit* deals with this subject.
11   The fourth usage, in 13:4, also speaks of strong desire, however, in a more negative sense: "Love . . . is not jealous (*zeeloi*)"

The KJV translates the word *zeloute* as "covet earnestly," which carries the connotation of overwhelming or consuming desire. *Zeloute* is derived from the word zeo which means to burn, glow, or boil. Metaphorically it means to boil with passion. Those wanting to be used in the exercise of spiritual gifts must have a strong desire to be used by God in this manner. Spiritual gifts are not for the complacent or nonchalant, but for those passionate about meeting the needs of others and advancing God's kingdom in the earth.

Further, in order to be used in the manifestation of spiritual gifts, the missionary must also learn to hear and respond to the Spirit's inner directives. Jesus ministered through the power of the Spirit, but only after He had heard the voice of His Father concerning the matter, spoken to Him through the Spirit (John 5:19, cf. Luke 4:1). The same can be said of Peter (Acts 10:19; 11:12), Paul (13:2; 16:6-10), and others in the New Testament church (8:29; 9:10-16). And the same must be said of us today, if we are to truly minister in the Spirit's power.

Spiritual gifts are released through obedience and faith. The Spirit of God comes to anoint and release spiritual gifts through us only as we respond in obedience to His Word and to His inner promptings. Allow me to illustrate what I mean. The Scriptures teach that the Spirit stands ready to come and supernaturally aid us in prayer (Rom. 8:26-27). Before He comes, however, we must first act in obedience to God's Word and the promptings of His Spirit and begin to pray. If we never obey and pray, how can the Spirit come to help us? If we, however, will act in obedience and begin to pray, all the while opening ourselves up to the influence of the Spirit, He will come to our aid and intercede through us "with groanings too deep for words" (Rom. 8:26).

The same principle can be applied to witnessing. The Spirit will anoint and enable us to effectively communicate Christ to the lost (Acts 1:8); however, we must begin the process by first acting in obedience to His Spirit and His Word and begin witnessing to someone. The sad truth is that many Christians, including

Pentecostal missionaries, have been filled with the Spirit, and yet they have never become effective witnesses for Christ. How can this happen? It is because they consistently refuse to obey the Word and the Spirit and begin witnessing to those with whom God brings them into contact. The Spirit will come to our aid only as we obey His directives. The principle then is this: We must first obey, and then the Spirit will come to anoint and enable us in ministry.

The anointing that comes as a result of an act of obedience must then be released through a corresponding act of faith. It is therefore vital that, when opportunities to minister present themselves, the Spirit-filled missionary be prepared to act with bold faith. Such acts of faith work much as does an electrical switch, releasing the power to accomplish the work. Just as the great potential that resides in the electrical lines is released to do its work only when the switch is flipped, in the same manner, the anointing to preach, prophesy, or heal the sick is released by an act of faith on the part of the minister.

Peter acted in bold faith when he commanded the lame man, "In the name of Jesus Christ the Nazarene—walk!" and then seized him by the hand and raised him up (Acts 3:6-7). Similarly, Paul acted in faith when he shouted to the crippled man in Lystra, "Stand upright on your feet" (14:10). Both acts resulted in the release of instantaneous miracles.

When a ministry opportunity presents itself and the missionary discerns the Spirit's voice prompting him to intervene in the situation, he has a choice. He can obey the Spirit's voice, or he can ignore it. If he obeys, the anointing will increase; if he disobeys, it will dissipate. Once the missionary obeys the Spirit's voice and begins to minister, he or she must then move confidently in the realm of faith. It will be through a Spirit-directed act of faith that the anointing will be released, the spiritual gift manifested, and the need met.

- CHAPTER 14 -

EVIDENTIAL
TONGUES

Classical Pentecostals have historically held that speaking in tongues is the "initial physical evidence" of one's being baptized in the Holy Spirit.[1] In proving their point they usually cite five incidences in Acts where people are initially filled with (or baptized in) the Spirit, pointing out that in three of these instances speaking in tongues is explicitly mentioned (2:4, 10:46; 19:6), and in the other two it is strongly implied (8:17-19, 9:17-18 with 1 Cor. 14:18).[2]

---

1   The statement from the Assemblies of God "Statement of Fundamental Truths," entitled "The Initial Physical Evidence of the Baptism in the Holy Ghost," is typical for most classical Pentecostal churches: "The baptism of believers in the Holy Ghost is witnessed by the initial physical sign of speaking with other tongues as the Spirit of God gives them utterance (Acts 2:4). The speaking in tongues in this instance is the same in essence as the gift of tongues (1 Corinthians 12:4-10, 28), but different in purpose and use."

2   Two early Pentecostal treatments of evidential tongues are Carl Brumback, *"What Meaneth This? A Pentecostal Answer to a Pentecostal Question* (Springfield, MO: Gospel Publishing House, 1947), 191-246, and Ralph M. Riggs, *The Spirit Himself* (Springfield, MO: Gospel Publishing House, 1977). Two works representing a more contemporary treatment of the same subject are *Where We Stand: The Official Position Papers of the Assemblies of God* (Springfield, MO: Gospel Publishing House, 1997), 146-150, and Anthony D. Palma, *The Holy Spirit: A Pentecostal Perspective* (Springfield, MO: Gospel Publishing House, 1999), 133-160.

Non-Pentecostals, however, cry, "Foul," claiming that
Pentecostals err at this point in that they employ a faulty
hermeneutic in interpreting Acts, that is, the hermeneutic of
historical precedent. These interpreters maintain that normative
doctrine (i.e., doctrine which is both universal and timeless) cannot
be legitimately derived from historical narratives. Others, a little
more conciliatory, say that, while normative doctrine can be derived
from historical narratives, it must always be tied to the original intent
of the author. Gordon D. Fee, for instance, says that "in the
hermeneutics of biblical history [meaning Acts] the major task of the
interpreter is to discover the author's (I would add, the Holy Spirit's)
intent in the recording of that history."[3] If this is the case, then before
Pentecostals can legitimately claim that speaking in tongues is the
normative sign of Spirit baptism, they must first demonstrate that
Luke in Acts intended to teach the doctrine. The purpose of this
chapter is to address this important issue. We will also investigate
some other insights on the subject as they relate to the subject matter
of this work.

AUTHORIAL INTENT AND TONGUES

In the preceding chapters I have sought to demonstrate that
Luke's primary intent in writing Acts is encapsulated in Acts 1:8. He
thus wrote with both *pneumatological* ("But you will receive power
when the Holy Spirit has come upon you . . .) and *missiological* (". . .
and you shall be My witnesses . . . even to the remotest part of the

---

3   Gordon D. Fee, *Gospel and Spirit: Issues in New Testament Hermeneutics*
(Peabody, MA: Hendrickson Publishers, 1991), 90. Certain New Testament scholars
have challenged this statement, saying that there is no scriptural warrant for such a
position: i.e., Gordon L. Anderson, "Pentecostal Hermeneutics, Part II," *Paraclete* 28,
no. 2 (Spring 1994): 16-18; J. Rodman Williams, *Renewal Theology: Systematic
Theology from a Charismatic Perspective: Three Volumes in One*, vol. 2, *Salvation, the
Holy Spirit and Christian Living* (Grand Rapids, MI: Zondervan Publishing House,
1990), 182.

earth") intent. Luke wrote primarily to show that the empowering presence of the Spirit is a necessary prerequisite for effective witness at home and abroad, and thus to encourage his readers to be filled with the Spirit in order to prepare themselves for missional witness. If my thesis is correct, then it appears that Luke did not, in fact, write Acts with the purpose of teaching that speaking in tongues is the normative sign of Spirit baptism—at least that was not his primary intent.

Some would say that this is the end of the matter. Acts, therefore, cannot teach that tongues is the normative sign of Spirit baptism. But is it the end of the matter? I think not, since it logically follows, that, if Luke was so singularly concerned with his readers being empowered for witness, he would also be equally concerned with their understanding just how the empowering experience occurs. To make certain they did, he included in his narrative, not one, but three explicit examples of believers being initially filled with the Spirit, evidenced by speaking in tongues and prophetic witness (Acts 2:4; 10:46-47; 19:6).[4] In narrative form Luke is saying, "See, here is what you too can expect to happen when you are filled with the Spirit." To the argument that tongues cannot be considered the normative sign of Spirit baptism because in two out of the five instances where people are initially filled with the Spirit in Acts, Luke does not specifically mention speaking in tongues, he would likely have responded, "Aren't three clear examples enough? If three will not convince you, would four, or five?" Thus, while it cannot be demonstrated that it was Luke's *primary* intent to teach that tongues is the normative sign of Spirit baptism, it can be reasonably deduced that it was his clear *secondary* intent. By citing three specific examples of believers speaking in tongues as a consequence of receiving the Spirit, Luke intended to teach readers (including both his original readers and those who would subsequently read his work) about the proper mode of Spirit baptism, which included

---

4   See the authors comments in Chapters 4, 8, and 10.

speaking in tongues. Robert P. Menzies comments, "The normative character of evidential tongues thus emerges, not from Luke's primary intent, but rather as an implication from Luke's prophetic pneumatology . . ."[5]

The same argument that is advanced to teach that speaking in tongues cannot be considered the normative accompaniment to Spirit baptism could also be made concerning water baptism and the new birth. It could be said that, since in Acts the rite is not mentioned after every stated instance of people being saved, then it cannot be considered normative that all new believers are required to be baptized in water. Most evangelical churches, nevertheless, still rightly contend that water baptism is normative for all new believers. As with Spirit baptism, Luke assumes that a few strategic mentions of water baptism are sufficient; therefore, he does not have to redundantly state that water baptism occurred after every instance of people coming to Christ.[6] He simply assumes that the reader will know that those who are converted are then baptized in water. The same can be said about Spirit baptism. Since Luke mentions speaking in tongues in a few strategic instances, he simply assumes that the reader will know that all who are baptized in the Holy Spirit speak in tongues. Anthony Palma points out that since Spirit baptism is a divinely performed act, while water baptism is a humanly performed act, the examples of Spirit baptism carry even more weight than the examples of water baptism.[7]

---

5 Robert P. Menzies, *Empowered for Witness: The Spirit in Luke-Acts* (Sheffield, Eng.: Sheffield Academic Press, 2001), 252.
6 Cases where water baptism is mentioned include 2:38, 41; 8:12-13, 16, 36, 38; 9:18; 10:47-48; 16:15, 33; 18:8, 25; 19:5; and 22:16. Cases where water baptism is not mentioned include 2:47; 5:14; 9:42; 11:21; 13:12; 14:1; 17:12, 34; and 19:18.
7 Palma, 95.

WHY TONGUES?

"But," some would ask, "why tongues? Why not some other physical or spiritual manifestation? Could not any other spiritual gift serve just as well as tongues?" Many charismatic interpreters contend that this is the case.[8] Others have claimed as evidence such manifestations as weeping, dancing, "falling under the power," seeing a vision, receiving a blessing, or manifesting a particular spiritual gift. Still others have surmised that the effect of Spirit baptism is totally internal and requires no external sign whatsoever. However, Luke in Acts never presents any of these manifestations (or non-manifestations) as being the verifying sign of Spirit baptism. The only confirmatory sign he presents is speaking in tongues (Acts 10:44-46). According to Douglass A. Oss, other than speaking in tongues, "no other manifestation associated with Spirit-Baptism in Acts is explicitly presented as evidence of the authenticity of the experience."[9]

In response to the question, Why tongues? we ask another: Could it be that God chose speaking in tongues as the sign of Spirit baptism because of its uniquely symbolic value? As with no other gift, speaking in tongues bears witness to the deeper meaning and purpose of Spirit baptism, that is, empowerment for missional witness. I say this for three reasons. The first two have to do with the symbolic value of speaking in tongues, the third has to do with its evidential value.

---

8   For a charismatic approach to initial evidence see Williams, 211-212. Williams says that tongues is the "primary activity consequent to the reception of the Holy Spirit"; however, it is not the only or necessary evidence.

9   Douglas A. Oss, " Pentecostal/Charismatic View," in *Are Miraculous Gifts for Today?: Four Views,* ed. Wayne A. Grudem (Grand Rapids, MI: Zondervan Publishing House, 1996), 261.

THE PROCLAMATIONAL
SYMBOLISM OF TONGUES

First, the "speaking" or oral aspect of speaking in tongues has symbolic value as to the purpose of the Spirit baptism. Jesus said, ". . . you will receive power . . . and you shall be My witnesses" (Acts 1:8). It seems that God has carefully selected a speaking sign to remind the speaker, as well as those who hear him or her speaking, that the purpose of Spirit baptism is empowerment to speak (that is, to preach) the gospel. No other gift testifies to the proclamational purpose of Spirit baptism as does speaking in tongues (except possibly prophecy which, as we will discuss later, lacks the evidential value of tongues). In Chapter 4 we discussed the vocational purpose of Spirit baptism. Speaking by the Spirit's inspiration thus reminds us that the receiver's primary Christian vocation will be to proclaim Christ to the lost in the power of the Spirit.

Menzies has demonstrated that in every instance in all of Luke-Acts where individuals are filled with the Spirit, the result is Spirit-inspired speech or insight.[10] The Spirit-inspired speech, of course, is not in tongues only, for speaking in tongues is but the sign of Spirit baptism; the substance is Spirit-empowered witness. In each instance in Acts where people spoke in tongues, the tongues were soon followed by Spirit-inspired proclamation of the gospel in the local vernacular (2:4, cf. v. 14; 10:46; 19:6).

The KJV translates Acts 1:8, "you shall be witnesses *unto me*" (italics added), indicating that the Spirit-baptized believers will not only be witnesses *for* Christ (i.e., on His behalf), they will be witnesses unto or *about* Him (i.e., Christ will be the subject of their witness). Throughout Acts, Christ was the central object of the

---

10   Menzies, *Empowered,* 202, 226.

missionaries' message.[11] When one is filled with the Spirit he or she is empowered to more convincingly proclaim Christ to the world.[12]

It is not without significance, however, that in Acts speaking in tongues is always mentioned as occurring immediately upon reception of Spirit baptism, and before proclamation. The implication is that tongues is the "initial" sign of Spirit baptism; prophetic witness is the functional result.

THE LINGUISTIC SYMBOLISM OF TONGUES

Not only does the "speaking" aspect of speaking in tongues have symbolic meaning as to the purpose of the experience, the "tongues" (or language) aspect also has symbolic meaning. God undoubtedly chose a linguistic sign because of its missiological symbolism. On the Day of Pentecost the newly Spirit-baptized disciples spoke in the languages of at least fifteen different Gentile nations (Acts 2:5-11). Numerous commentators have recognized the missional symbolism of their speaking in these languages.[13] Today, when someone is filled with the Spirit, evidenced by Spirit-inspired speaking in tongues, he or she is (or at least should be) made aware of the missiological (I could say, Pentecostal) purpose of the gift, that purpose being empowerment for witness "to the remotest part of the earth." Speaking *in tongues* reminds us that the gift of the Spirit is about enablement to proclaim the gospel to "every tribe *and tongue and people and nation*" (Rev. 5:9, emphasis added).

---

11   cf. Acts 2:22-36; 3:12-26; 4:2, 8-12, 33; 5:29-32, 42; 8:5, 35; 9:19, 22, 27; 10:34-38; 11:20; 13:23-39; 16:31; 17:2-3, 18; 18:5, 25, 28; 19:8; 20:21-22, 24; 22:6-10; 24:24; 26:22-23; 28:23, 31.

12   As in the ministry of Philip, this proclamation can be either to the multitudes (Acts 8:5) or one-on-one (8:35).

13   F. F. Bruce, *The Book of the Acts,* rev. ed. (Grand Rapids, MI: William B. Eerdmans Publishing Co., 1988), 53; Stanley M. Horton, *What the Bible Says About the Holy Spirit* (Springfield, MO: Gospel Publishing House, 1976), 143; John R. W. Stott, *The Message of Acts: The Spirit, the Church and the World* (Leichester, Eng.: Inter-Varsity Press, 1990), 68.

Pentecostal missiologist, John V. York, in addressing the issue of evidential tongues, quotes Don Richardson: "Seen in the context of Jesus' ministry and His clearly articulated plans for the whole world, the bestowal of the miraculous outburst of *Gentile* languages could have only one main purpose: . . . the evangelization of all peoples."[14] York further comments that most debates concerning the issue of evidential tongues are conducted outside of a missional context (something Luke could have never imagined). Throughout Acts, speaking in tongues is firmly couched in the context of the fulfillment of the mission of God. York comments:

> As long as there is a hurting and broken world divided primarily along lines of language and ethnicity, I hope Pentecostals will increase their emphasis upon speaking in tongues. It would be an untold tragedy to back away from that part of our heritage that most directly gives evidence of God's determination to bless all nations through Christ, the seed of Abraham (Gal. 3:6).[15]

The Evidential Value of Tongues

There is a third reason God may have chosen speaking in tongues as the sign of Spirit baptism: speaking in tongues has unique evidential value. All must agree that, historically speaking, tongues was *the* initial physical sign of Spirit baptism. It was at Pentecost that Christ's followers were first filled with the Spirit and "began to speak with other tongues as the Spirit was giving them utterance" (Acts 2:4). All must further agree that speaking in tongues has clear evidential value, as is demonstrated in Acts 10:45-46: "All the circumcised believers who came with Peter were amazed, because the

14   Don Richardson, *Eternity in Their Hearts* (Ventura, CA: Regal Books, 1981), 157, quoted in John V. York, *Missions in the Age of the Spirit* (Springfield, MO: Gospel Publishing House, 2000), 186.
15   York, 186.

gift of the Holy Spirit had been poured out on the Gentiles also, for [Gk.: *gar*, because] they were hearing them speaking with tongues and exalting God."[16]

Note how, in these verses, Luke, in the form of a parenthetical aside, explains to his readers how Peter's Jewish companions knew that the Gentiles had received the Spirit. It was because they heard them speaking with tongues and exalting God. Luke inserted this explanatory comment so his readers would know that they, too, could expect to speak in tongues and exalt God (bear prophetic witness) when they were baptized in the Holy Spirit.[17]

Some may ask, since prophecy is a speaking gift just as tongues is, and since in Acts the believers spoke in tongues "and prophesied" when they were filled with the Spirit, could not prophecy serve just as well as tongues as the initial sign of Spirit baptism? Although prophetic witness can be considered a normative result of Spirit baptism, it does not carry the same evidential weight as speaking in tongues, since the supernatural character of prophecy is more difficult to assess than tongues. Menzies asks,

> ... how is one to distinguish inspired intelligible speech from that which is uninspired? Although we may all be able to think of instances when intelligible speech was uttered in a manner which indicated the inspiration of the Spirit (spontaneous, edifying, appropriate), the point is that judgements of this kind are rather tenuous and approximate. ... Tongues-speech, however, because of its unusual and demonstrative character (the very reason it is both often maligned or over-esteemed), is particularly well suited to serve as "evidence." In short, if we ask the question

---

16   For a discussion on the Greek word, *gar,* see Robert W. Graves, "The Use of *gar* in Acts 10:46," *Paraclete* 22, no. 2 (Spring 1988): 15-18. Commenting on the illative (inferential) use of *gar*, Graves states, ". . . only a divinely assigned cause-effect pattern would justify Luke's use of *gar* in Acts 10:46 and explain the unargued acceptance of the Gentiles simply because they had praised God in other tongues" (17).
17   See the discussion on "Parenthetical Commentary" in Chapter 1, 24-26.

concerning "initial physical evidence" of Luke, tongues-speech uniquely "fits the bill" because of its intrinsically demonstrative character.[18]

Menzies suggests another benefit of the doctrine of evidential tongues: "The doctrine calls us to retain a biblical sense of expectancy, for it reminds us that the manifestation of tongues is an integral part of the Pentecostal gift . . ."[19] He further states, "Above all, the manifestation of tongues is a powerful reminder that the Church is, by virtue of the Pentecostal gift, a prophetic community called and empowered to bear witness to the world."[20]

HISTORICAL TESTIMONY

The worldwide growth of the Pentecostal movement stands as a testimony to the wisdom of its classical doctrinal formulation concerning the baptism in the Holy Spirit evidenced by speaking in tongues. In a paper presented to the Twenty-third Annual Meeting of the Society for Pentecostal Studies in Guadalajara, Mexico, Vinson Synan noted that "the Pentecostal churches that have held strongly to this teaching [initial evidence] have surpassed all others in church growth and missionary success in the period since World War II."[21] To illustrate his point, Synan compared the growth of three churches/church groups which accepted the initial evidence teaching with the growth of three similar churches/church groups who rejected the teaching (see Fig. 14.1 below).

Synan first compared the growth of Church of God in Christ with the growth of the church from which it separated as a result of a Pentecostal outpouring in its midst in 1908. The separation came

18   Menzies, 250-251.
19   Ibid., 255.
20   Ibid.
21   Vinson Synan, "The Role of Tongues as Initial Evidence," in *Conference Papers on the Theme, To the Ends of the Earth, Presented at the Twenty-third Annual Meeting of the Society for Pentecostal Studies* (November 11-13, 1993), 18.

over the issue of evidential tongues. In March of 1907 Charles H. Mason from Memphis, Tennessee, visited the Azusa Street revival in Los Angeles, California. There he was powerfully baptized in the Holy Spirit with the evidence of speaking in tongues. When he returned to his church in Memphis, he began to preach the Pentecostal message. As a result of the revival that followed in 1908, the holiness denomination to which he belonged split into two groups of roughly the same size. By 1992 the segment of the church that rejected the initial evidence teaching, the Church of God in Christ (Holiness), had grown to only 15, 000 members. During the same period the church that embraced the doctrine, the Church of God in Christ, had grown to 3.7 million members.[22] Next, Synan compared the growth of the Assemblies of God (AG), U.S.A., with that of the Christian and Missionary Alliance (CMA), which in many ways can be viewed as the spiritual father of the AG. From the CMA and its founder, A. B. Simpson, the AG inherited, among other things, its openness to the power of the Spirit, (i.e., divine healing and power encounters), many of its theological formulations (i.e., the fourfold gospel), and its missionary passion and strategy (i.e., indigenous church principles).

In 1906-1907 a Pentecostal revival swept through the ranks of the CMA, with many of its members and leaders being filled with the Spirit and speaking in tongues. The leadership of the church ultimately took a noncommittal stand concerning the doctrine of evidential tongues, expressed in the formula "seek not, forbid not." This stance effectively ended the Pentecostal renewal in the CMA. It was at this point that many who had been baptized in the Holy Spirit left the ranks of the church. Some who left later helped to found the AG in 1914, including such notables as Daniel W. Kerr, J. Roswell and Alice Reynolds Flower, Carrie Judd Montgomery, Noel Perkin,

---

22   By 2002 the COGIC had grown to 5,499,875 members and adherents according to the *Yearbook of American and Canadian Churches: 2004: Equipping Leaders: Theological Education,* ed. Eileen W. Lindner (Nashville, TN: Abington Press, 2004).

GROWTH OF CHURCHES EMBRACING AND
OPPOSING EVIDENTIAL TONGUES
(FIGURE 14.1)

	(early 1900's) Adherents	(1992) Adherents[23]	Comparison
Church of God in Christ (Holiness)	Same as COGIC	15,000 members	
Church of God in Christ	Same as COGIC (Holiness)	3.7 million members	247 x COGIC (Holiness)
Christian and Missionary Alliance		**US:** 265,863 **World:** 1.9 million	
Assemblies of God		**US:** 2.2 million	8.3 x CMA
		World: 25 million	13.1 x CMA
Holiness Churches Opposing Tongues		**World:** 5.4 million	
Pentecostals Espousing Tongues		**World:** 205 million *denominational* Pentecostals	38 x holiness churches
		World: 420 million *total* Pentecostals	77.8 x holiness churches

John W. Welch, Frank M. Boyd and W. I. Evans.[23] The AG adopted many of the policies and practices of the CMA into its own church structure. According to William W. Menzies, the AG inherited from the CMA its "Bible institute program, ecclesiology, the missionary

---

23   Gary B. McGee, "All for Jesus: The Revival Legacy of A. B. Simpson," in *Enrichment Journal* Website, available <http://enrichmentjournal.ag.org/199902/082_all_for_Jesus.cfm> (December 28, 2004).

vision, the emphasis on divine healing, much of its early hymnology, and even a significant portion of its early leadership.[24] Says Gary B. McGee, "[The CMA] profoundly effected the early course of the [AG] Council."[25] The primary difference between the two groups was their differing beliefs concerning evidential tongues. Synan noted that "by 1992 the CMA had grown to only 265,863 members in its U.S. church and an estimated 1.9 million members around the world.[26] On the other hand the Assemblies of God, which has strongly maintained the [initial evidence] teaching from its founding, had grown to 2,170,890 members in the U.S. with an estimated worldwide constituency of 25 million members."[27]

Synan then compared the growth of the worldwide constituencies of the holiness churches that early in the twentieth century opposed the initial evidence position with the growth of the classical Pentecostal churches who embraced it. By 1992 the total membership of the holiness churches that opposed the teaching numbered 5.4 million worldwide compared to 205 million in the denominational Pentecostal churches who espoused it. Including independent Pentecostals and charismatics, the number of Pentecostals worldwide had grown to 420 million. Synan concludes his analysis with this challenge:

> In the end, the teaching of tongues as initial evidence has played a major role in recent church history. The Pentecostal experience and the doctrine explaining it has galvanized the most explosive movement among Christians since the days

---

24   William W. Menzies, *Anointed to Serve* (Springfield, MO: Gospel Publishing House, 1971), 28.

25   McGee, "All For Jesus."

26   CMA now reports "more than 2 million" members and adherents worldwide according to their official website, available <http://www.cmalliance.org> (December 27, 2004).

27   By 2003 the Assemblies of God had 2,729,562 members and adherents in the US and an additional 48 million members worldwide according to the official Assemblies of God website, available <http://ag.org/top/about/statistics.cfm> (December 27, 2004).

of the Reformation. It is unthinkable that the Pentecostal movement could have developed as it did without the initial evidence position[28]

Initial evidence is more than a denominational distinctive. It has served as a key to unlocking the blessings of God in the lives of millions of Christians worldwide. During my twelve years as a missionary in Africa, it has been my great privilege to personally pray with thousands of African believers to receive the Spirit, evidenced by speaking in tongues. I have seen their lives dramatically changed as a result of receiving this wonderful gift from heaven. Many have testified to a new passion to preach the gospel. Some have immediately sensed the desire to enter full-time ministry and have entered into Bible school in preparation for that ministry. I have also witnessed the launching of a dynamic church planting movement as a result of Pentecostal renewal coming to a formerly dormant national church. As a result, in just ten years over one thousand churches have been planted and thousands have come to know Christ as Savior.

Now is not the time for the Pentecostal church to back off from the clear teaching of Scripture. It is the time for the church to renew its efforts and proclaim the Pentecostal message far and wide. The nations await the message of Christ, and Christ awaits the prayer of the church: "Send Your Spirit, O Lord, and fill us, and empower us to take Your Name to the nations in Pentecostal power!"

CONCLUSION

In this book we have examined the essential role of spiritual empowerment in the work of missions. We have observed the Spirit's power at work in and through the first century missionaries. By observing and comparing the teachings of Luke in Acts and Paul in his epistles, we discovered that both writers viewed the empowering

28   Synan, 19.

work of the Spirit and the manifestation of spiritual gifts as indispensable components of all missionary work.

We now end our study by asking a final question: What should our response be to these findings? Should we not be convicted of our complacency concerning the role of the Spirit in our lives and in the mission of the church—and should we not be moved to do better? Historically, non-Pentecostals have, by and large, ignored the empowering role of the Spirit in missions. While this is tragic, it is even more tragic that many Pentecostals have, in recent years, done little better, at times giving little more than lip service to the doctrine of Spirit baptism. This neglect has lead to a crisis of experience in the Pentecostal church worldwide. Today most (if not all) Pentecostal denominations report that only a minority of their membership has been baptized in the Spirit evidenced by speaking in tongues.

This crisis of experience has, in turn, led to a crisis of theology. With less and less of their members claiming the Pentecostal experience, more and more Pentecostals are questioning their defining doctrines of subsequence and evidential tongues. Pentecostals, who have long been accused of theologizing from their experience, now, like many non-Pentecostals, are tempted to begin theologizing from their non-experience. If this trend is not properly addressed, and reversed, it will result in an even further crisis of experience in the church, and ultimately in a crisis of missionary effectiveness in the field.

What then is the answer? We must seek God for a fresh outpouring of the Spirit on the church. This outpouring must be undergirded by a proper understanding of the experience of Spirit baptism as a means of empowerment for missional witness, both locally and globally. Such an outpouring could fittingly begin with the Pentecostal missionary force in the field, since these workers will likely be most aware of their need for divine empowering to accomplish their work. It could then possibly spread in two directions: onward to the nations through the national churches these missionaries would influence, and then backwards across the oceans to the church at home.

It is my belief that the western Pentecostal church's hope lies, at least in part, in the emerging missionary movements of its daughter churches in Africa, Asia, and Latin America. These churches are much more oriented to supernatural experience than their parent churches in the west. Rather than following the lead of the west, these churches must assert themselves, and stand firm in the area of Pentecostal doctrine and experience. Lacking much of the wealth and technology available to the western church, the emerging missionary movements in the Two-Thirds World are more acutely aware of their complete dependence on the power and provision of God. Like the first church, they must commit themselves to "stay in the city until [they] are clothed with power from on high" (Luke 24:49). Brothers and sisters, we are counting on you!

Finally, we must all renew our commitment to the original vision of Christ for His church, that is, that it would take the gospel to the nations in Pentecostal power (Acts 1:8). We must never lose sight of the fact that the work of missions is, in the final analysis, not a work of man but a work of God. Did not Jesus say, "I will build my church"? (Matt. 16:18). We must be ever mindful of the fact that the task of global missions is accomplished "not by might nor by power, but by My Spirit, says the LORD of hosts" (Zech. 4:6). May the Pentecostal church, and the church worldwide, once again, as at the beginning, cry out to the Lord of the Harvest, "Empower us, O Lord, for global mission."

EPISODES IN ACTS

Definitions:

Episode: ....A story which is complete in itself but is itself part of a larger story.

Episodic Series: ....A series of events which form a complete story in themselves but are part of a yet larger story.

Episode	Text	Date
EPISODIC SERIES 1: Beginnings in Jerusalem		
Introductory words (Summary)	1:1-4	
1. Final instructions	1:5-8	
2. The ascension of Christ	1:8-11	
3. In the upper room	1:12-26	
4. Pentecost: <u>The First Jerusalem Outpouring</u>	2:1-42	A.D. 28
Summary Statement 1	2:43-47	
5. Healing at the Beautiful Gate	3:1-4:3	
Summary Statement 2	4:4	
6. The trial and release of Peter and John	4:5-22	

Episode	Text	Date
7. <u>The Second Jerusalem Outpouring</u>	4:23-31	
Summary Statement 3	4:32-35	
8. Barnabas/Ananias and Sapphira	4:36-5:10	
Summary Statement 4	5:11-16	
9. Apostles imprisoned, threatened, and released	5:17-41	
Summary Statement 5	5:42	
10. The seven are chosen	6:1-6	
Summary Statement 6	6:7	
11. Stephen's capture, sermon, and martyrdom	6:8-7:60a	
12. Saul is introduced	7:60b-8:3	
Summary Statement 7	8:4	

EPISODIC SERIES 2: Outreach in Samaria

13. Philip's revival in Samaria and	8:4-24	
14. <u>The Samaritan Outpouring</u>	8:14-17	A.D. 31
15. Philip and the Ethiopian	8:25-39	
16. Philip preaches from Azotus to Caesarea	8:40	

EPISODIC SERIES 3: Saul's Conversion and Early Ministry

17. The conversion of Saul	9:1-9	
18. The commissioning and empowering of Saul		
19. <u>The Damascene Outpouring</u>	9:10-19	A.D. 32
20. Saul in Damascus	9:20-25	
21. Saul in Jerusalem	9:26-30	
Summary Statement 8	9:31	

EPISODIC SERIES 4: Peter's Ministry in Greater Judea

22. Peter's ministry in Judea	9:32-43	
23. <u>The Caesarean Outpouring</u>	10:1-48	A.D. 34
24. Peter reports to Jerusalem	11:1-18	

Episode	Text	Date

EPISODIC SERIES 5: Intervening Events

25. The church at Antioch	11:19-26	
26. A great famine	11:27-30	
27. Peter arrested and delivered	12:1-19	
28. Herod judged by God	12:20-23	
Summary Statement 9	12:24	

EPISODIC SERIES 6: Paul's First Missionary Tour

29. Paul and Barnabas sent out and		
30. The Antiochian Outpouring	13:1-4a	A.D. 45
31. Ministry in Cyprus	13:4b-12	
32. Ministry in Pisidian Antioch	13:13-43	
33. Driven out of Antioch	13:44-51	
Summary Statement 10	13:52	
34. Ministry in Iconium	14:1-5	
Summary Statement 11	14:6:6-7	
35. Ministry in Lystra and Derbe	14:8-20	
36. Strengthening the churches	14:21-26	
37. "Missions convention" in Antioch	14:27	
Summary Statement 12	14:28	

EPISODIC SERIES 7: The Jerusalem Council

38. The council at Jerusalem	15:1-29	
39. Report and ministry in Antioch	15:30-34	
Summary Statement 13	15:35	

Episode	Text	Date

EPISODIC SERIES 8: Paul's Second Missionary Tour

40. Dispute over John Mark	15:35-41	
41. Timothy is chosen and circumcised	16:1-3	
Summary Statement 14	16:4-5	
42. The Holy Spirit directs the missionaries	16:4-12	
43. Ministry in Philippi	16:13-40	
44. Conversion of Lydia	16:13-15	
45. Demonized girl delivered	16:16-18	
46. Paul and Silas delivered from prison	16:19-40	
47. Ministry in Thessalonica	17:1-9	
48. Ministry in Berea	17:10-15	
49. Ministry in Athens	17:16-34	
50. Ministry in Corinth	18:1-17	
51. Journey back to Antioch	18:18-23	

EPISODIC SERIES 9: Paul's Third Missionary Tour (Ephesus)

52. The story of Apollos	18:24-28	A.D. 53
53. Ministry in Ephesus	19:1-20:1	
54. The Ephesian Outpouring	19:1-7	
55. Missionary outreach to Asia	19:8-10	
56. Challenging sorcery	19:11-19	
Summary Statement 15	19:20	
57. Disturbance in Ephesus	19:20-20:1	

EPISODIC SERIES 10: Journey to Jerusalem

58. Travels through Macedonia, Greece, Troas	20:1-6	
59. Ministry in Troas (Eutychus healed)	20:7-12	
60. Journey to Miletus	20:13-16	
61. Farewell to Ephesian elders	20:17-38	
62. Journey to Jerusalem	21:1-13	
63. Prophecy of Agabus	21:10-14	

Episode	Text	Date

EPISODIC SERIES 11: Trials

64. Paul at Jerusalem	21:15-23:10	
65. Report to James and the Elders	21:17-26	
66. Paul seized in the Temple	21:27-36	
67. Paul's defense in the Temple	21:37-22:30	
68. Paul before the Jewish Council	23:1-10	
69. Vision of the Lord in the night	23:11	
70. Plot to kill Paul, transfer to Caesarea	23:12-35	
71. Paul before Felix	24:1-27	
72. Paul before Festus	25:1-22	
73. Paul before Agrippa	25:23-26:32	

EPISODIC SERIES 12: Journey to Rome

74. Journey to Rome	27:1-8	
75. Shipwreck	27:9-44	
76. Ministry at Malta	28:1-10	
77. Snakebite	28:1-6	
78. Healing of Publius and others	28:7-10	
79. Journey through Italy to Rome	28:11-15	

EPISODIC SERIES 13: Ministry in Rome

80. Ministry in Rome	28:16-31	
81. To the Jewish leaders	28:16-29	
82. Two full years of unhindered preaching	28:30-31	

- A P P E N D I X   2   -

SPIRITUAL GIFTS IN ACTS

REVELATION GIFTS IN ACTS

CATEGORY		EVENT	REFERENCE
Readiness to receive healing revealed	⊛	Revelation is given at the Beautiful Gate.	Acts 3:4
	⊛	The Spirit reveals the lame man's faith to Paul.	Acts 14:8-11
Motive of a person's heart revealed	⊛	Ananias and Sapphira's deception is revealed.	Acts 5:3-6, 7-11
	⊛	The intention of Simon's heart is revealed to Peter.	Acts 8:18-23
Seeing into the spiritual realm	⊛	Stephen sees into heaven.	Acts 7:55-56
Divine guidance received	⊛	Philip receives guidance.	Acts 8:26-30
	⊛	Ananias has a vision.	Acts 9:10-17
	⊛	Peter testifies in Jerusalem concerning the Spirit's guidance.	Acts 11:12
	⊛	Paul is directed by the Spirit to Macedonia.	Acts 16:6-10
	⊛	The Spirit directs Paul to go to Jerusalem.	Acts 19:21
The presence of visitors revealed	⊛	The presence of Visitors is revealed to Peter.	Acts 10:19

God's will revealed	● God's will for the Gentiles is revealed to Peter.	Acts 10:9-17
	● Peter testifies concerning His revelation.	Acts 10:27-29
	● The Lord tells Paul he will go to the Gentiles.	Acts 22:21
	● It is revealed to Paul that He must go to Rome.	Acts 23:11
God's intention revealed	● God reveals to Paul His intention to blind Elymas.	Acts 13:9-12
	● James' wisdom discourse is given at the Council in Jerusalem.	
Divine comfort given	● The Lord speaks to Paul in a night vision	Acts 18:9-10
Future events revealed	● The Holy Spirit reveals to Paul what awaits him in Jerusalem.	Acts 20:22-23
	● The Spirit reveals to Paul that the voyage will be with great loss.	Acts 27:9-10
	● God reveals the fate of the ship to Paul	Acts 27:21-26
	● The believers warn Paul "through the Spirit."	Acts 21:4
Warning of danger given	● The Spirit warns Paul to leave Jerusalem.	Acts 22:17-18

PROPHETIC GIFTS IN ACTS

CATEGORY		EVENT	REFERENCE
Speaking in tongues	◉	Tongues at Pentecost	Acts 2:4
	◉	Tongues and prophetic speech at Caesarea	Acts 10:46
	◉	Tongues and prophetic speech at Ephesus	Acts 19:6
Prophetic proclamation	◉	Peter's pneuma discourse	Acts 2:14
	◉	Peter's second pneuma discourse	Acts 4:8
	◉	Bold proclamation following the Second Jerusalem Outpouring	Acts 4:31
	◉	Powerful proclamation in Jerusalem	Acts 4:33
	◉	Stephen's pneuma discourse	Acts 6:10;
	◉	The persuasive preaching of Saul (Paul)	7:1-53 Acts 9:22
	◉	Paul and Barnabas' bold proclamation in Iconium	Acts 14:3
	◉	Paul's bold proclamation in Ephesus	Acts 19:8
Predicting the future	◉	Prophecy of Agabus	Acts 11:28
	◉	Prophets warn Paul in Tyre	Acts 21:4
	◉	Agabus prophesies in Caesarea	Acts 21:10
Launching a missionary journey	◉	The Holy Spirit speaks through prophets in Antioch	Acts 13:1-4
Women prophets	◉	Philip's four daughters	Acts 21:9

POWER GIFTS IN ACTS

CATEGORY		EVENT	REFERENCE
Signs and wonders	•	Wonders and signs through the apostles	Acts 2:43
	•	Signs and wonders	Acts 5:12-13
	•	Stephen performs great wonders and signs	Acts 6:8
	•	Philip performs signs, casts out demons, and heals the sick	Acts 8:6-8
	•	God grants Paul and Barnabas signs and wonders	Acts 14:3
	•	Paul and Barnabas testify concerning signs and wonders	Acts 15:12
Healing	•	A cripple is healed	Acts 3:6-7
	•	Many healed and delivered	Acts 5:13-16
	•	Philip performs signs, casts out demons and heals the sick	Acts 8:6-8
	•	Simon observes signs and miracles	Acts 8:13
	•	Ananias heals Saul	Acts 9:17-18
	•	Peter heals Aeneas	Acts 9:34-35
	•	Lame man in Lystra is healed	Acts 14:8-10
	•	Paul is healed in Iconium	Ac. 14:19-20
	•	Paul testifies about his healing by Ananias	Acts 22:13
	•	Paul heals the father of Publius and many others	Acts 28:8-9
Demonic deliverance	•	Many are healed and delivered	Acts 5:13-16
	•	Philip performs signs, casts out demons, and heals the sick	Acts 8:6-8
	•	Paul casts a demon out of a slave girl	Acts 16:16-18

Praying with others to receive the Holy Spirit	◉	Apostles lay hands on the Samaritan converts to receive the Holy Spirit	Acts 8:17
	◉	Ananias prays for Saul to receive the Spirit	Acts 9:17-18
Undesignated miracles	◉	Saul proves that Jesus is the Messiah	Acts 9:22
Raising the dead	◉	Peter raises Dorcas from the Dead	Acts 9:40-42
	◉	Eutychus is raised by Paul	Acts 20:9-10
Extraordinary miracles	◉	Peter's shadow heals the sick	Acts 5:15
	◉	Extraordinary miracles of healing and exorcism are done by Paul	Acts 19:11-12
	◉	Paul is delivered from a snake bite	Acts 28:3-5

- GLOSSARY OF TERMS -

apologia: (n.) a formal or reasoned defense of a doctrine or idea

diaspora: those Jews who were dispersed from the Holy Land after the Babylonian captivity

epochal: (adj.) having to do with the beginning of a new and important period of history, having to do with epochs or ages

eschatological: (adj.) having to do with the study of the end times

ethne: (n., Greek) the nations, also translated "Gentiles" in the English New Testament

hermeneutics: the science of interpretation; the study of the principles of biblical interpretation and exegesis

missiological: (adj.) having to do with the study of missions

ontological: (adj.) the study of the ultimate nature of being of a thing

parousia: (n.) the second coming of Christ

pneumatological: (adj.) having to do with the study of the doctrine of the Holy Spirit

raison d'etre: (n., Fr.) reason for being; justification for existence

soteriological: (adj.) having to do with the study of the doctrine of salvation

- S E L E C T E D   B I B L I O G R A P H Y -

Allen, Clifton J., ed. *The Broadman Bible Commentary*. Vol. 10,
    Acts—1 Corinthians, by T. C. Smith. Nashville, TN: The
    Broadman Press, 1970.

Allen, Roland. *Missionary Methods: St. Paul's or Ours*. Grand Rapids,
    MI: William B. Eerdmans Publishing Co., 1962.

Anderson, Gordon L. "Baptism in the Holy Spirit, Initial Evidence, A
    New Model." In *Enrichment Journal* Website. Available
    <http://enrichmentjournal.ag.org/200501
    /200501_071_BaptismHS.cfm> (December 26, 2004).

_____. "Pentecostal Hermeneutics, Part II." *Paraclete* 28, no. 2,
    Spring 1994.

Arrington, French, L. *The Acts of the Apostles: An Introduction and
    Commentary*. Peabody, MA: Hendrickson Publishers, Inc.,
    1988.

_____. "Acts of the Apostles." In *The Full Life Bible Commentary
    to the New Testament*. Edited by French L. Arrington and
    Roger Stronstad. Grand Rapids, MI: Zondervan Publishing
    House, 1999.

_____. "Luke." In *The Full Life Bible Commentary to the New
    Testament*. Edited by French L. Arrington and Roger
    Stronstad. Grand Rapids, MI: Zondervan Publishing House,
    1999.

Assemblies of God, *Where We Stand: The Official Position Papers of
    the Assemblies of God*. Springfield, MO: Gospel Publishing
    House, 1997.

Atter, Gordon F. *The Third Force*. Peterborough, Ont.: The College Press, 1965.

Barclay, William. *The Letters to the Corinthians*, rev. ed. Louisville, KY: Westminister John Knox Press, 1975.

_____. *The Daily Study Bible: The Acts of the Apostles*, rev. ed. Edinburgh, Eng.: The Saint Andrew Press, 1976.

Barrett, David. "The Worldwide Holy Spirit Renewal." In *The Century of the Holy Spirit: One Hundred Years of Pentecostal and Charismatic Renewal*, 1901-2001. Edited by Vinson Synan. Nashville, TN: Thomas Nelson Publishers, 2001.

Bennett, Dennis and Rita Bennett. *The Holy Spirit and You: A Study Guide to the Spirit-Filled Life*. Plainfield, NJ: Logos International, 1971.

Blumhofer, Edith L., Russell P. Spittler, and Grant A. Wacker. *Pentecostal Currents in American Protestantism*. Urbana, IL: University of Illinois Press, 1999.

Boer, Harry R. *Pentecost and Missions*. Grand Rapids, MI: William B. Eerdmans Publishing Co., 1975.

Bonnke, Reinhard. *Mighty Manifestations: The Gifts and Power of the Holy Spirit*. Eastborne, Eng.: Kingsway Publications, 1994.

Booth, Wayne C., Gregory Colomb, and Joseph M. Williams. *The Craft of Research*, 2nd. ed. Chicago, IL: University of Chicago Press, 2003.

Brandt, R. L. *Gifts for the Marketplace*. Tulsa, OK: Christian Publishing Services, 1989.

Bridges, James K. "Introduction." In *Pentecostal Gifts and Ministries in a Postmodern Era*. Edited by James K. Bridges. Springfield, MO: Gospel Publishing House, 2004.

Bruce, F. F. *The Book of the Acts*, rev. ed. Grand Rapids, MI: William
    B. Eerdmans Publishing Co., 1988.

Brumback, Carl. *What Meaneth This? A Pentecostal Answer to a
    Pentecostal Question.* Springfield, MO: Gospel Publishing
    House, 1947.

Burgess, Stanley M. and Gary B. McGee. *Dictionary of Pentecostal
    and Charismatic Movements.* Grand Rapids, MI: Regency
    Reference Library, Zondervan Publishing House, 1988.

Burgess, Stanley M. and Eduard M. van der Maas. *The New
    International Dictionary of Pentecostal and Charismatic
    Movements*, rev. ed. Grand Rapids, MI: Zondervan
    Publishing House, 2002.

Carpenter, Harold R. Mandate and Mission: *The Theory and Practice
    of Assemblies of God Missions.* Springfield, MO: CBC Press,
    1989.

Coleman, Robert E. *The Master Plan of Evangelism.* Old Tappan, NJ:
    Fleming H. Revell Co., 1972.

Cox, Harvey. *Fire from Heaven: The Rise of Pentecostal Spirituality
    and the Reshaping of Religion in the Twenty-First Century.*
    Reading, MA: Addison-Wesley Publishing Co., 1995.

Dalton, Robert Chandler. *Tongues Like as of Fire: A Critical Study of
    Modern Tongue Movements in the Light of Apostolic and
    Patristic Times.* Springfield, MO: Gospel Publishing House,
    1945.

Deere, Jack. *Surprised by the Power of the Spirit.* Grand Rapids, MI:
    Zondervan Publishing House, 1993.

Dempster, Murray A., Byron D. Klaus and Douglas Petersen, eds.
    *Called and Empowered: Global Mission in Pentecostal
    Perspective.* Peabody, MA: Hendrickson Publishers, Inc.,
    1991.

_____, eds. *The Globalization of Pentecostalism: A Religion Made to Travel*. Oxford, UK: Regnum Books International, 1999.

Dixon, Thomas. "'Celebration Ephesus' in Historic Turkish Ruins Celebrates Major Spiritual Breakthrough." *Charisma NOW* Website. Available <http://www.charismanow.com/a.php? ArticleID= 2185> (September 8, 2004).

Dunn, James D. G. *Baptism in the Holy Spirit: A Re-examination of the New Testament Teaching on the Gift of the Spirit in Relation to Pentecostalism Today*. Philadelphia, PA: The Westminister Press, 1970.

_____. "The Gift of the Spirit." In *The Theology of Paul the Apostle*. Grand Rapids, MI: William B. Eerdmans Publishing Co., 1998.

_____. "The Church." In *The Theology of Paul the Apostle*. Grand Rapids, MI: William B. Eerdmans Publishing Co., 1998.

Ervin, Howard M. "Hermeneutics: A Pentecostal Option." *Pneuma* 3, no. 2, 1981.

_____. *Spirit Baptism: A Biblical Investigation*. Peabody, MA: Hendrickson Publishers, Inc., 1987.

Fee, Gordon D. *Gospel and Spirit: Issues in New Testament Hermeneutics*. Peabody, MA: Hendrickson Publishers, Inc., 1991.

_____. *God's Empowering Presence: The Holy Spirit in the Letters of Paul*. Peabody, MA: Hendrickson Publishers, Inc., 1994.

_____. *Paul, the Spirit, and the People of God*. Peabody, MA: Hendrickson Publishers, Inc., 1996.

_____. *Listening to the Spirit in the Text*. Grand Rapids, MI: William B. Eerdmans Publishing Co., 2000.

Fee, Gordon and Douglas Stuart. *How to Read the Bible for All Its Worth,* 2nd. ed. Grand Rapids, MI: Zondervan Publishing House, 1993.

Gee, Donald. *Spiritual Gifts in the Work of the Ministry Today.* Springfield, MO: Gospel Publishing House, 1963.

_____. "Spiritual Gifts in World Evangelization." In *Azusa Street and Beyond: Pentecostal Missions and Church Growth in the Twentieth Century.* Edited by L. Grant McClung, Jr. South Plainfield, NJ: Bridge Publishing, 1986.

Goff, James R., Jr., and Grant Wacker. *Portraits of a Generation: Early Pentecostal Leaders.* Fayetteville, AR: University of Arkansas Press, 2002.

Gordon, A. J. *The Holy Spirit and Missions.* Harrisburg, PA: Christian Publications, Inc., 1968.

Graves, Robert W. "The Use of gar in Acts 10:46." *Paraclete* 22, no. 2, Spring 1988.

Greig, Gary S. and Kevin N. Springer, eds. *The Kingdom and the Power: Are Healing and Spiritual Gifts Used by Jesus and the Early Church Meant for the Church Today?* Ventura, CA: Regal Books, 1993.

Grudem, Wayne A. "The Doctrine of the Church." In *Systematic Theology: An Introduction to Biblical Doctrine.* Leichester, Eng.: Inter-Varsity Press, 1994.

_____, ed. *Are Miraculous Gifts for Today? Four Views.* Grand Rapids, MI: Zondervan Publishing House, 1996.

Guthrie, Stan. *Missions in the Third Millennium: 21 Key Trends for the 21st Century.* Waynesboro, GA: Paternoster Press, 2000.

Harris, Ralph W., gen. ed. *The Complete Biblical Library.* Vol. 5. *Acts by Stanley M. Horton.* Springfield, MO: The Complete Biblical Library, 1991.

Hayford, Jack. *The Beauty of Spiritual Language: Unveiling the Mystery of Speaking in Tongues.* Nashville, TN: Thomas Nelson Publishers, 1996.

Hodges, Melvin L. *The Theology of the Church and Its Mission: A Pentecostal Perspective.* Springfield, MO: Gospel Publishing House, 1977.

_____. *The Indigenous Church and the Missionary.* South Pasadena, CA: William Carey Library, 1978.

_____. *The Indigenous Church.* Springfield, MO: Gospel Publishing House, 1990.

Hollenweger, Walter J. *Pentecostalism: Origins and Developments Worldwide.* Peabody, MA: Hendrickson Publishers, Inc., 1997.

Holy Bible (The). *Updated New American Standard Bible.* La Habra, CA: The Lockman Foundation, 1995.

Horton, Stanley M. *What the Bible Says about the Holy Spirit.* Springfield, MO: Gospel Publishing House, 1989.

_____. *The Book of Acts: The Wind of the Spirit.* Springfield, MO: Gospel Publishing House, 1996.

Hovenden, Gerald. *Speaking in Tongues: The New Testament Evidence in Context.* Sheffield, Eng.: Sheffield Academic Press, 2002.

Jacobsen, Douglas. *Thinking in the Spirit: Theologies of the Early Pentecostal Movement.* Bloomington, IN: Indiana University Press, 2003.

Jepson, J. W. *What You Should Know About the Holy Spirit.* Springfield, MO: Gospel Publishing House, 1986.

Jeter, Hugh. *By His Stripes: A Biblical Study on Divine Healing.* Springfield, MO: Gospel Publishing House, 1977.

Joel News Website. 5 October 1999. Available
    <http://www.joelnews.org/news- en/jn294.htm#eph1>
    (September 8, 2004).

Johns, Donald A. "Some New Directions in Hermeneutics of
    Classical Pentecostalism's Doctrine of Initial Evidence." In
    *Initial Evidence: Historical and Biblical Perspectives on the
    Pentecostal Doctrine of Spirit Baptism.* Edited by Gary B.
    McGee. Peabody, MA: Hendrickson Publishers, Inc., 1991.

Keener, Craig S. *The Spirit in the Gospels and Acts: Divine Purity and
    Power.* Peabody, MA: Hendrickson Publishers, Inc., 1997.

_____. *Three Crucial Questions About the Holy Spirit.* Grand
    Rapids, MI: Baker Book House, 1999.

_____. *Gift and Giver: The Holy Spirit for Today.* Grand Rapids,
    MI: Baker Academic, 2001.

Klaus, Byron D. "The Mission of the Church." In *Systematic
    Theology,* rev. ed. Stanley M. Horton, ed. Springfield, MO:
    Logion Press, 1995.

Kraft, Charles H. *Christianity with Power: Your Worldview and Your
    Experience of the Supernatural.* Ann Arbor, MI: Vine Books,
    1989.

Kraft, Marguerite G. *Understanding Spiritual Power: A Forgotten
    Dimension of Cross-Cultural Mission and Ministry.*
    Maryknoll, NY: Orbis Books, 1995.

Ladd, George Eldon. *The Gospel of the Kingdom: Scriptural Studies in
    the Kingdom of God.* Grand Rapids, MI: William B.
    Eerdmans Publishing Co., 1959.

Lampe, G. W. H. *The Seal of the Spirit.* London, Eng: Longmans,
    Green, 1951. Quoted in F. F. Bruce. *The Book of the Acts,* rev.
    ed. Grand Rapids, MI: William B. Eerdmans Publishing
    Co., 1988.

Lawrence, J. B. *The Holy Spirit in Missions.* Atlanta, GA: Home
        Missions Board Southern Baptism Convention, 1947.

Lawrence, Carl. *Rwanda: A Walk Through Darkness . . . into Light.*
        Gresham, OR: Vision House Publishing, 1995.

Lim, David. *Spiritual Gifts: A Fresh Look.* Springfield, MO: Gospel
        Publishing House, 1999.

Lindner, Eileen W., ed. *Yearbook of American and Canadian
        Churches: 2004: Equipping Leaders: Theological Education.*
        Nashville, TN: Abington Press Churches, 2004.

Lloyd-Jones, D. Martin. *Joy Unspeakable.* Eastbourne, Eng:
        Kingsway, 1984. Quoted in David Shibley. *Once in a
        Lifetime: Seizing Today's Opportunities for World Harvest.*
        Kent, Eng.: Sovereign World, 1997.

Ma, Sonsuk and Robert P. Menzies, eds. *Pentecostalism in Context:
        Essays in Honor of William W. Menzies.* Sheffield, Eng.:
        Sheffield Academic Press, 1997.

Marshall, I. Howard. *Luke, Historian and Theologian.* Grand Rapids,
        MI: Zondervan Publishing House, 1970.

Martin, David. *Pentecostalism: The World is Their Parish.* Malden,
        MA: Blackwell Publishers, 2002.

McConnell, C. Douglas, ed. *The Holy Spirit and Mission Dynamics.*
        Pasadena, CA: William Carey Library, 1997.

McGee, Gary B. *This Gospel Shall Be Preached: A History and
        Theology of Assemblies of God Foreign Missions to 1959.*
        Springfield, MO: Gospel Publishing House, 1986.

_____. *This Gospel Shall Be Preached: A History and Theology of
        Assemblies of God Foreign Missions Since 1959.* Springfield,
        MO: Gospel Publishing House, 1989.

_____. *People of the Spirit: The Assemblies of God*. Springfield, MO: Gospel Publishing House, 2004.

_____. "All for Jesus, the Revival Legacy of A. B. Simpson," in *Enrichment Journal* Website. Available <http://enrichmentjournal.ag.org/199902/082_all_for_Jesus.cfm> (December 28, 2004).

Menzies, Robert P. *Empowered for Witness: The Spirit in Luke-Acts*. Sheffield, Eng.: Sheffield Academic Press, 2001.

Menzies, William W. *Anointed to Serve: The Story of the Assemblies of God*. Springfield, MO: Gospel Publishing House, 1971.

_____. "Synoptic Theology, An Essay on Pentecostal Hermeneutics." *Paraclete*, 13, no. 1, Winter 1979.

_____. "The Methodology of Pentecostal Theology: An Essay on Hermeneutics." In *Essays on Apostolic Themes: Studies in Honor of Howard M. Ervin Presented to Him by Colleagues and Friends on His Sixty-fifth Birthday*. Edited by Paul Elbert. Peabody, MA: Hendrickson Publishers, Inc., 1986.

Menzies, William W. and Robert P. Menzies, *Spirit and Power: Foundations of Pentecostal Experience*. Grand Rapids, MI: Zondervan Publishing House, 2000.

Miller, Dezil R. *Power Ministry: How to Minister in the Spirit's Power*. Springfield, MO: Africa's Hope, 2005.

_____. *From Azusa to Africa to the Nations.* Springfield, MO: Assemblies of God World Missions: Africa Office, 2005.

_____. *In Step with the Spirit: Studies in the Spirit-filled Walk*. Springfield, MO: AIA Publications, 2008.

_____. *Teaching in the Spirit*. Springfield, MO: Africa Theological Training Services,

_____. *Acts: The Spirit of God in Mission.* Springfield, MO: AIA
        Publications, 2011.

_____. *The Kingdom and the Power: The Kingdom of God: A
        Pentecostal Investigation.* Springfield, MO: AIA Publications,
        2009.

_____. *Experiencing the Spirit: A Study of the Work of the Holy
        Spirit in the Life of a Believer.* Springfield, MO: AIA
        Publications, 2009.

_____. *The 1:8 Promise of Jesus: The Key to World Harvest.*
        Springfield, MO: PneumaLife Publications, 2012.

Moreau, Scott A., Gary R. Corwin, and Gary B. McGee. *Introducing
        World Missions: A Biblical, Historical and Practical Survey.*
        Grand Rapids, MI: Baker Academic, 2004.

Oss, Douglas A. "Pentecostal/Charismatic View." In *Are Miraculous
        Gifts for Today?: Four Views.* Edited by Wayne A. Grudem.
        Grand Rapids, MI: Zondervan Publishing House, 1996.

Palma, Anthony D. *Baptism in the Holy Spirit.* Springfield, MO:
        Gospel Publishing House, 1999.

_____. *The Holy Spirit: A Pentecostal Perspective.* Springfield,
        MO: Logion Press, 2001.

Paton, David and Charles H. Long, eds. *The Compulsion of the Spirit:
        A Roland Allen Reader.* Grand Rapids, MI: William B.
        Eerdmans Publishing Co., 1983.

Penney, John Michael. *The Missionary Emphasis of Lukan
        Pneumatology.* Sheffield, Eng.: Sheffield Academic Press,
        1997.

Pinnock, Clark H. *Flame of Love: A Theology of the Holy Spirit.*
        Downers Grove, IL: Inter-Varsity Press, 1996.

Pomerville, Paul A. *The Third Force in Missions: A Pentecostal Contribution to Contemporary Mission Theology.* Peabody, MA: Hendrickson Publishers, Inc., 1985.

_____. *Introduction to Missions.* Irving, TX: International Correspondence Institute, 1987.

Rea, John. *The Holy Spirit in the Bible: All the Major Passages About the Spirit, A Commentary.* Lake Mary, FL: Creation House, 1998.

Reddin, Opal L., ed. *Power Encounter: A Pentecostal Perspective.* Springfield, MO: Central Bible College, 1989.

Richardson, Don. *Eternity in Their Hearts,* rev. ed. Ventura, CA: Regal Books, 1984.

Riggs, Ralph M. *The Spirit Himself.* Springfield, MO: Gospel Publishing House, 1977.

Rommen, Edward, ed., *Spiritual Power in Missions: Raising the Issues.* Pasadena, CA: William Carey Library, 1995.

Sanders, J. Oswald. "The Spirit–The Breath of God." In *Spiritual Maturity.* Chicago, IL: Moody Press, 1969.

Schatzmann, Siegfried. *A Pauline Theology of Charismata.* Peabody, MA: Hendrickson Publishers, Inc., 1987.

Scroggie, W. Graham. *The Unfolding Drama of Redemption: The Bible as a Whole.* Vol. 2, 2nd. ed. Grand Rapids, MI: Zondervan Publishing House, 1976.

Shelton, James B. *Mighty in Word and Deed: The Role of the Holy Spirit in Luke-Acts.* Peabody, MA: Hendrickson Publishers, Inc., 1991.

Shibley, David. Missions *Addiction: Capturing God's Passion for the World.* Lake Mary, FL: Charisma House, 2001.

_____. *Once in a Lifetime: Seizing Today's Opportunities for World Harvest*. Kent, Eng.: Sovereign World, 1997.

Stott, John R. W. *Baptism and Fulness of the Holy Spirit*. Downers Grove, IL: Inter-Varsity Press, 1964.

_____. *The Message of Acts: The Spirit, the Church and the World*. Leichester, Eng.: Inter-Varsity Press, 1990.

Stronstad, Roger. *The Charismatic Theology of St. Luke*. Peabody, MA: Hendrickson Publishers, Inc., 1984.

_____. *Spirit, Scripture, and Theology: A Pentecostal Perspective*. Baguio City, Philippines: Asia Pacific Theological Seminary Press, 1995.

_____. *The Prophethood of All Believers: A Study in Luke's Charismatic Theology*. Irving, TX: ICI University Press, 1997.

_____. *Signs on the Earth Beneath: A Commentary on Acts 2:1-21*. Springfield, MO: Life Publishers International, 2003.

Sumrall, Lester. *The Gifts and Ministries of the Holy Spirit*. New Kensington, PA: Whitaker House, 1993.

Synan, Vinson. *The Spirit Said "Grow": The Astounding Worldwide Expansion of the Pentecostal and Charismatic Churches*. Monrovia, CA: MARC, 1992.

_____. "The Role of Tongues as Initial Evidence." In *Conference Papers on the Theme 'To the Ends of the Earth' Presented at the Twenty-third Annual Meeting of the Society for Pentecostal Studies*, November 11-13, 1993.

_____, ed. *The Century of the Holy Spirit: 100 Years of Pentecostal and Charismatic Renewal*. Nashville, TN: Thomas Nelson Publishers, 2001.

Tannehill, Robert C. *The Narrative Unity of Luke-Acts: A Literary Interpretation.* Vol. 1, *The Gospel According to Luke.* Philadelphia, PA: Fortress Press, 1991.

_____. *The Narrative Unity of Luke-Acts: A Literary Interpretation.* Vol. 2, *The Acts of the Apostles.* Philadelphia, PA: Fortress Press, 1994.

Turner, Max. *The Holy Spirit and Spiritual Gifts.* Peabody, MA: Hendrickson Publishers, Inc., 1996.

Wacker, Grant. *Heaven Below: Early Pentecostals and American Culture.* Cambridge, MA: Harvard University Press, 2001.

Wagner, C. Peter. *Confronting the Queen of Heaven.* Colorado Springs, CO: Wagner Publications, 1999.

_____. *The Acts of the Holy Spirit: A Modern Commentary on the Book of Acts.* Ventura, CA: Regal Books, 2000.

Williams, Don. Signs, *Wonders, and the Kingdom of God: A Biblical Guide for the Reluctant Skeptic.* Ann Arbor, MI: Vine Books, 1989.

Williams, J. Rodman. *Renewal Theology: Systematic Theology from a Charismatic Perspective: Three Volumes in One.* Vol. 2, *Salvation, the Holy Spirit and Christian Living.* Grand Rapids, MI: Zondervan Publishing House, 1990.

Williams, Joseph M. *Style: Toward Clarity and Grace.* Chicago, IL: The University of Chicago Press, 1995.

Wilson, Everett A. *Strategy of the Spirit: J. Philip Hogan and the Growth of the Assemblies of God Worldwide, 1960-1990.* Suffolk, Eng.: Regnum, 1997.

Wimber, John. *Power Evangelism.* San Francisco, CA: Harper and Row Publishers, 1986.

Womack, David A., ed. *Pentecostal Experience: The Writings of Donald Gee.* Springfield, MO: Gospel Publishing House, 1994.

York, John V. *Missions in the Age of the Spirit.* Springfield, MO: Logion Press, 2000.

SCRIPTURE INDEX

OTHER BOOKS BY DENZIL R. MILLER

Power Ministry: How to Minister in the Spirit's Power (2004)
(also available in French, Portuguese, Malagasy,
Swahili, Kinyarwanda, and Chichewa)

*Empowered for Global Mission: A Missionary Look at
the Book of Acts* (2005)

From Azusa to Africa to the Nations (2005)
(also available in French, Spanish, and Portuguese)

Acts: The Spirit of God in Mission (2007)

In Step with the Spirit: Studies in the Spirit-filled Walk (2008)

*The Kingdom and the Power: The Kingdom of God:
A Pentecostal Interpretation* (2009)

*Experiencing the Spirit: A Study of the Work of the Spirit
in the Life of the Believer* (2009)

Teaching in the Spirit (2009)

*Power Encounter: Ministering in the Power and
Anointing of the Holy Spirit: Revised* (2009)
(also available in Kiswahili)

*You Can Minister in God's Power: A Guide for
Spirit-filled Disciples* (2009)

*The Spirit of God in Mission: A Vocational Commentary
on the Book of Acts* (2011)

*Proclaiming Pentecost: 100 Sermon Outlines on
the Power of the Holy Spirit* (2011) (Associate editor with Mark Turney,
editor) (Available in French, Spanish, Portuguese, and Swahili)

Globalizing Pentecostal Missions in Africa (2011)
(Editor, with Enson Lwesya)

The 1:8 Promise of Jesus: The Key to World Harvest (2012)

All books are available online at www.DenzilRMiller.com

Published by PneumaLifePublications
3766 N Delaware Ave.
Springfield, MO 65803
USA3

Printed in the United States of America

www.ingramcontent.com/pod-product-compliance
Lightning Source LLC
Chambersburg PA
CBHW051942090426

42741CB00008B/1233